AN INTRODUCTION TO
SOCIAL HOUSING

AN INTRODUCTION TO SOCIAL HOUSING

Paul Reeves

A member of the Hodder Headline Group
LONDON • SYDNEY • AUCKLAND

First published in Great Britain in 1996 by
Arnold, a member of the Hodder Headline Group,
338 Euston Road, London NW1 3BH

Whilst the advice and information in this book is believed to be true
and accurate at the date of going to press, neither the author nor the
publisher can accept any legal responsibility or liability for any errors
or omissions that may be made.

British Library Cataloguing in Publication Data
A catalogue record for this book is available from the British Library

ISBN 0 340 66197 6

Typeset in 10/12 pt Times by
Anneset, Weston-super-Mare, Avon
Printed and bound in Great Britain by
J W Arrowsmith Ltd, Bristol.

To Marlena, with love

Contents

List of figures and tables

Front cover illustration: Trowbridge Estate, Hackney. Part of Hackney Council's Comprehensive Estates Initiative.

Figures

Tables

Acknowledgements

Especial thanks are due to the following, without whom this book would not have been possible. I have acknowledged them in sequence with my career in housing; but first, my thanks to Marlena, to whom this book is dedicated, without whose love, support and understanding it would have been impossible to contemplate writing this volume.

At Cambridge City Council, I thank John McGibbon, who was Housing Advisory Officer, and who broke me into housing aid and homelessness work with a sense of ironic humour; also Sandra Cole, Gaile Walker, Sue Reeves, Richard Darlington and David Poole, City Housing Manager, and all other staff with whom I worked. Thanks also to the lecturers at what was then Essex Institute of Higher Education, who gave me a valuable insight into the field of social housing in teaching towards the Institute of Housing Professional Qualification; and to my colleague, Reg Bek, for driving us there every Wednesday for 3 years.

At the London Borough of Southwark, I thank Ian Jones, then Chief Policy and Development Officer, Marie Price, Judith Harrison, and especially Jim Dickson. At London Borough of Greenwich, Rona Nicholson, and especially Peter Quinn.

At Hammersmith and West London College, my thanks are due to Chris Griffiths, Housing Programme Area Leader, Chris Mounsey, Eileen Speight, and all other housing and related lecturers from whom I have learned so much. At the University of Westminster, Peter Harvie, Senior Lecturer in Law, who started me off in university lecturing; also Keith Jacobs and the rest of the housing team, for their interest and support.

I should also like to thank the staff and committee members of Bush Housing Association and Garden City Homes Housing Association, from whom I have learned much about the voluntary housing movement.

The articles all come from *Public Service and Local Government* (*PSLG*), and the book would not have been possible without consent to republish them. Thanks especially to Kathy Stansfield, past Editor, and to all who contributed to the articles; I hope I have not misrepresented them to the point of legal action!

Paul F. Reeves MA (Cantab), MCIH, PGCE(HE)
1996

Introduction

This is a book about social housing, and the changes which have occurred in the field, up to the mid-1990s. Social housing relates to the activities of both local authorities and housing associations in providing and managing homes for those who cannot compete in the market to satisfy what is a basic human requirement. Much has been written about the subject, and this book cannot realistically provide more than an overview; but this is what is needed as an initial framework within which to fit more detailed analysis.

I have worked as a housing officer in a variety of local authorities, performing functions such as the assessment of homeless persons, giving housing advice, and developing new initiatives to provide homes for rent and sale, and I have undertaken consultancy work on policy and practice issues. I have lectured on a wide range of housing and related areas at Hammersmith and West London College, a large inner city college of further and higher education, and at the University of Westminster. This period, which stretches from the early 1980s to the mid-1990s, has been a process of education, where the larger picture has emerged as a series of discoveries: it took many years for me to gain an overall perspective.

One of the reasons this book has been written is that it is extremely difficult to appreciate the overall context of housing, but such an appreciation is vital if those working in the field are to make a real and lasting contribution to the future of social housing provision and management. This is because all the strands are interlinked. Those working in a specific section or area of a housing provider or management organisation, unless occupying positions of senior management, and perhaps not even then, are necessarily concerned with performing their particular function to the best of their ability, within the rules which apply, and this may prevent the development of a wider perspective. There is need for a book to tie the strands together, and it is hoped that readers will find that this book does so, and thereby helps them to acquire that broad perspective.

Students of housing, at all levels, often feel daunted at the sheer scale of the subject, and its seeming complexity. The terminology of housing finance, law and development is enough to frustrate enthusiasm and comprehension by itself. There are very many good and detailed texts dealing with various aspects of the area, but comparatively few that are written in a user-friendly style, which can provide a gentle induction and foster further curiosity. Again, it is hoped that this book will do something to remedy this problem.

By way of introduction, the flavour of the chapters is given below. I also wrote very many articles for *Public Service and Local Government*, a magazine which was designed principally for those working for councils, to update them on new initiatives, and it was my mission to present housing changes in a non-complex manner, as far as this was possible, for the informed generalist. Several of these articles are featured at the end of each chapter. The intention is that the reader, having considered the arguments presented in the chapter, will read these articles as a way of summarising and pointing up the issues, and, through answering some of the questions which are set out at the end of each articles as thinking-points, clarify their own views and, hopefully, wish to take matters further. The busy reader may read the articles first, and defer a study of the main text for later. You bought the book – it is yours to use as you wish!

Chapter 1, entitled 'A Changing Environment', defines social housing and charts its course since the last century, identifying the main stimuli of policy, from well-meaning philanthropism and concern over public health, through the production of mass housing and planned settlements, to today's concerns of privatisation and the challenges of homelessness and community care. Themes discussed include the sale of council houses, always a controversial issue since the instigation of the Right to Buy in 1981 under the Tory government of Margaret Thatcher. Housing finance, far from being a merely dry subject full of figures and difficult concepts and acronyms, even if it is partly these things at times, is related to general macro-economic policy. Housing associations have changed in character and context since their inception in the nineteenth century, and are vital actors in providing affordable homes; and they are introduced as today's prime social housing movers. Housing need and homelessness are and have been key concerns of council providers since the formation of housing departments, and the issue is set in the context of central government policy, which has not always been easy to reconcile with the aims of those working on the ground. Finally, the rise of the customer care ethos is charted, rightly so, as rents are increasingly the main source of funding for services and even capital projects in some areas.

Chapter 2 is concerned to demystify housing finance, by defining it in everyday terms before launching into a history of its development. Many of the concepts are obvious when compared to the operation of current bank accounts, and the sort of spending activities most of us do. I have worked in the field, and it is my prime conviction that much of the complexity has been generated by professionals who wish to reinforce their status through mystique, or to bamboozle those who have chosen to assist those who so desperately need housing; and if that sounds combative, so be it. The construction and management accounts of local authorities and housing associations are discussed, and the personal subsidy system founded on Income Support evaluated, so that the reader can see ways in which the labyrinth might be reformed.

Chapter 3 deals with homelessness, although the legislational sands are rapidly shifting. But there is an underlying question: whatever the technical nature of the legal or organisational response might be, what is the most socially responsible and humane way to treat the issue? Can it be right that so many face years in bed and breakfast and other expensive, inappropriate and often downright unpleasant forms of temporary housing, whilst the building industry lurches from recession to recession, and the cost of providing decent permanent housing would be less in the long run? Homelessness is disgusting in a so-called civilised society, and this is the central point which should emerge. The chapter outlines the quite disgraceful policies and practices adopted towards these people, who deserve better.

Chapter 4 examines the housing association movement, which has become the major provider of new-build affordable housing, supplanting the role of councils in this respect. Housing associations' legal and organisational framework is discussed, and the range of functions, running through providing housing for rent and for sale, managing other owners' stock, and acting as advisers and development agents, is outlined. Their activities are set within the context of Housing Corporation policy (the Housing Corporation being a quango which often has an uneasy relationship with the bodies it funds and oversees), and the legal status of their tenants, which differs radically from that enjoyed in the public and private sectors, is examined. It is vital that those concerned in any way with housing should thoroughly understand the nature of this movement, its strengths and limitations, because in very many senses it is the future; but, at their best, housing associations are partners with others.

Chapter 5 discusses councils and their tenants. An overview of local government is given. It has often been the unwilling and sometimes deserved target of central government economies and policy changes, and much controversy surrounds its role both as a provider and enabler.

For much of the century, local government has been the undisputed provider of essential services and housing, but its role in both of these is under threat, as governments have sought to introduce a greater degree of private input into the areas with which it deals. These are interesting times for the bureaucrats and local politicians who run them, and for those who live in accommodation owned and managed by the private sector. There is little doubt that councils will continue to have an important role in this field, even if as facilitators through sources of finance and through their strategic town and country planning functions. An understanding of their past role is essential to chart the possibilities for future involvement, and this chapter may help those in these organisations who may be going through a crisis of identity. Housing is just one of the areas where the question of the appropriateness of public ownership and regulation arises, but if not these organisations, who? Is it correct to leave the destiny of the provision of what is a basic human requirement, which too many find difficulty in obtaining, to the vagaries of private investment, or even in the control of well-meaning, unelected committees of good people labouring under the weight of regulations devised by the government's quango?

Chapter 6 unravels the minefield of planning and development issues. Strategic planning is vital to the production of a well-ordered and humane environment, and its absence as in Victorian England and in too many parts of the less developed world even today, makes a powerful case for a rational town and country planning system.

It is vital that would-be developers understand the necessary constraints imposed by planning authorities, even if their role sometimes seems unnecessarily prescriptive. But the planning system also contains creative solutions to meeting housing need, through planning deals in which social housing developers can share in the profits of private developers, and through the judicious use of planning circulars and advice offered by central government. The role of local authorities as planning enablers of housing will grow as public financial resources are increasingly constrained.

Development is intimately linked with finance, but also with good design standards and the awareness of customer needs and preferences. I make no apology for concentrating on housing associations as the prime actors in the production of social housing, and on the constraints under which they work; and I recommend that this chapter be read in conjunction with that on finance issues, although this is very much a shifting scene.

The last chapter takes a hard look at the development of a commercialistic ethos in the social housing arena. The change of either has been stimulated by the increased reliance on private finance and the need to convince lenders of the viability of organisational strategies, as well as by the continued emphasis on home ownership, and the involvement of those owning private property in tackling housing needs and wants. The organisational structures of many local authorities and housing associations resemble those of corporate businesses, and many of the tools of private enterprise, for example business planning, total quality management and cash planning targets, and the information technology paraphernalia which goes with this, have been integrated into the work of socially based organisations.

Specific themes include that of compulsory competitive tendering, which has forced councils to compete with private organisations for the right to provide hitherto publicly provided services and therefore to adopt some of their methodologies. Large-scale voluntary transfer, involving the sale of public housing assets to housing associations, which have had to raise private money to acquire stock, has increased the commercial aspect of social housing. Local housing companies, which were being tested as this book was written, represent a desperate attempt by councils to stay in the role of providers and managers of social housing by avoiding public expenditure constraints; and housing associations are increasingly engaging with private landlords as managing agents on behalf of councils struggling to provide decent temporary housing for those to whom they have a responsibility under homelessness legislation. Thus, commercial practices are changing the role and nature of the world in which those who work for associations and councils live, perhaps irrevocably.

I hope that this book will stimulate thought amongst students, policy-makers and practitioners about what can and should be done in the interests of those who rely upon social housing. It is designed principally for students of housing courses, ranging from those taking Housing Access courses, the BTEC National Certificate in Housing Studies and the Higher National Certificate, and those studying towards housing and housing-related degrees, but I hope that the general reader will find it useful in informing opinion, and perhaps action as well.

Paul Reeves
London, 1996

1 A changing environment

1.1 What is social housing?

This book seeks to examine the way in which housing need has been addressed by a variety of agencies, including local authorities, housing associations, and even the private sector. The term 'social housing' has been in vogue only since the mid-1980s, and is used to describe any accommodation which is provided for those who cannot compete in the marketplace to provide their own roof. Social housing agencies, it seems, have at least this in common, although they differ widely in character. Later chapters discuss the dimensions of social housing provision in detail, but it is necessary to present an overview to provide an orientation, and to engage in a debate as to the nature of this form of housing provision.

A few years ago – perhaps as short a time ago as the late 1980s – it would not have occurred to most lower-cost housing providers that they were essentially an arm of the welfare state, in the sense that social security is. Today, it is easy to forget that as recently as the 1970s, council housing was generally available, after a wait, to all who wanted it, that local authority tenure was regarded as as much a choice as deciding to buy a house, rather than as a last resort. It is clear that council and housing association tenure is regarded in some quarters as an adjunct to the social security system, as is shown in one of the articles at the end of this chapter, 'Welfare housing and the Minister' (p. 30) where the then Minister of Housing, Sir George Young, defended the emphasis on personal subsidy and a move away from central support to lower building costs and thus rents generally on the grounds that it is better to use limited public finance to support the building of new homes for the poorest than to use it to depress rents generally.

Indeed, some have resisted use of the term 'social housing' to pick out council and housing association provision on the grounds that this appellation somehow stigmatises the occupants as 'welfare cases'. In the United

States of America, welfare housing is a commonly accepted term and denotes accommodation provided by welfare agencies, generally the city or federal authorities, on the basis of poverty rather than any other defining characteristic of housing need, whereas some so-called social housing providers in the UK continue to wish to be seen as meeting the needs of a broader cross-section of society than this. In 1993, the Labour Party decided against the term because it considered that it limited the role of such providers unduly. The term has entered the language; however, once one attempts to justify the term, it becomes increasingly difficult to arrive at a meaningful definition.

Social housing is generally thought of as relatively low-cost housing; that is, housing that the occupant should easily be able to afford, whether supported by state benefits wholly or partially or not at all. Until the late 1970s, the term – if it had been used then – would have applied almost exclusively to housing for rent provided by councils and, to a tiny extent, by associations. By the mid-1990s, with over one-quarter of the cash available to housing associations via the Housing Corporation being devoted to the grant support of housing for sale, such a definition would be unduly narrow.

Shared ownership and other forms of low-cost home ownership, promoted mainly through the housing association movement, have become increasingly important in providing homes for those who cannot raise the finance either to pay often high private rents or to enter the property market on a conventional basis. Now that housing organisations that are charities are allowed to provide such housing without conflicting with their aim of having to provide for those in 'necessitous' circumstances (the 'needy'), it seems that there is a case for regarding this form of provision as 'social'.

There is also a case for regarding some forms of private sector activity as providing social housing, albeit sometimes in a rather indirect or less obvious fashion. Since the mid-1980s, many councils have leased (rented) properties from private individuals for a short term, usually for less than 3 years, to use for housing homeless persons on a temporary basis until other solutions can be found. Housing associations also operate as management agents for private sector landlords, enabling those in severe housing need to satisfy their requirements in the short term. Renovation grants have been made available to owners of flats above commercial properties, which have been subsequently let to associations or managed by them for use as temporary housing. Those housed become tenants of the local authority or association, and as such could be regarded as 'social tenants' even though the property is not in public or association ownership, and in some cases,the full market rent, plus a management charge, is passed on to them and covered by housing benefit.

This brings the issue of subsidy into the discussion. Those people in private rented accommodation in the circumstances outlined above usually receive housing benefit. There is a very strong correlation between homelessness and poverty, since housing is a relatively expensive commodity, especially in areas such as London, where house prices are high in relation to average incomes, and where there is relatively strong demand for private rented tenure. Housing benefit is part of the income support system, designed to provide persons with sufficient income to live at just above an officially defined poverty level. Does it therefore follow that anyone receiving some form of state subsidy is a social housing client, regardless of whether the property has been built, or even provided, by an agency generally acknowledged to be in the social housing business, as previously defined? This is a tempting argument, until it is recognised that the majority of mortgage-holders also fall into this category in so far as they receive what amounts to a subsidy on their interest rate via the Mortgage Interest Tax Relief system. It is unlikely that anyone would wish to include most owner-occupiers in the category of social housing clients.

It seems, then, that it would be wrong to classify persons as social housing clients purely on the basis of whether they receive some form of personal subsidy. Is it, then, any more realistic to simply equate social housing with the sum of homes provided by councils and housing associations, whether built or acquired permanently or temporarily by them? If so, one has to countenance the designation of a wealthy tenant who still lives in a council flat, which may have been acquired at a time when housing need was not the primary determinant of allocation, as a social housing client purely because he or she happens to have that form of tenure.

One could say, in this instance, that the tenant is exercising a choice to remain in the social accommodation, and that that tenant is not therefore 'really' a social housing tenant. If this is admitted, and if the flat is inalienably a 'social home', one is driven to the conclusion that the person really should not be there, justifying moving them either by persuasion or coercion. This argument is highlighted in the article 'Welfare housing and the Minister'.

The former route has been attempted by many social housing landlords, through the media of 'portable discount' or 'tenant incentive' schemes, cash sums to help tenants purchase a home on the open market; and such people have been prioritised for shared ownership schemes in an attempt to release further social lettings without building unnecessarily. Indeed, this strategy has formed a central plank of central government housing policy in the 1990s. The latter route has not yet been attempted: there is no lawful clause in council or association tenancies which makes earnings or wealth beyond a given level grounds for possession. Yet if one were to be totally consistent, to say that social housing is that provided for those who cannot compete in the market, one would be driven to this somewhat draconian policy, unless one weakened the definition. Unless, that is, one simply and only looked at the status of the occupant at the time of entry into the system, in which case, what of those who entered before income (or the lack of it) was an issue in the provision of state or state-assisted housing?

Does one weaken the definition further to identifying it with housing provided from a time (to be defined presumably either by fiat or by historians) when, generally speaking, income was the dominant criterion upon which eligibility was decided? If so, from when? A problem arises here in so far that in general, local authorities have never imposed an income qualification on potential tenants at the point of entry; there is no statutory bar to such a qualification, although where it has been attempted it has long since been abandoned, owing largely to the controversy or complexity entailed. Some housing associations try to impose such a qualification as they claim it is in line with their charitable status; and shared ownership schemes such as Do It Yourself Shared Ownership do in fact impose a bar on those who can afford to buy conventionally. But income qualifications are currently rare in the social housing arena. This, it seems, cannot be the defining characteristic of social housing.

There appears to be no will on the part of providers to treat council and association provision as simply an arm of the social security system. To means-test tenants (or low-cost owners for that matter) on a regular basis to determine their continued eligibility has never been seriously proposed: what of those with fluctuating incomes? For how long would one have to sustain an income of a level judged by some bureaucrat or statute to be sufficient to buy or rent privately to become liable to eviction? Would one have a reciprocal right to re-enter social housing if one's income fell significantly in respect to the cost of housing? And what of the human consequences of frequent moves to satisfy a money-oriented view of state and voluntary housing? For as long as there is no will to identify this form of provision with welfare benefits, one must question the use of the term 'social housing' in this context.

Perhaps, then, social housing is so called because of the nature of its providers. The common view is that councils and housing associations are heavily subsidised by the public purse, and that therefore their products are equivalent to state provision. Maybe it is this that justifies the social housing label. Unfortunately this is not accurate. Whilst it is true that councils do receive some revenue subsidy to help with their running costs, the amount is declining and these days related largely to the cost of housing benefit, which applies to social and non-social tenants. Increasingly, the bill for housing running costs is laid collectively at the door of tenants through their rents – and that frequently includes meeting the loss incurred by granting rent rebates to poorer tenants.

Where councils still build, they have increasingly to borrow privately, like a company, and use money received from the sale of council homes to their tenants, to whom they are no longer allowed to grant mortgages. Where is the justification for identifying as a social housing organisation an organisation which has to operate, more or less, like a business and which receives minimal subsidy?

At this point it may be objected that council rents are much lower than commercial rents, and it is this which sets them apart from others as 'social' landlords. This is largely accidental. Councils have been building houses since the turn of the century. Rents are low largely because many of the loans taken out to build have been repaid, and costs are generally pooled

– that is, divided – amongst all tenants. Thus low rents are a historical accident – and they increased rapidly during the 1980s as a result of subsidy
withdrawal.

Although legislation states that council rents must be 'reasonable', there
is no table of limits, and in fact no clear definition of what 'reasonable'
means in this context. Is there anything unreasonable about market rents?
If there were, presumably some form of rent regulation would have been
retained for assured tenancies.

It is certainly true that housing associations used to charge 'fair' rents
which were much lower than market rents. Indeed, the whole purpose of
the pre-1988 housing association grant arrangement was to ensure that associations were able to conform to the fair rent regime. But this has been
abandoned, following the 1988 Housing Act, which has lowered grant rates
and forced associations to borrow privately, thus elevating new rents to levels which sometimes approximate to those found in the private sector and
which are in many cases unaffordable to those not in receipt of housing
benefit or on higher than average incomes. Fair rents have risen sharply in
the 1990s as rent officers have taken account of market factors when
reassessing such rent levels. Thus it would be wrong to identify social housing uncritically as 'low rent' housing or 'subsidised' housing.

The idea may be advanced that there is something distinctive about the
constitution of social housing providers that sets them apart from all others and justifies the label: that they were created by the central state to do
a specific job, to provide state (or social) housing. Councils are notoriously
creatures of statute, creations of Parliament, their powers and duties completely circumscribed by legislation. Housing associations are hidebound by
regulation and legislation, and monitored by the state's quango, the
Housing Corporation. But councils do not have to provide housing – the
1989 Local Government and Housing Act made this explicit – and housing
associations are purely voluntary bodies, and do not have to exist. Private
landlords are no less prisoners of legislation: they have to abide by the complexity of landlord–tenant law. Thus the view that councils and associations
are the state's housing providers is simplistic – even more so against the
background of compulsory competitive tendering, which entails the contracting out of services traditionally provided by councils, including the
housing function. The ability of public authorities to provide housing
directly varies with changes in legislation which follow political realign-
ments at the centre, and another article, 'Politics, property and people'
(p. 34), highlights the different policy orientations of the major political parties in the early 1990s. However, as the article makes clear, any proposal
for reviving public sector construction has to be weighed against broader
economic conditions and their management.

One of the distinctive features of social housing seems to be that it is
allocated on the basis of need rather than effective demand (that someone
can pay for it). Being able to afford it is not the main criterion for getting
it; at least, it should not be. Factors such as poor existing accommodation,

overcrowding and homelessness are far more significant. In other words, the commodity is rationed by some mechanism which is set apart from the market. In a sense, it is there to correct, or in recognition of, a dysfunction in the market economy. It is perhaps this feature which truly justifies the term 'social housing'. But this is true only at the point of entry. Consistency demands that, if we wish to hang on to need as the defining characteristic, we have to accept that some tenanted council housing is not social housing: that some tenants are social housing tenants and some are not. This is extremely clumsy, and could be stigmatising.

It seems, then, that the search for a clear, unambiguous definition of social housing which avoids the simplicity of simply equating it with that which housing associations and councils provide is doomed to failure. However, by exploring the notion, we have identified several interesting aspects of that provision. They can be summarised as follows:

- It is provided by councils and housing associations, either directly or indirectly.

- It is provided in the main to those who cannot compete in the marketplace at the point of entry, even though there are generally no 'income qualifications' imposed.

- It is provided on the basis of need rather than effective demand.

- Its occupants may be eligible for personal subsidy. It so happens that this is increasingly the case.

- It was at one time associated with heavy public sector subsidy.

- It can be for rent or for sale on 'low-cost' terms.

It is essential to think critically about the definition of the terms used in this area, like any other subject, before using them. 'Social housing' is a term very easily and loosely used, but the concepts which it embodies are far too important to be gathered up in this simple way. Thinking about the terms in this way can help clarify one's thinking about the issue, and help one examine one's own stance towards it. No practitioner should have a neutral, uncritical view about something as vital as housing need and the way it has been addressed. It is part of the purpose of this book to foster such critical thinking, which is why we have started by examining a commonly held set of beliefs surrounding a glibly used, certainly overused, phrase.

1.2 Changes in social housing provision

It is the aim of this section to briefly chart the history of social housing provision and to identify significant themes. Greater emphasis will be placed on its more recent history: there are several excellent texts which deal with its origins. The central lesson is that such provision can be seen as attempts to resolve a series of perceived housing 'crises', and that it is impossible to understand policy unless one tries to get inside the mindset of the actors. This is easier said than done, because the analyst is trapped within the set of assumptions and modes of behaviour which constitute the society, or that portion of it, within which he or she lives. All historical interpretation, even that of the comparatively recent past, beyond the mere recitation of dates, owes as much to the creative imagination as to analysis, and cannot therefore be said to have the hard cutting edge of a natural science. Therein lies much of history's appeal.

1.2.1   Crisis 1: fear of diseases

Following the agricultural and industrial 'revolutions' during the eighteenth and nineteenth centuries respectively, the population of Britain increased rapidly, and became more concentrated in towns and cities. The agricultural revolution, characterised by enclosure – the rationalisation of land-holdings, improvement of crop yields, mechanisation, and consequent reduction in labour demand – led to 'push' migration: ex-agricultural workers seeking employment and homes in urban areas. The industrial changes of the early nineteenth century, with the replacement of the 'domestic' by the 'factory' mode of industrial organisation, served to further reduce the importance of the village as an economic unit, and gave great impetus to urban growth, especially in regions rich in exploitable natural resources such as coal and iron ore. Increasing urbanisation was accompanied by falls in mortality rates, which had become noticeable as far back as the seventeenth century, as a consequence of improved nutrition and medical techniques. By the second half of the nineteenth century, the process of urbanisation, in terms of both population distribution and economic character, was well advanced.

The social consequences of this wholesale geographical change were enormous, not least in housing terms. The towns and cities which mushroomed on the back of industrial expansion were universally ill-planned, if planned at all. Workers were housed in appalling conditions, apart from notable exceptions such as settlements provided by various philanthropic industrialists such as the soap magnate Lever (Port Sunlight on Merseyside) and the chocolate manufacturer Cadbury at Bournville, near Birmingham. There was no state provision: existing private rented accommodation became fearfully overcrowded, and housing built by factory owners was frequently wholly inadequate to meet even basic shelter needs.

Back-to-back terraced housing sharing a party wall to the rear, with little in the way of light or ventilation, was a typical product of the age. A consequence of insanitary, overcrowded housing was disease, often of a communicable variety: witness the cholera epidemic in London in the 1840s, and numerous outbreaks of typhoid, often originating from the poorer areas of cities. A lack of basic sewerage, and simple lack of segregation of incompatible land uses, aided the problem. By the 1870s, policy-makers, drawn from the rich and powerful, had begun to perceive that there was a serious public health problem associated with squalid living conditions, and were greatly exercised by the fear that such diseases might spread from the poorer areas to their somewhat more salubrious districts. This fear, rather than any concern for the health of working people, stimulated several Acts of Parliament which attempted to lay down basic housing design standards to try to avoid some of the root causes of disease.

Examples include the 1874 Artisan's Dwelling Act, which sought to outlaw the back-to-back, and numerous public health acts which attempted to lay down overcrowding standards. These Acts led to the demolition of considerable areas of slums, without any rehousing duty, leading to yet worse overcrowding, and an escalation of private rents in response to housing shortages.

There was some philanthropic provision in the wake of this approach – for example, those blocks built by the Guinness Trust in London – but the response was quite inadequate in relation to the scale of the problem, and provided accommodation only for the 'deserving' poor in stable work who could afford the rent without assistance. This can be identified as the start of the voluntary housing movement exemplified by today's housing associations. It is not my intention to provide an in-depth historical analysis – a bibliography is provided for the interested reader – but the upshot of this activity was to create a *cordon sanitaire* between the 'great unwashed' and the better-off, who, with improvements in transportation, were seeking housing out of the inner city, out of the zone of transition 'invaded' by migrants seeking employment and living in rooming-houses converted from the homes of the great and the good by speculators.

The 1890s saw the first wave, albeit a small one, of local authority building, notably on the part of Chamberlain's Birmingham City Council, and the newly formed London County Council. Courtyard blocks in Bethnal Green are still standing and are an interesting testament to these reforms. These blocks were built as a public health measure, and were vastly superior to anything provided by the private sector for working people. But, as stated previously, the initiative was relatively insignificant because of a general belief that the state should not intervene in housing provision except where absolutely necessary – a *laissez-faire* attitude which permeated Victorian thought.

By 1914, the crises of poor housing conditions and inadequate supply still existed, although the precedent set by some local authorities at least started a line of thought suggesting that there was a place for social housing provision.

1.2.2 Crisis 2: fear of revolution

The 1914–18 war was a European catastrophe: conscription had mobilised the working men of its nations in a futile struggle for hegemony. It also saw the end of tsarist Russia, swept away by a violent *coup d'état* by the

Bolsheviks in 1917, which was given foundation by significant mass discontent resulting not only from the Russian war strategy but also from previous abortive land reforms under the reformer Stolypin and from the lack of basic foodstuffs, together with other privations. At home, the Liberal government of Lloyd George sought to lay the foundations of state welfare by devising a national pensions scheme and promised 'homes fit for heroes' for the returning troops – those who were left. It is an indictment of the public health standards and inadequate housing provision of the time that over 30 per cent of conscripts were found unfit for military service. 'Homes fit for heroes' was as much a panic reaction to events in Russia as a thought-out housing strategy to genuinely assuage the conditions of the urban poor. Luckily the Allies were victorious; one hates to imagine what the consequences for the government and the ruling classes in general would have been if the disillusioned troops had returned not only to the squalor which they had left, but also to a demoralised, defeated nation. Presumably there would have been the sort of anarchy which reigned in Germany between 1918 and 1920.

During the war, the government had sought to assuage housing discontent on occasions such as in its response to the 1915 Glasgow rent strike, when private landlords sought to hike up rents in the absence of bread-winners. This led to the first attempts at rent control, perhaps motivated by the desire to keep war production going.

The scale of the war and the resources needed to fight it entailed national planning in many areas previously untouched by the state: food rationing, state factories to produce munitions, and plan-making in general on a scale previously unguessed at. State intervention had become a necessity to co-ordinate the war effort; perhaps it was the necessities of war which made the notion of state involvement respectable, albeit still to be treated with suspicion.

In 1919, the first Housing Act was passed, which gave councils the power to apply the product of a penny rate towards the construction of municipal housing to generous standards, with the state providing the difference. This was the beginning of subsidised housing. Housing produced was revolutionary: the so-called Tudor Walters houses, named after a committee established by Parliament to establish housing design standards, were some of the largest yet seen, with separate living and dining rooms, kitchens and inside bathrooms and toilets. These have been amongst the quickest to be sold under the Right to Buy, surely an indication of popularity! The influence of Ebenezer Howard and the Garden City movement should be mentioned, in that his ideas informed aspects of the Tudor Walters brief regarding house design and estate layout. However, from the early 1920s onwards, these standards were diluted by successive governments; subsidies were reduced, and it was generally thought that the rise of owner-occupation, brought about by the expansion of the building societies movement from 1925 through enabling legislation, would make large-scale local authority provision unnecessary. The immediate threat of revolt had been avoided by a package of welfare measures including a modicum of state housing: the crisis had passed.

1.2.3 Crisis 3: war damage

Owing to aerial bombardment, the 1939–45 war entailed destruction on a massive scale. Inner city areas, with their close mix of essential factories and dense housing, were targeted in an attempt to destroy the industrial base and so disable Britain's war effort, forcing the country to sue for peace. Towards the end of the war, and for a period afterwards, a major housing policy aim was the construction of temporary accommodation to house those displaced by enemy action. This was facilitated in the main by the provision of prefabricated dwellings, fabricated in factories and assembled on site. Some of these still remain, and are often popular with their inhabitants.

The war provided an opportunity not only for ingenious stop-gap approaches such as prefabs, but for the wholesale clearance of insanitary inner city slum areas, the reconstruction of existing towns and cities along planned lines, and the creation of wholly new settlements or developments around small existing cores, planned to meet contemporary social and economic requirements. The Second World War had spawned a massive bureaucracy, and had made public planning on a vast scale respectable; and Beveridge's health and welfare state reforms were unquestionably a consequence of the perceived success of state planning in a crisis. It could also be argued that, once set in motion, such a machine is hard to stop, and the rehousing and planning programmes of the 1940s and 1950s are to some extent a reflection of the momentum built up during the war years.

The construction of new and expanded settlements following the 1947 New Towns Act such as Stevenage, Harlow and Hemel Hempstead, the slum clearance and municipal building projects of the 1950s and 1960s, and a comprehensive town and country planning system must be seen as part of a package of state-ism following largely from the crisis management of the war years. Other aspects included nationalisation of key industries, the emergence of a modern welfare state and the proliferation of government and its agencies, which now reached into every aspect of life. State planning had and provision had become respectable, and a consensus developed across party lines that this was the only rational way to organise the nation's affairs.

The uniformity of planned towns, the design of tower blocks and estates, the construction of a rationalised road network to meet the needs of a new, mobile population, and the expansion of local government powers and duties can be seen as the tangible proof of the trend towards centralism consequent upon the management of conflict. Such momentum has been dissipated only in the last two decades of the twentieth century.

By the mid-1960s, it was generally considered that the crisis of insufficient housing and poor conditions had largely been solved. Once more, it

was felt that the growth in incomes consequent on economic growth and
the burgeoning of owner-occupation would ensure that decent housing was
within the reach of all.

1.2.4   Crisis 4: the discovery of homelessness

The issue of homelessness was highlighted after the Second World War
through the squatting of ex-service camps and seaside holiday flats during
the winter, as well as vacant flats in fashionable areas of London, in
response to housing shortage. But it was the screening of the television play
Cathy Come Home in 1967 and the subsequent founding of SHELTER, the
national campaign for the homeless and badly housed, which spurred
national awareness of the problem, although it took 10 years for legislation
forcing local authorities to house at least the more vulnerable homeless to
come about.

Prior to the passage of the 1977 Housing (Homeless Persons) Act, homeless persons were dealt with by welfare departments, the forerunner of
social services; the issue was seen as a social rather than a housing shortage problem. Many authorities housed mothers and their children in hostels apart from their spouses, subjecting inmates to cruel and unnecessary
rules, thereby prompting protests and defiance which caught national attention in several cases. For example, the squatting by husbands in a homeless
persons' hostel run by Kent County Council made national headlines and
provoked television and radio coverage, engendering a movement to abol-
ish separate hostels and leading to that council abandoning its policies.

Campaigning organisations like SHELTER, SHAC (Shelter Housing Aid
Centre, now part of SHELTER) and CHAR (Campaign for the Homeless
and Rootless) have been greatly helped by the development of the mass
media, which are able to sensationalise an issue and bring it to a vast audience. Homelessness has always been an issue, but it is hard to understand
why the mid-1970s should have produced such a significant reform unless
that move is seen as a government reaction to public disquiet fuelled by
the media. Over the intervening years, it is an issue which has remained
current, providing material for television documentaries and dramas,
although some of the programmes have served to foster stereotypical views
of 'the homeless', especially in relation to single-parent families, leading to
ill-informed policy initiatives and needless reviews of the legislation without adequate statistical back-up. It is the widespread public realisation of
the squalor of bed and breakfast establishments as much as the unacceptable cost of using this last resort which has led governments to steer local
authorities away from this provision and towards the greater utilisation of
self-contained private accommodation.

Homelessness relates to a number of factors, some of which relate to societal changes, although these have often been overstressed. It is a combination of earlier family-formation, rising expectations, changing lifestyles and
the high price of private rented and owner-occupied accommodation,

together with inadequate output of affordable housing, which explains the phenomenon rather than personal inadequacy or fecklessness, as will be argued later. A clear indication that policy initiatives are driven by what policy-makers believe to be public perception can be obtained by considering the street-sleeping initiatives of the early 1990s, designed to eliminate the highly visual, disturbing and media-friendly phenomenon of people of all ages, some very young, sleeping in shop doorways in the capital. Rudimentary hostels, a degree of life-skills training and some move-on accommodation were provided; and the 1989 Children Act imposed a new duty on social services authorities to find accommodation for vulnerable young people, especially those discharged from care institutions. Could the government have been shamed into concern not only by the work of pressure groups such as National Children's Homes, Barnardos, SHELTER and Save the Children, but by the BBC's Esther Rantzen and her championship of homeless youngsters in London in the immensely popular *That's Life* programme?

It is sad but probably true to say that, in today's society, situations do not become issues, and issues do not become crises, until they are packaged as such by the media. Unfortunately, although fashions and interest in events change, the underlying problems do not, and the danger in policy-making as a reaction to the vagaries of public opinion stimulated by the box in the corner is that solutions will be quick-fix, designed for maximum visual impact, and therefore probably temporary or inadequate in nature through not having been adequately thought through.

1.2.5 Crisis 5: an economy out of control

During the late 1970s, there were a series of economic crises caused mainly by currency destabilisation, and exacerbated by industrial action following the erosion of the value of money in real terms by double-figure inflation. The 'winter of discontent' of 1978, characterised by strikes in the public services, led to the collapse of the Labour administration, and to a perception that economic management required re-examination.

It was a desire on the part of governments of varying political complexions to stabilise the economy by controlling expenditure which led to the introduction of the 'cash limits' system, whereby each head of public expenditure is given spending ceilings on an annual basis, replacing a 'volume-based' system where the amount of central cash was determined by measured need rather than provision being determined by cash available. Planning within such constraints, and shrinkage in real terms of several public sector programmes, has been a hallmark of economic policy since the late 1970s.

Cash limiting was legitimised by the monetarist theories of Milton Friedman, which view money as any other commodity: it loses its value under conditions of excess supply. Governments have used various levers to attempt to restrict the amount of money in circulation, to avoid the

Fig. 1.1 Victorian terraces, Cricklewood, London

Fig. 1.2 Systems-built concrete housing, Swansea

hyperinflation and consequent economic destabilisation of earlier decades by seeking to influence interest rates, increasing indirect taxation and limiting public sector programmes.

In housing terms, the desire to control inflation through monetary measures has found expression in a sustained reduction in public housing capital programmes since the early 1980s, cuts in real terms in revenue account

Fig. 1.3 Tower blocks, West London

subsidies frustrated only by a soaring housing benefit bill, reduced housing association grants with consequent reliance on private sector finance, very tight spending permission and borrowing constraints, and increasingly severe limitations on councils' ability to spend capital receipts realised from the enforced sale of council housing under the Right to Buy. Consequences have included increased rents, often at rates exceeding inflation, in both council and housing association sectors, longer waiting lists, greater housing stress including homelessness, and latterly attempts to restrain social security spending, including moves to cap housing benefit. Housing policy can be understood only against the background of collective fear of inflation, and the rejection of electorally unpopular fiscal controls over the money supply such as raising direct taxation.

A general belief that limited public funds could produce more if used by organisations either within the private sector or adopting business methodologies has grown up with the public sector cash restraint already referred to. The belief that private enterprise is inherently more efficient than state institutions has been expressed through privatisations, compulsory competitive tendering for council functions, the transfer of council housing to housing associations which have adopted business methodologies and structures and which engage with the private sector, and latterly the creation of local housing companies which remove public housing organisations from the constraint of the public sector borrowing requirement but which also underline belief in the business culture.

Fig. 1.4 Bed and breakfast hotels, Kensington

1.3   Recent themes in social housing

The scene having been set for housing developments over the past century, it is necessary to focus on trends and themes over the past decade or two to understand the present position of social housing policy and provision.

The 1980s was a decade of great change in the social housing arena. A number of dominant themes became apparent, of interlinking significance.

1.3.1   Council house sales

The 1980 Housing Act will be remembered principally for introducing the Right to Buy, enabling public sector tenants of 3 years standing to purchase their homes at a discount starting at 33 per cent. The legislation is now contained within Part 5 of the 1985 Housing Act. Subsequently, discounts have been increased, a form of shared ownership introduced (now abandoned), and latterly a rent-to-mortgage scheme implemented to consolidate the initiative. By 1994, nearly one and a half million households in the UK had taken advantage of this right, helping to boost owner-occupation to 67 per cent of all tenures by that year. This has been one of the largest privatisations to take place. By 1992 1.45 million sales had taken place, but that year saw the lowest number of sales since the start of the programme. Billions of pounds have been raised as a result, many authorities have become debt free as a result of applying receipts from sales to paying off housing and other loans, and the social geography of some urban areas has changed beyond recognition. The Right to Buy has confirmed council tenure as housing of last resort: much of the most popular stock has already been sold.

The Right to Buy and associated policy has had mixed success. Take-up by tenants of houses, especially in shire districts, was initially strong: the early 1980s saw significant house price rises, and many were attracted by the thought of buying their home, waiting for a few years until the liability to repay part of the discount lapsed, selling the house at a considerable surplus and trading up. The Right to Buy must therefore have increased the personal wealth of many, and assisted the 'filtering up' process. Flats were a less attractive proposition, with their relatively lower resale values, and liability to pay service charges which were frequently higher than expected. The policy response, under the 1985 Housing Act and the 1986 Housing and Planning Act, was to increase the discount floor to 40 per cent and the maximum to 70 per cent, as well as to increase the discount floor on houses to the current 32 per cent after only 2 years' public sector tenure; but bad publicity over the lack of a resale market, compounded by the cost of major repairs, has led to a slump in this area despite the financial inducements mentioned above.

The 1984 Housing and Building Control Act, incorporated under the 1985 Housing Act, introduced a right to shared ownership, whereby tenants who could not afford to raise a mortgage to cover the difference between the discounted valuation and any deposit that could be raised could purchase a minimum 25 per cent interest in the property and pay rent to reflect the council's remaining interest. Having purchased the initial share, the tenants could buy remaining portions in 'tranches' of a minimum of 12.5 per cent (a process known as staircasing), with the option to buy the remainder or 'staircase out' in due course when income allowed a further mortgage advance. Take-up was disappointingly low, and the scheme was abandoned as a result of the 1993 Leasehold Reform, Housing and Urban Development Act.

This 'low-cost home ownership' initiative was replaced by Rent to Mortgage in 1994 as a result of the same Act. Essentially, this involves the tenant acquiring their home on payment of an amount supportable by rent payments converted into mortgage instalments. The process of working out the size of loan which any given revenue sum (for example, rental amount) can support (that is, treating that sum as an instalment of principal and interest) is known as capitalisation. The difference between the valuation minus Right to Buy discount and the capitalised sum is treated as an interest-free loan, repayable on the death of the purchaser, or on resale. No rent or any other consideration is payable in respect of the difference, and the purchaser assumes the rights and obligations of a full owner-occupier. Only secure tenants who are not on housing benefit and would not be eligible for it if they applied are able to take part in the scheme, which is also subject to property value limits. By the end of 1994, only two Rent to Mortgage transfers had taken place, although some £400 000 had been spent by the Department of the Environment on publicity for the scheme.

It is generally accepted that the Right to Buy and associated initiatives have run out of steam. No 'right to rent' has been implemented for those unlucky enough to default on mortgages taken out to finance their share of owner-occupation!

1.3.2   Local authority housing finance

As suggested previously, it is important to connect housing finance with the general management of the economy. Although cash limiting was introduced across the public sector in 1976/77, the system established under the 1980 Local Government, Planning and Land Act represented a significant development. Councils now had to bid for spending permission, more tightly constrained than previously, against a framework of a nationally determined cash limit. Their plans for capital spending programmes – Housing Investment Programme submissions – were to be judged against a system of housing needs scores, the Generalised Needs Index (GNI). Tight constraints on borrowing levels were introduced, and a system of scheme cost limits to attempt to secure value for money – the Admissible Cost Limit regime – was used to further restrict loan subsidy available, signalling the end of generous Parker Morris standards (*see* p. 214) as authorities attempted to stay within limits. Parker Morris had been abandoned as a mandatory condition of subsidy the previous decade.

The new system also addressed the issue of capital receipts, boosted by the Right to Buy. Previously, under voluntary sales schemes, there were no restrictions on reinvestment. Now, local authorities could use only 50 per cent of receipts to support capital works in the first year realised, the rest being held in bank accounts and released only gradually over a number of years, a process known aptly as the cascade.

The intention was to prevent large-scale public expenditure, which it was thought would fuel inflation, and to encourage councils to redeem debts. The proportion of receipts which could be used in any one year declined over the next nine years to only 20 per cent. Against a background of credit control, this made it increasingly difficult to deliver feasible house building programmes and prompted a rush of creative accountancy measures to avoid the regulations. Because the rules on capital expenditure were so strict, authorities tried to redefine many activities – for example certain forms of improvement – as revenue to maximise their use of receipts. Every year, new circulars were issued by the Department of the Environment (D.o.E.) to plug loopholes: every year ingenious solutions were found, until finally a revised regime was enacted in 1990 as a result of the 1989 Local Government and Housing Act, which explicitly defined what councils could and could not count as capital. The same Act further restricted the use of receipts, so that henceforth, councils could use only 25 per cent of their housing receipts and 50 per cent of land sales towards capital projects, with the rest being frozen or applied to debt redemption. The cascade was thereby abolished, and the end of large-scale municipal housing development signalled.

Council Housing Revenue Accounts (HRAs) had remained in similar form since their inception in 1936. (Council finance is dealt with in Chapter 2.) The 1985 Housing Act merely incorporated the old system, although subsidy changes were legion. Subsidy to help councils repay loan debt and meet management and maintenance costs, with the object of keeping rents down, was based on estimates based upon actual council expenditure and income, and started to fall away with the increasing significance of interest from Right to Buy receipts. This had the effect of liberating council rent policy from central influence. The system became highly complex, with arcane methods of settling subsidy on different forms of scheme. The more complex it became, the easier it was to use to municipal advantage. At the time, it was also possible to make contributions to the HRA from the rates fund, an internal subsidy which helped keep rents comfortably within the reach of most tenants; and rent rebate losses were met virtually pound for pound by separate Department of Health and Social Security payments.

In an attempt to batten down subsidy settlements, the government erected a wholly new, simplified system from 1990, under the 1989 Local Government and Housing Act. The HRA was more tightly redefined, with greater provision for central interference and control as to levels of input (for example, restrictions on the amount of interest which could be credited) and, significantly, the ending of rate fund contributions; the new HRA was to be a business-type account funded largely by rents. (No wonder no attempt was made to fix rent levels centrally, although this had been tried in 1974 under the abortive 1972 Finance Act, which attempted to force councils to charge 'fair rents', in general higher than hitherto.) This exclusion was known as 'ring-fencing', although it was one-way: under certain circumstances, councils found themselves forced to make payments from their HRA to their General Fund (a term that will be explained in Chapter 2 – *see* p. 41). Now, who was subsidising whom?

The new subsidy system established under the same Act provoked much criticism. 'HRA subsidy' would now be based not on actual but on notional deficits on the basis of government assumptions about income and expenditure, crucially rents and management and maintenance costs. The separate Rent Rebate Subsidy was abolished, as the 'notional' HRA used for calculation purposes now included assumed losses incurred by granting rent rebates. Since this was now just another figure on the debit side, overestimates of income meant that many authorities now received nothing whatever towards their rebate losses, meaning that poorer tenants were effectively being subsidised by their better-off neighbours. The housing benefit system as applied to council tenants had changed from being a part of the national income support network to a version of the local Poor Law regime as applied in the nineteenth century! Government justified this by urging that the discipline of the new regime stimulated cost-effectiveness and efficiency. However, rents in many authorities soared as a result of these changes.

The late 1980s also saw the abandonment of the old domestic property rate system in favour of the personal community charge or 'poll tax', which was levied on individuals. It was implemented in Scotland in 1989 and England and Wales the following year, but violent protests and mass non-payments led to its abandonment 3 years later, and the resurrection of an updated rates system – the council tax – just 3 years later. Restrictions on Revenue Support Grant (which supports general council expenditure) and the 'capping' of (setting an upper limit on) community charge and council tax bills by the government led to cuts in services in many areas, and reductions in expenditure on housing aid and homelessness services, traditionally funded from councils' General Fund.

By 1993, the above-mentioned restrictions had prompted over 30 authorities to give up their role as housing providers, and sell their assets wholesale to housing associations under 'large-scale voluntary transfer' arrangements. They also led to pressure for the formation of 'local housing companies', whereby local authority housing could be excluded from the realm of public expenditure controls.

Rather more successful, after a fiasco in 1983, was the unification of rent rebate and rent allowance systems, social security and other cases under a single rule, ending the 'better-off' problem. Prior to that date, because of different methods of assessing housing benefit claimants on supplementary benefit (later Income Support) and others, many found themselves marginally better off out of work than in. Local authorities were now given the lion's share of processing and decision-making responsibility. The system was further refined in 1988 under the 1986 Social Security Act. Since then, largely owing to the deregulation of private sector rents, and a new financial regime for housing associations forcing them to charge higher rents for properties constructed after April 1989, the housing benefit bill has reached worrying proportions. Housing benefit expenditure almost trebled from around £4 billion in 1986/87 to around £11 billion (projected) in 1995/96 (source: *Social security: The government's expenditure plans 1992–93 to 1994–95*, Cm 1914). In the late 1980s, attempts were made to cap housing benefit payments, but these were abandoned, and replaced by limits on housing benefit subsidy payable to local authorities. The size of the bill prompted renewed efforts to cap payments in the mid-1990s, and part of the receipts from large-scale voluntary transfers were commandeered and used to meet some of the costs. There remains great uncertainty over how to stabilise this expenditure.

1.3.3 Housing associations

The 1980 Housing Act conferred secure tenancies on the vast majority of housing association tenants. The movement was then much less significant than now. Tenants were guaranteed fair rents considerably below market levels. Grants were structured to ensure that associations could guarantee these rent levels, and revenue subsidies were given to further assist them. Public sector loans on preferential terms were made to further ensure affordability. This financial assistance was forthcoming from the Department of the Environment. The Housing Corporation had a registration, regulative and promotional role only. In 1981, housing association tenure accounted for just 2 per cent of total tenure, roughly 420 000 households.

Just 11 years later, the sector had increased by almost 50 per cent, so that by December 1992 there were around 655 000 households accommodated in this sector, against a 24 per cent decline in council tenure over the same period (source: *Housing and construction statistics*). The decade saw dramatic changes in the nature and scope of the voluntary housing movement, largely as the result of the 1988 Housing Act. This abolished fair rents for new properties developed after February 1990, and introduced a wholly new grant regime, not based on the principle of securing fair rents, but resting instead on the basis of strictly applied national cash limits and reduced grants, to be mixed in the main with private finance. Grants were made on the basis of ideal costings based on an assessment of typical regional building costs, and set at the beginning rather than the end of the development, thereby transferring the risk of cost overruns and thus higher than expected rents to the associations. The Housing Corporation became the grant-making authority, with an annual budget voted by Parliament, and was reformed, being given new powers and duties connected with scheme appraisal and supervision.

The upshot of the 1988 Act reforms was generally higher rents for new tenancies, a steep learning curve for association development staff and committees, which now had to deal with high finance, and a reduction in space standards as associations struggled to produce affordable housing within tight limits, often having to use their reserves to guarantee this end. Associations began to develop more home ownership schemes, partly motivated by the need to cross-subsidise rented developments.

Rising rents have trapped many tenants in poverty, such that they would have to earn significantly more than income support to find themselves any better off, after taking travel and other costs into account. There is a clear connection here between the housing benefit bill and the new financial regime.

During the 1990s, despite housing associations being seen as the new providers of social housing, output actually declined. Whilst informed commentators stressed the need for up to 100 000 new homes in the sector annually, figures were consistently below this.

The 1980s and 1990s also saw the movement being seen by central government as the natural successor to local authorities in ownership and management, with large-scale voluntary transfers of stock, and particularly the invitation to bid for housing management contracts under compulsory competitive tender. It is difficult to see how the movement can truly provide affordable social housing in the long term without a radical overhaul of the system; perhaps the rising benefit bill will yet force reconsideration.

1.3.4   Housing needs and homelessness

In 1980 council tenure was generally perceived as a genuine choice rather than housing of last resort, but because of the factors already mentioned, by the end of the 1980s it had become severely rationed. The tendency for greater precision in allocation had been given impetus by a series of reports, including the 1969 Cullingworth Report, which urged authorities to adopt priority systems, but the dominant route of obtaining public sector tenancies at the beginning of the decade was the waiting list. Since then, most councils have implemented 'points systems' which attempt to weigh the relative housing needs of applicants to decide who gets what, where and when. Some have now abandoned this method, as homelessness has increased and forced their hand. Many housing associations now use similar priority methods.

The 1957 Housing Act forced councils to consider the needs of specific groups, although not in any specific order, when deciding allocation. These included large families, homeless households, those with special housing needs and people in unsatisfactory accommodation. The development of points systems stimulated great investment in information technology to resolve this issue. During the 1970s it became apparent that some ethnic groups were being treated less favourably than others in some areas, and the 1976 Race Relations Act has been used on occasions to redress indirect and sometimes direct discrimination in this respect.

But the greatest pressure has come in the form of the need to resolve homelessness. The 1977 Housing (Homeless Persons) Act, whilst it did not directly entail that local authorities favour homeless people above others in granting their tenancies, had this effect in practice. In proof of this, Department of Environment Annual Expenditure Plans reveal that whereas in 1982/83 homeless households took up only 19 per cent of new tenancies, this figure had risen to 46 per cent less than 10 years later in 1991/92. In brief, the Act imposed new duties on councils to investigate the circumstances of those found to be homeless, and in priority cases to secure suitable accommodation, which in most cases meant ensuring that priority was given to this group either in the form of direct rehousing or via nominations to housing associations. It also led to the wholesale use of often unsatisfactory and relatively expensive temporary accommodation stopgaps such as bed and breakfast. Giving housing aid and advice became an important local authority function, both to investigate and to prevent homelessness, and the Act rapidly generated reams of case law and controversy. On the back of largely unsubstantiated claims of abuse of the system, of 'queue-jumping' and fecklessness, the government instituted a review of the legislation in 1993. This entailed that all housing applicants, whether homeless or applying through more conventional routes such as points systems, should be treated equally, with the implication that many homeless households would have to spend time in temporary accommodation as a matter of course before their cases could be considered alongside others for rehousing.

The housing practitioner should ask whether increasing homelessness is really a function of changing societal attitudes or rather the continued decline in the availability of affordable accommodation. Around two million council homes have been sold, with restrictions on the use of cash receipts for replacement. Other financial constraints have spelt the virtual end of new council provision, although there are sound arguments to support renewed support for such construction: see the Article 'Politics, property and people' (p. 34) for further discussion. In 1982/83, 27 000 council homes were completed, with the number declining to just 7000 in 1991/92. The housing association movement is producing fewer homes every year. Owner-occupation, despite creative initiatives such as shared ownership, is still relatively expensive, and there have been many repossession casualties of the rapid interest rate rises of the late 1980s and early 1990s. All this is against the background of a boom–bust cycle in the economy. The UK population has been virtually static over the past decade: increased homelessness cannot be blamed on population or household-formation changes. In 1982, well into the course of the new legislation, 76 471 households were accepted as homeless in the UK: 9 years later, this figure had risen to 178 133 (source: D.o.E., Scottish Office, Welsh Office). Numbers in temporary accommodation in England alone had risen over the same period from 9340 to 59 930 over the same period (source: *Homelessness statistics,* D.o.E.). The cost to the nation is enormous: in the early 1990s, it was estimated that it cost on average £15 000 to keep a family in bed and breakfast for a year. Official statistics reveal that in 1992, 42 per cent of households accepted had become homeless because parents, friends and relatives were no longer willing to accommodate them, surely revealing overcrowding and housing shortage. Only 17 per cent of such acceptances related to relationship breakdowns; it is therefore otiose to blame the increases on changes in social behaviour.

Against this background, it seems odd that so much store should be placed upon the rationalisation of lettings policies to achieve a 'fairer' distribution. Rearranging the deck chairs on a sinking liner will do little or nothing to save the ship.

Although the Children Act 1989 has done something to relieve the plight of young homeless people, especially those released from care, the legislation is exclusive rather than inclusive. The homelessness figures do not reflect the needs of single people, childless couples and others who do not fit into the neat pigeonholes of priority need; thus the problem is much worse than that recorded. Squatting and travelling is often a response to lack of accommodation through traditional routes rather than a genuine lifestyle choice.

In summary, the consequences of the rise of homelessness in terms of human misery and cost to society are clearly unacceptable, and policy decisions will have to be taken sooner rather than later to resolve the issue. A solution will not come about simply by redefinition.

1.3.5   Tenants as customers and custodians

Prior to the 1980 Housing Act, there was no standard agreement for local authority tenants. Rights were far fewer, management was more paternalistic, and evictions easier. The 1980 Act delivered a number of improvements via its Tenant's Charter provisions, standardising contracts, conferring greater rights to redress, and introducing the Right to Buy. These rights were enhanced by the 1985 Housing Act, and widened further by subsequent amendments to that Act. There are now rights to information in a clear format, and to tenant involvement, to the extent that several co-operatives have been formed which have taken over the management and sometimes the ownership of local authority stock, facilitated to an extent by agencies such as the Priority Estates Project, the Tenants Participation Advisory Service, and many housing association agencies dedicated to co-operative formation and advice. The Citizen's Charter of the early 1990s stimulated further enhancements to such rights. Tenants have also been given a say in the transfer of their homes to other organisations, and latterly in the nature of contracted-out management arrangements under compulsory competitive tender, if not in the final selection of contractor. It seems that tenants are now to be regarded as customers, with the full range of rights one would expect as a consequence of paying for a service.

It is difficult to say exactly why these changes have come about, but easier to justify them. First, owing to the revised subsidy arrangements for council housing, tenants' rents are in a majority of cases the dominant source of income for running the housing service; justice therefore demands that tenants' have a greater say in service delivery. Second, the increase in tenants rights has been used to foster privatisation through the Right to Buy, and to sanction transfers to housing associations and housing action trusts through their votes. Encouragement to collectively opt out of the council domain was also given impetus under the Tenant's Choice element of the 1988 Housing Act, although this initiative has hardly borne fruit.

Although tenants now have more information than ever before, there is no logical link between this and action. Indeed, it could be argued that the central failings of municipal housing may be hidden beneath the welter of information contained within Council Performance Indicators, reports provided to tenants on the annual performance of their landlords in 1990 as a result of the 1989 Local Government and Housing Act. Such reports have been used as much to calibrate revenue and capital support as for their own sake – as indicators of performance for users; but at least the nature of such organisations is made more accessible. Given the necessity for council tenants to be consulted on management changes and ownership, this is an essential rather than an optional extra.

1.4 Summary

Social housing, then, has to be viewed against a broader background. Housing policy is not the central concern of government, and is subservient to economic policy. It is, however, a major element of public expenditure, and control over its capital and revenue aspects is therefore seen as crucial. If present trends continue, it is unlikely that there will be very much council housing outside inner cities and poorer rural areas, and that which there is will cater exclusively for the needy. Housing association rents will continue to rise to the point where the issue of housing benefit forces a rethink over the relationship between rent levels, private finance and grant levels. Homelessness will continue to be an issue, as supply falls short of need, and as private landlords increasingly seek more remunerative homes for their capital investment, a trend which has continued throughout the 1900s. Local authorities will eventually hand over their management roles to private contractors, sometimes formed by council staff, rather as has happened in many areas over refuse contracting, even though 80 per cent of bids were won by local authorities in the first round. All in all, unless there is a radical ideological shift, it is likely that the social housing sector will be smaller and much more residualised than now. Much depends upon political orientation, although in the mid-1990s there appeared to be a consensus developing in many areas, and broad agreement between the main parties over the future development of social policy, perhaps standardised by considerations of European Union regulation.

Another of the articles, at the end of this chapter, 'Social housing and the economic cycle' (p. 32), suggests that a reversal of the trend against municipal housing construction and greater assistance to associations in providing new housing might serve to strengthen the economy by evening out the cycle of recession and boom which has damaged the economy over the past decades. The stabilisation of the economy is a laudable aim, but need not necessarily be brought by public sector cash restraint, if such activity could promote economic growth both directly and indirectly. The social benefits which would arise from a greater commitment to the provision of affordable homes would more than justify renewed investment in the social housing sector.

Articles

1. 'Welfare housing and the Minister'

2. 'Social housing and the economic cycle'

3. 'Politics, property and people'

Welfare housing and the Minister

In his recent lecture at the London School of Economics ('Housing: the big issues', 4 March 1993), the Minister of Housing, Sir George Young, emphasised the welfare aspects of social housing. He suggested progressively replacing bricks and mortar subsidy with personal subsidy, on the grounds that it is better to use limited public finance to support the building of more new homes to house the poorest than to use it to depress rents generally, regardless of ability to pay. Affordability would relate to net rents – what tenants actually pay – rather than gross rents – rents prior to the application of personal subsidy. Subsidy in the form of housing benefit would go to those in greatest need, with higher rents encouraging others to seek homes in the marketplace. This argument was used to justify continued reduction in Housing Association Grant (HAG) rates and restraint on Housing Revenue Account (HRA) subsidy.

It might seem reasonable to target subsidy on the poorest rather than those able to do without it, and it certainly sits well with a low direct tax policy and restraint on public expenditure to curb inflation. As a further point, if local authority and housing association management practices can be improved to the extent that high standards of housing are guaranteed in those sectors, it seems unfair that their tenants should get away with generally low rents because of an over-generous bricks and mortar subsidy system, whilst many private sector tenants pay far more for lower standards. And it is certainly true that not all council tenants are poor.

If housing benefit were to take the strain of more realistic rents, why should policies stressing output at the cost of gross affordability not garner general support? More homes are surely required.

Several factors undermine this approach. Aspects of the housing benefit system have been proven to generate a poverty trap whereby one has to earn a considerable amount above income support for there to be any financial advantage in working as compared with complete dependence upon state assistance. This is due partly to the steep withdrawal rate of housing benefit: 65p for every £1 earned above the income support level. But government could ill afford to reduce this taper; to do so would add considerably to the public expenditure burden. In the presently depressed labour market, it is otiose to suggest that the poverty trap can be overcome by simply getting a well-paid job, and the government's opposition to a minimum wages policy further reduces the incentive to obtain work. The poor cannot be blamed for not wanting to become poorer. An inescapable consequence of reliance on personal housing subsidies is to keep people out of work, doing nothing to stimulate economic recovery and reinforcing an unhealthy dependency culture. There is therefore little justification for moving the balance of support towards personal subsidy, without wholesale revision of that system, which is not proposed.

What if such a policy were developed? One can envisage its logical outcome. Social housing would be treated as any other welfare benefit: qualification, both at the point of entry and for continued assistance, would depend upon the occupant's income and wealth at any one time. Presumably tenants would have to leave when their income exceeded a point related to their ability to afford market accommodation.

Anything else would be inconsistent with the total package of means-tested welfare benefits. Would living in social housing whilst earning above a given income be treated as fraud in the same way as cheating the social security system? Surely any other approach would be inconsistent.

However, such a policy would be obviously inhumane. The cost and emotional upheaval of enforced removal precludes the treatment of housing in the same way as cash benefits; and the argument surely demands the means-testing of mortgage interest tax relief, which would be politically infeasible. It is therefore completely unreasonable to opt for a subsidy system biased towards personal benefits.

Where does this leave the problem of output maximisation under conditions of limited public finance? A number of options exist to produce more affordable housing without over-concentration on personal subsidy. Why not allow housing suppliers to build on freely given land owned by government departments and possibly the crown, and to convert unused government buildings into homes at nil acquisition cost? With the contraction of the armed forces, Ministry of Defence properties could be freely granted for social housing purposes to councils and housing associations. Subsequent pooling of costs with other new-build projects would mean generally lower rents. There should be a land and property audit to at least allow examination of these options.

Such a policy would provide cheap housing which could be allocated partly on the basis of financial circumstances without trapping people in poverty, and would assist in the social and economic regeneration which is so badly needed today.

PSLG, April 1993

Addendum (October 1995)

Since this article was written, the Treasury announced that housing benefit will be 'capped' from January 1996, at levels considered reasonable. The capping is intended to encourage landlords in the private sector to reduce rents to affordable levels. This may reduce the size of the national social security bill – a concern highlighted in the article. Additionally, the government considered the introduction of rent controls on new housing association rents: the 'X factor', such that rents could rise only by the RPI (Retail Price Index) plus X per cent. Again, this was seen as a way of reducing social security expenditure, but has implications for housing association grant levels. If rents are limited, will grants rise to ensure that development costs can be financed, without false economies on the quality of the properties produced?

In 1995, the Minister for Housing was David Curry MP. Sir George Young was moved to the Treasury, and then to Transport, as Minister of State.

Questions

1. Why did Sir George Young suggest replacing bricks and mortar subsidies with personal subsidies?
2. What is the housing benefit poverty trap?
3. What is the logical outcome of treating social housing as part of the social security system?

Social housing and the economic cycle

Many commentators in the field of social housing and economics now agree that the boom–bust cycle which has characterised the post-war UK economy has been accentuated by the behaviour of the owner-occupied market. Remedies are less clear, but recent important research, including that undertaken by the Joseph Rowntree Foundation (Wilcox, 1993), suggests that a revitalisation of the private rented sector and greater commitment to social housing construction and renewal may form part of the recipe for economic stabilisation.

The contribution of owner-occupation to a damaging roller-coaster of booms and slumps has several aspects. The abolition of double mortgage tax interest relief in 1987 helped stimulate an upsurge in house purchase shortly before that move, abetted by relatively low interest rates and rising real incomes. This served temporarily to stimulate a credit boom not only in mortgage lending but generally, as the paraphernalia which goes with home-founding was often funded through loans. Additionally, equity leaked in the form of trading profits being used to buy consumer durables, stimulating a short-term consumption boom and injection of cash into the economy, and so inflationary tendencies for the later 1980s. Many of those purchasing did so not for nesting but investing.

Thus there was a degree of overheating in the economy, and Treasury attempts to reverse inflation by reducing the money supply and curbing credit took the form of interest rate increases, leading in turn to problems in business investment, and a wave of repossessions and default. Effective demand for house purchase fell, and a new phenomenon of negative equity turned what had seemed like certain wealth accumulation into a trap.

Lessons have been learnt from calamity. That lower interest rates and a growing perception that the recession is ending have not given rise to a significant upturn in the property market yet is evidence that houses are seen as homes rather than investments, and the over-consumption on the scale of the 1980s might be avoided in the 1990s. Nevertheless, ownership is still seen as an attractive, if not the only natural, form of tenure for security and potential capital gain, and considerable pent-up demand indicates that there may be a property boom shortly, with consequences already itemised. Memories are short, and perceptions not aided by a renewed government promotion of owner-occupation.

How, then, can the stimulus of the private rented sector and social housing help avoid the consequences of boom and bust? The relative shortage of private rented homes – private renting makes up less than 8 per cent of all tenures – forced those for whom it would be a logical choice – the young and economically mobile – into ownership, artificially inflating demand. An enhanced, attractive private rented sector would not only aid labour mobility but also cream off excess demand, thus avoiding excessive boom.

Because rents are paid from current income rather than credit, a buoyant private rented sector would not force interest rates up as demand for borrowing would not be subject to the sort of stimulus seen before. What is required is the fiscal stimulation of the sector through tax allowances to make it an attractive investment proposition without entailing outrageous rents. This would provide additional tax revenue. The building industry would also be revived by new building, conversions and improvements, again producing revenue for the Exchequer and jobs. This argument is based on the assumption that there are sufficient customers who would find the relative freedom of renting attractive, and also on the existence of accessible alternative investments for those forgoing ownership and the possibility of accumulating equity.

The social rented sector could also play a key part in economic stabilisation, although less directly. It is unlikely that this sector will be seen again as a genuine tenure choice rather than as a form of social support, as the notion of state support for preference rather than need is unfashionable and hard to justify. Therefore it is unlikely to be seen as a genuine alternative to owner-occupation. Its role economically would be to divert construction away from over-producing homes for ownership, which helped stimulate the last boom, whilst ensuring that the construction industry remains viable, along with the production of homes for private renting, with obvious economic advantages. A desirable side-effect of this would be the shortening of waiting lists and the elimination of much homelessness.

A case has been made for enhancing both private and social rented sectors for sound macro-economic reasons, but sight must not be lost of the principal reason for concern over housing issues, namely, that decent housing at affordable levels should be available to all, regardless of chosen type of tenure. Unfortunately, the argument for greater rented provision is likely to be won on an economic rather than an ethical basis, but the social end justifies its winning.

PSLG, July/August 1993

Questions

1. How does the instability of the house sales market affect the general economy?
2. Is it unrealistic to treat owner-occupation as an investment? If so, why?
3. How could the revival of the private and social rented sectors avoid the negative consequences of the boom–bust cycle?

Politics, property and people

The 1990 party conference season provides a timely opportunity to highlight the three main contenders' housing strategies. The Tories want 'Choice for all in housing', Labour see 'opening doors', while the Liberal Democrats are in waiting with 'housing: A time for action'. Brave-sounding titles on bold documents.

Expansion of housing choice underscores the Conservative proposals. Chris Patten, Secretary of State for the Environment, says owner-occupancy should be encouraged, and tenants should be given greater choice by breaking the council monopoly in renting, mainly by attracting private landlords by making letting more profitable. The Right to Buy, deregulation, the landlord tax-break Business Expansion Scheme and the 1988 Act Tenants' Choice measures are billed as beacons showing the way. The conversion of councils from providers to 'enablers' will continue, with an increased role for housing associations backed by predominantly private finance; although 'because there will still be generous government grants for development, rents will be held at levels within the reach of groups traditionally catered for by housing associations', which implies commitment to Exchequer assistance, albeit limited assistance.

Labour councils are criticised for poor management: Conservatives believe that the threat that tenants will choose other landlords under the 1988 provisions has forced such authorities to rethink their approach. The 87 per cent vote in favour of voluntary transfer in Newbury is cited as evidence that tenants welcome increased choice. Not surprisingly, Housing Action Trusts are given scant mention.

As for finance, use of capital receipts for enforced debt repayment is seen as financial prudence, and protests from some (Labour) councils are countered by indicating questionable cash management shown in 'unacceptably high levels of arrears'. The line on homelessness is that councils could save on bed and breakfast by reducing voids (empty properties) – it is mainly seen as a resource management problem, although social changes are partly blamed. It is claimed that more generous income support and housing benefit measures will somehow reduce youth homelessness. Finally, planning authorities are urged to take local need for cheaper housing into account when formulating policies.

Labour posits a 'fresh approach' to increase choices for those in housing need and 'create greater flexibility between owning and renting to banish the barriers between owners and tenants'. This will come through introducing new rights for all tenants, tackling homelessness by providing 'affordable' housing for all, increasing the supply of different types of good-standard accommodation, and reforming housing finance in order to increase help to tenants and poorer owners.

The government record on homelessness and declining social housing construction is slated, along with the impact on mortgages of a high interest rates policy. Part of the cost of reviving social housing would be met by letting councils use all their capital receipts for new building, although beyond this, for all the talk of 'meeting the challenge', Labour is cagey over promising extra Exchequer funding, taking on board the tax implications, and perhaps electoral credibility. Housing associations, however, will be receiving greater support through the Housing Corporation channelling funds from the Public Works Loan Board, presumably on favourable terms. The old antagonism towards voluntary housing seems to be dead.

Labour considers private tenants have been bruised by the 1988 Act, with expensive assured tenancies and restricted security. Reform means a new 'secure tenancy' conferring conditions similar to those of council tenants, with rights to affordable rents. Clearly, Labour does not see the private sector as a major vehicle of housing policy!

The Liberal Democrats see more scope for councils and housing associations in building, acquiring, improving and maintaining housing to meet the needs of those on low incomes – and make no bones that sufficient public cash should be forthcoming to meet these objectives. Thus greater levels of subsidy will be available to ensure that local authority and association rents are at levels which most can afford without receiving housing benefit.

A recent speech by Paddy Ashdown bravely passed this considerable bill to the taxpayer: but all credit to the Liberals in identifying low-cost housing as the solution to present levels of homelessness and housing stress. A major plank of Liberal policy is a commitment to 'housing cost relief', to replace housing benefit and mortgage interest tax relief systems, giving financial help for housing costs equitably – something long overdue, if posing interesting challenges to civil servants. A new sector of the rented market will be created attracting less subsidy than traditional council or voluntary provision – but higher rents would be offset by housing cost relief according to income.

In summary, no party is offering unequivocal support to councils as providers, and only the Liberals are willing to promise significantly higher levels of central investment in social housing. The policies differ widely, but it seems that housing has received the high profile it deserves. Let's hope it isn't forgotten amongst other pressing concerns at election time.

PSLG, November 1990

Addendum (October 1995)

Since the article was written, the property market has continued to slide, and the current Housing Minister, David Curry, has made it clear that he does not believe that owner occupation is superior to renting. Mortgage interest tax relief has been limited to 15 per cent on the first £30 000 borrowed, and is to be cut back further, although the role of housing associations in providing homes for owner-occupation is still supported, especially through the DIYSO (Do It Yourself Shared Ownership) initiative. The Business Expansion Scheme came to an end in March 1995. A White Paper was published in that year, setting out the government's agenda, including extending the Right to Buy to housing association properties in the form of a cash sum to tenants to buy their homes known as the Voluntary Purchase Grant, rules concerning the formation of local housing companies, to which council homes may be transferred, and wholesale revision of the homelessness legislation. The other parties have changed their housing policies marginally, with Labour admitting that the private rented sector has a significant role to play in meeting housing need, and offering support in the event of a Labour government, and supporting the notion of housing companies, but disagreeing with the government's stance on homelessness.

Questions

1. What were the main stated aims of Conservative housing policy in 1990?
2. What were the main accusations levelled at Labour-run housing authorities by the Conservative Party, and do you consider them to be reasonable?
3. In what major respects did the Labour and Liberal housing agendas differ?

2 Finance and housing

2.1 Introduction

Housing finance is thought by many students and practitioners to be a difficult area. It is true that mistakes can be costly, and failure to appreciate the scope of the subject can lead to uncreative policies. It is also the case that the goalposts, if not the entire pitch, have been moved rather more frequently than practitioners would wish over the past decade or two. But this should not stop the determined inquirer from seeking light. It is the purpose of this chapter to illuminate the system as it applies to local authorities and housing associations, and point to possible areas of reform in both capital and revenue systems.

2.1.1 Definitions

The terminology of finance is often arcane in the extreme: it is not the language of everyday life, unless one works in the City, or a finance department of a housing association or council. The easiest way to approach the subject is to consider one's own bank account and day-to-day financial dealings.

2.1.1.1 Capital

Capital operations involve the creation and adding to the value of assets. An asset is defined in accountancy as anything which will last for more than 1 year. Capital expenditure therefore involves spending money to create or improve items which will last for more than 1 year – which are relatively durable. House purchase is an example of capital expenditure, as is buying a car (probably). Capital income is income derived from the sale of assets. The study of capital operations involves examining ways of raising money to undertake capital works, their sale, and the limitations imposed on organisations by central government on such activities.

2.1.1.2   Revenue

Revenue operations also involve spending and receiving money, but on current items. Current account income and expenditure nicely illustrates revenue operations. For example, spending money on a repair and paying wages are both revenue operations, as is paying capital and interest on a loan on a periodic basis. The study of revenue operations involves examining income and expenditure accounts, the use of interest from money received from asset sales, subsidies received internally and externally, and the scheduling of loans, amongst other things.

2.1.1.3   Financing Capital Operations

Financing capital expenditure can be done in several ways, most of which find their reflection in policies adopted by housing organisations. Supposing you wished to buy a car. You could save up sufficient money from wages until the requisite amount was reached, and then buy it. Or you could raise a loan from a bank or building society, buy the item, and then pay back principal and interest over a term of months or years. Or you could put down a deposit from your savings, and raise a loan to cover the remainder. Or you could part-exchange the vehicle for another one, and pay the balance of the value. The last option is not available to housing organisations.

A loan is money advanced, repayable over a period or *term*. The charge for borrowing money is called *interest*. The sum borrowed, the loan sum, is called the *principal*. There are a variety of loans available. Some require the repayment of equal amounts of interest and principal over the term; so-called conventional repayment mortgages are of this form. Some require the payment of interest only over the term, with the borrower paying a *premium* which is invested in an assurance policy that hopefully will cover the loan sum (or principal) when it *matures* at the end of the term. This is on a life assurance basis, and this form of borrowing is available only to people, as only mortals can die. Endowment mortgages are of this form. Some loans allow the borrower to make lower payments in the early years on the basis of charging a reduced interest rate. Later in the term, the interest which was not charged is added to the loan, and repayments increase. This is the so-called deferred interest type of loan, and has proved attractive to housing associations and first-time buyers with expectations of rising salaries alike. A further form of '*LOW-START*' loan is the index-linked loan where repayments start at levels below conventional repayment loans, and rise according to an index every year – say, the retail price index, or 5 per cent, whichever is the higher. The latter forms of loan tend to work out more expensive than conventional or endowment loans, since effectively

more interest is paid. The lender makes a relatively higher charge for defer-
ring part of the interest payment in the early years, or allowing the borrower to start on a low-payment basis.

Loans may be agreed on a fixed interest or variable interest rate basis.
Lenders may fix the effective rate of interest for a given number of years,
or even the entire term, on the basis of judging the likely trends in interest rates over the years, although such rates have been shown to be rather
unstable over the past decades, rising to around 15 per cent in the early
1990s, and falling to around 5 per cent by the mid-1990s. Or, in the case of
variable loans, they may alter the interest rate when rates are changed. Most
personal loans made by banks are fixed-rate loans. Interest is fixed at the
prevailing rate at the time. Repayment mortgages are generally of the variable variety, although in recent years many lenders have been prepared to
fix their rates for up to 10 years to attract new business, although the rate
does change beyond an agreed date. Much skill and judgement is needed
by treasurers when considering which sort of loan to go for.

Lending institutions include banks, City institutions (which lend on the
basis of money raised through share issues) and building societies. As we
shall see, there is a vast variety of such institutions which can be and have
been approached and used by local authorities and housing associations;
and it is true to say that such institutions now have a great deal more knowledge of associations than before the financial reforms which affected the
movement in 1989.

Loans can be repaid on a month-by-month basis, or any other period
agreeable to lender and borrower. It is also possible to repay them early
from capital resources (savings, or money realised from the sale of assets).
In this case, the lender may impose a penalty for early repayment, though
not necessarily. If a borrower does so, clearly they will forgo any interest
on money held on deposit, which might have been used for other things.
However, they will no longer have to find money to repay the loan, or at
least the part redeemed (repaid). It is a matter of working out which would
be the best strategy – and that depends upon current interest rates, in comparison to the interest rate fixed on the loan (unless it is variable).

Loans are either secured, part-secured or unsecured. A *secured* loan is a
loan which involves the lender taking a *legal charge* on property owned by
the borrower – for example, the very thing bought by the money loaned.
A legal charge gives the borrower a right to sell the asset in the event that
the borrower *defaults* (fails to pay) on their repayments, to ensure that the
amount advanced is recouped. Charges may be *fixed* on a specific property
or properties, or *floating* – over an unspecified number of properties, to the
value of the loan. A mortgage is actually a fixed charge on a property and
not the loan itself. Those buying their house by means of loans from banks
and building societies give the lender a legal charge over their property –
in other words, they give the lender a mortgage, not the other way about.
That is why the person borrowing money for house purchase in this way is
called the *mortgagor* and the lending institution the *mortgagee* (compare

'lessor', the person granting a lease, or landlord, and 'lessee', the recipient of a lease, or tenant).

2.1.1.4　Subsidies

Subsidies are vital to social housing, but what are they? Many practitioners and students find the subject difficult, because of the multiplicity of types and rules applying to them, but in essence the concept is simple. A subsidy is assistance towards the capital or revenue costs of an individual or organisation, usually from outside, to ensure that the cost of the service or product to the consumer is reduced from what it would have been were no assistance available. Capital subsidies include assistance towards the cost of building or renovation works. Revenue subsidies include financial help towards running costs or current expenditure, including loan repayments. Subsidy can be further broken down into object' subsidy – to bring down the price of a product or service, regardless of who lives in the dwelling or uses the service – and 'subject' subsidies (often referred to as personal or individual subsidies) – targeted at those using the services, and usually paid on the basis of a means test – in respect of income.

As will be seen, the object of both forms of subsidy in the social housing world is to bring rents down to affordable levels, although there is debate about whether cash help should be directed towards objects or subjects. Other home-dwellers also receive help: owner-occupiers who have a mortgage currently receive what is effectively a reduction in interest rates through the medium of mortgage interest tax relief.

2.2　Local authority finance

Local authorities are creations of Parliament. Their powers and duties are specified by Acts of Parliament, and that includes their ability to raise and spend money, in housing and non-housing spheres. This is in line with the intuition that they spend public money, and that they should therefore be accountable. It is the purpose of this section to outline briefly the essential aspects of local authority finance, both generally and specifically in relation to housing. It is not intended to be an exhaustive treatment: several excellent texts referred to in the bibliography give more detailed information.

2.2.1　General functions

Local authorities provide a range of services for those who live within their areas. What they do rather depends upon their constitution and scope. There are three principal forms of council: county councils, district councils, and unitary authorities. Unitary authorities combine the functions of the first two. Exact functions will be discussed later in this book, but it is instructive to consider some of the key functions of each type of authority.

District councils are responsible for:

• housing

• planning control

• leisure and recreation

• some highway duties

• refuse collection

• environmental health.

County councils are responsible for:

• social services

• education

• strategic planning

• some highways

• libraries.

Both types of local authority undertake capital and revenue expenditure in connection with their powers and duties.

Housing is treated separately for accounting purposes, and has been since 1936; but other functions are funded from a central budget known as the General Fund. These functions are paid for by a combination of council tax (locally raised income from householders), redistributed Unified Business Rates (UBR) (raised from commercial occupiers and divided up from a central collection fund in proportion to the number of inhabitants in each district) and subsidy from central government known as Revenue Support Grant (RSG). Every year, local authorities have to make bids for RSG on the basis of anticipated budgetary requirements, taking account of expected locally generated income and of estimates of what they will receive from the UBR pool. The total amount of RSG available is cash-limited: that is, there is a finite pool available, and it is divided on the basis of bids, but also on government estimates of what each local authority should spend to deliver a standard level of service to its population. Limits are also placed on councils' ability to raise local income via increased council taxes, and several authorities have been 'capped', meaning that their council taxes have been limited centrally in response to what the government considers to be overspending, or excessive budgets.

Council tax is collected by and RSG is paid to district authorities and unitary authorities. County councils, town councils and parish councils, amongst others, along with the police services, and other emergency services receive part of the proceeds from the collecting authorities in the form of a 'precept', the amount of which is made clear via publicity from district authorities directed at local residents.

The General Fund is supposed to pay for services which are or could be required by all residents in the area. Local authority housing has its own account because the services provided by it are specific to tenants, who are a subclass of residents; and it is no longer possible to make contributions from the General Fund to council Housing Revenue Accounts, as was the case prior to 1990. Some housing services clearly benefit more than just local authority tenants – for example, housing aid and homelessness services – and these can be funded from the General Fund, as is private sector housing benefit, which is grant-aided by the Department of Social Security (DSS).

2.2.2   Overview of housing current expenditure

Housing revenue expenditure is conducted through the Housing Revenue Account (HRA). The form of this is prescribed by legislation: the 1985 Housing Act, as amended by the 1989 Local Government and Housing Act. Principal income items include gross rents (without taking account of Housing Benefit (Public Sector), service charges, interest from local authority-granted mortgages and on principal from sales of land and housing, and 'Housing Revenue Account subsidy' from central government. Major expenditure items include management and maintenance expenses, loan charges, and losses incurred by granting rent rebates – reductions in local authority rents now referred to as Housing Benefit (Public Sector), although this is not expenditure at all, rather forgone income. It is no mere accountancy device that rent rebates, as they are still referred to in finance departments, are treated in this way: this is crucial in the subsidy calculation.

Local authorities borrow money from a variety of sources including banks and building societies and the Public Works Loan Commissioners, the government acting as lender of last resort, and place it in a central council finance pool known as the Consolidated Loan Fund – money held for use by its various service departments. Housing departments cannot borrow as they cannot be 'legal persons' as a corporation can be, and cannot therefore enter into a contract. So the council as a legal entity then 'lends' money to its service departments, including the housing department, at a rate of interest reflecting its own liabilities, known as the Consolidated Loan Fund rate. This is repaid through the Housing Revenue Account.

2.2.3   Overview of housing capital expenditure

Section 40 of the 1989 Local Government and Housing Act defines capital expenditure as 'the acquisition, reclamation, enhancement or laying out of land, roads, buildings, other structures and machinery'. Broadly this equates to buying, improving or increasing the value of, or building, the things referred to in the quote. It accords with the accountancy definition of capital expenditure as any expenditure which creates assets that which will have a life of at least 1 year. The definition was deliberately tightened to plug loopholes in the expenditure rules which had been used by some councils to dodge capital controls during the 1980s.

Every year, councils must submit a Housing Strategy and Investment Programme (HSIP) which is included in a general bid for permission to spend on a variety of capital programmes across the board, but which is laid out in two documents. One, the Housing Strategy Statement, outlines the council's perception of housing need in its area and how it intends to meet it both directly and through other agencies; the other involves a 3-year projection of capital requirements to meet the programme, with 2 years past expenditure recorded, along with programme outputs (for example, the number of houses built, the extent of stock improvement). Estimates of cash receivable from sales of council property under the Right to Buy and sales of land must also be given.

The Department of the Environment is responsible for evaluating bids to incur expenditure. It has to work within a cash limit for social housing, which has to be divided between housing association and local authority expenditure. It does so partially on the basis of the HSIP submissions, but principally according to its own estimates of relative need in various parts of the country calibrated through a measure known as the Generalised Needs Index; however, bids have been evaluated increasingly on the basis of ministerial judgement as to the efficiency of authorities.

Some people believe that local authorities bid for cash grants to help them provide council housing. This is not generally so. What they in fact get is permission to spend up to a certain amount, and, within that, permission to do so partially on the basis of obtaining credit (largely borrowing). Limits are imposed principally because the government believes that the control of public expenditure, however financed, is a key element in controlling the money supply, and thus inflation. (This is the monetarist doctrine).

To simplify: prior to the start of each financial year, councils are issued with so-called Annual Capital Guidelines (ACGs) which tell the council what the government believes the authority needs to spend to realise its capital programmes. It assumes that part of this sum will be financed from cash received from asset sales (capital receipts) – at least, that part which the authority is allowed to use for this purpose (25 per cent of housing receipts and 50 per cent of land receipts (as at 1995)). Sales levels, of course, have to be assumed at that stage. The rest, it is assumed, will have to be borrowed, and each council receives a 'Basic Credit Approval' (BCA) in respect of programmes that it has devised, and 'Supplementary Credit Approvals' (SCA) to borrow to undertake projects devised centrally (e.g. under the Single Regeneration Budget – perhaps to comprehensively redevelop an inner-city estate). The latter can be granted at any time of the year; however, there is a global cash limit on all credit approvals, so the more that is allocated as SCA, the less is allocated as BCA. Sometimes it is said that SCAs are 'top-sliced' from the Credit Approvals budget – it means the same thing.

Worked example: Notional District Council, Credit Approval, 1997/98

From the Department of the Environment

To: Housing Director, Notional DC
From: A. Civil-Servant, D.o.E.
Date: 1 March, 1997

Dear Housing Director,

I am pleased to inform you of your credit approval limits for the coming year, and to outline the assumptions upon which they are based.

This year, the Department has, for the purposes of clarification, decided to refer specifically to housing capital requirements, and issue credit approvals accordingly.

Having analysed your Housing Investment Programme bid, the Department has resolved the following:

1. ANNUAL CAPITAL GUIDELINE (ACG) (the amount the department considers you need to spend to build and improve your stock, and to support other providers): £40 million
2. EXPECTED USABLE CAPITAL RECEIPTS
   As you know, you are allowed to use 25 per cent of proceeds from house sales under the Right to Buy, and 50 per cent of proceeds from housing land sales. This sum is deducted from the ACG, as it is assumed that you will use it for capital purposes, before your credit approval is assessed.

Expected housing receipt:	£10 million
Usable portion:	£2.5 million
Expected land receipt:	£5 million
Usable portion:	£2.5 million
Total usable amount:	£5 MILLION

Credit approval: The Department will allow you to incur credit this year to the sum of ACG minus expected usable receipts, and assumed Revenue Contributions to Capital Outlay (RCCO) – i.e. cash saved from your Housing Revenue Account towards capital expenditure. That is, £40 million minus £5 million (Usable receipts) minus £1 million (RCCO), i.e. a total of £34 million.

Of this, £10 million will be granted this year as a Basic Credit Approval, to be raised to undertake work specified in your Housing Strategy Statement. However, in line with changed housing policy, the remainder (£24 million) is granted as a Supplementary Credit Approval, to be borrowed to finance projects specified by this

Department which it is considered will meet national housing objectives. In the case of *Notional District Council*, the Supplementary Credit Approvals will be focused on renovating the tower blocks on the Awful Estate in line with the Single Regeneration Budget initiative.

Your bid to grant-fund (Local Authority Housing Association Grant scheme) Central Housing Association in respect of 100 new units on the Awful Estate is approved in full, and will use £5 million of the BCA amount, to be reimbursed to you by the Housing Corporation.

The Credit Approvals are lower than the bid. This is partly because it is considered that local housing associations will be doing more building work this year, and because there is ministerial concern at inefficiencies noted in the manner in which the Housing Revenue Account has been conducted. A separate communication follows on this matter.

Yours sincerely

A. Civil-Servant

Councils must programme their capital works carefully. If they spend below their ACG, the next year it may be reduced for that reason. Overspending is unlawful. They do not know how many sales they will make, thus they can never be certain that they will have sufficient to complete all their programmes, even if they are fully contractually committed. They cannot roll forward spending permission to the following year. In practice, approvals have been so tight, and often so specific, that many local authorities have given up their role as developers and have turned to others, principally housing associations, to develop social housing to which councils then seek access. When they provide land or money to associations to do this, councils are termed 'enablers' rather than 'providers'.

2.2.4 Capital receipts

It may seem odd that councils are unable to use everything they make from house and land sales to finance new capital expenditure. Since the passage of the 1980 Housing Act, restrictions have been imposed on the amount of receipts which can be used in that way in any one year. The reason is to encourage, or force, councils to use the balance to pay off their debts, accumulated over many years, many of which are public sector loans. Additionally, it is a way of controlling local authority expenditure, and hence the amount of money in circulation, as previously stated.

The 1980 Housing Act introduced the Right to Buy: by the end of 1994, almost 1.5 million households had bought their council homes at discounts ranging from 32 to 70 per cent. Prior to the Act, some councils exercised their power to sell council houses to sitting tenants, and some even promoted council house sales. All the receipts could be ploughed back into council business, including the building of new houses. But the Right to Buy meant a massive surge in council receipts, and restrictions on spending were introduced to stop inflation caused by excess money circulating in the economy. Initially, councils could spend 50 per cent of the receipts in any one year, but had to carry the rest forward, although they were allowed to use 50 per cent of this amount the following year, plus 50 per cent of any new receipts. This rule was known as the cascade, as money realised from sales in previous years would eventually trickle down to following years' capital programmes. The percentage usable in any one year was steadily reduced in the 1980s, until by the last year of the system, 1989, the relevant percentages were 20 per cent of house sales and 50 per cent of land sales.

The cascade led to some weird and wonderful practices which served to increase the ability of local authorities to provide or enable social housing. Some councils preferred to use some of the money realised from sales to pay off debts, or to do repairs, or even to pay wages. If they did so, clearly they could not then use that money to build houses or undertake other capital works. Once spent, spent. However, capital spent in that way at least reduced indebtedness, and therefore pressures on rents.

However, students of the myriad regulations accompanying the 1980 Local Government, Planning and Land Act and associated legislation and circulars began to realise that money spent in this way could still be 'used' for capital purposes, even though it had been spent! This is because it had been spent in the 'wrong' way. If a local authority spent all of its capital receipt on revenue (for example, repairs programme), it could still 'carry forward' (in 1982) 50 per cent of the receipt spent in that way to the next year, as a so-called 'notional capital receipt'. But it was useless 'money': it could not be spent. Spending capital for revenue purposes might dampen rents, but it did not produce any more cash. One could not spend the notional receipts, borrow against them, or lend them. They might as well not have existed!

That is, until local authorities, realising that they faced capital starvation due to increasingly restrictive Housing Investment Programme settlements, began to lease equipment and homes rather than buy or construct, using revenue to pay for what would once have been financed through capital. Many local authorities took leases of up to 30 years on private sector properties or homes built by housing associations to augment their stock. The government of the day, in 1987, saw this as a blatant attempt to circumvent capital expenditure rules, and sought to restrain this activity by imposing a capital charge on the activity. Henceforth, if local authorities leased a property for 3 years or more, they would lose the ability to spend an amount broadly equivalent to the capital value of the property leased from the amount they were permitted to spend. It was thought that this would stop councils in their tracks. It did not. Councils simply counted the value of the properties against notional capital receipts! Thus wise councils forfeited no actual spending powers whatever.

The 1989 Local Government and Housing Act stopped all this by abolishing the cascade, and with it notional capital receipts. A new, stricter definition of capital was erected. Henceforth, councils would be permitted to spend only 25 per cent of capital receipts from house sales and 50 per cent from land sales in the year of sales. The remainder was frozen for the eventual repayment of debt. Nor could councils credit the interest from the frozen receipts fully to their HRA: in some years, the lion's share had to be paid into the General Fund, where it was not required to be used to pay off debts. In 1992/3, councils were briefly allowed to use all the receipts from sales that year as they wished, but by that time Right to Buy sales had already peaked, so the harvest was less impressive than it could have been. The door closed again from 1994.

Example to illustrate pre- and post-1990 Act systems

Pre-1990 Act

(This example assumes all receipts spent for capital purposes, and 20 per cent of that year's and previous years' receipts spent. No debt redemption. All housing receipts.)

Table 2.1 The cascade

Year	Receipts	Cumulative	Spent (20%)	Carried forward (80%)
1986	£1 000 000	£1 000 000	£200 000	£800 000
1987	£1 000 000	£1 800 000	£360 000	£1 440 000
1988	£500 000	£1 940 000	£388 000	£1 552 000
1989	£500 000	£2 052 000	£410 000	£1 642 000
Total spent on capital works:			£1 358 000	
Total remaining in bank (could be used to repay debt):				£1 642 000

If any part of the 20 per cent of receipts which were spent on capital works had been spent on debt repayment, that amount would have been carried forward as a notional capital receipt, and could have been set against the capital value of leased property to avoid incurring reduced ability to spend.

So, if in this example the council had spent the entire previous year's receipt (£1m) on debt redemption in 1987, it would have been able to carry forward 20 per cent of this (£200 000) as a notional capital receipt, to be set against leased properties in 1987 (say four, worth £50 000 each, leased for 29 years). It would have forfeited nothing from its ability to spend borrowed money, and therefore could have borrowed £200 000 to build, say, four houses at £50 000 each. Therefore, by using notional capital receipts, it would have increased its stock by four properties over and above what it could have if it hadn't repaid debt. And, of course, the HRA benefits through debt redemption, as expenditure on debt servicing is stabilised.

Post-1990

(In this example it is assumed that no cash has been carried forward from 1989. Local authority has debts and has been ordered to use 75 per cent of receipts to pay them off. Housing receipts only.)

Table 2.2 Post-1989 Act receipt rules

Year	Receipts	Spent on capital (25 per cent maximum)	Debt redeemed (75 per cent of receipts)
1990	£1 000 000	£250 000	£750 000
1991	£1 000 000	£250 000	£750 000
1992	£500 000	£125 000	£375 000
1993	£500 000	£125 000	£375 000
Total spent on capital works: £750 000			
Total used to redeem debt:			£2 250 000

It can be seen that the new system allows far less expenditure on capital operations than the old one, but that, since it enforces debt redemption, the effect could be to reduce HRA expenditure through lessening debt and therefore size of repayments.

Whether or not councils should be allowed to use all the money realised from sales is a perennial issue. On the one hand, it is much easier to use your own money to finance a project than borrowed money because you do not have to justify its use to a critical external party. On the other hand, if you use all the money realised from the sale of an asset to build further assets, you forgo the prudent move of paying off debts and improving your 'gearing' (ratio of assets to debts), something which private lenders look very carefully at. Pro and con arguments can be listed as follows:

In favour of unlimited spending power.

- It makes it easy to acquire funds.

- Councils can determine and meet their own priorities, locally decided.

- It's the councils' own money – why should their power to spend it be centrally restricted?

- Think of the homes, but also the construction jobs the spending could produce, not to mention the multiplier effects (furniture, carpets, etc. would need to be supplied from somewhere – there would be a stimulus to the local economy).

- If councils were to grant-aid local housing associations at the standard Housing Corporation rates, think of the number of homes that could be produced in conjunction with private loan finance.

Against these freedoms.

- Unlimited spending would boost public expenditure, which is generally inefficient.

- It would be a stimulus to inflation.

- Paying off local authority debt reduces the national debt, as most of the money local authorities borrowed was borrowed from the government in the first place. Therefore redemption can be used to finance tax cuts.

- If councils are forced to pay off debt, then they can pass on savings in loan charges to tenants in the form of lower rent rises, or even rent cuts in due course.

- Instead of using capital receipts fully, local authorities can use them to repay debt, and save up the money they would have spent on redeeming debt as Revenue Contributions to Capital Outlay (RCCOs).

2.2.5 The Housing Revenue Account

The Housing Revenue Account (HRA) of local authorities is specified in Part 6 of the 1989 Local Government and Housing Act. This amended the previous formulation, in the 1985 Housing Act, which had remained substantially unchanged since the 1936 Housing Act. The items which can be credited and debited are specified in detail in Schedule 4, Parts 1 and 2 of the 1989 Act. The account format was changed to reflect new subsidy arrangements, and to give the Secretary of State more leeway to influence local authority practices by importing assumptions into the account rather than relying upon the council's own estimates.

As subsidy is paid throughout the year, in a number of stages, and relates to that year's estimated expenditure, the inputs and outputs are clearly guesses at the stage when the projected accounts are presented. A summary of the account format is given below. Numbers relate to the 'Items' under which amounts can be credited or debited.

2.2.5.1 Credits to the account (Schedule 4, Part 1)

1. Gross rents – that is, estimated total rent yield, prior to rebating. Local authorities are free to set their own rents, but they must be 'reasonable' and bear some relation to the proportionate relationships of private sector rents in the area. Broadly, if private sector rents for two-bed properties are twice as much as for one-bed properties, say, this relationship should also obtain in the local authority sector.

2. Charges for services and facilities (including those which are legitimately charged to the General Fund – for example, the cost of homelessness and housing aid services, together with an element towards the

care aspect of the warden service).

3. HRA subsidy, about which more later.

4. Contributions made to the local authority (by third parties).

5. Housing benefit transfers. If a council houses someone, say temporarily, on behalf of another authority, then although the receiving council pays (or rather rebates) housing benefit, the referring authority is liable for that negative expenditure.

6. Transfers from the Housing Repairs Account. Many local authorities no longer keep such an account, although they have had the power to do so since 1936. Any surplus from such an account will be transferred to the HRA.

7. Reductions for bad or doubtful debts. This is money which the council expects to collect from bad debtors (for example, those in rent arrears who still owe money from previous years). If the figure is deemed to be unrealistically low, the Secretary of State can substitute another figure!

8. Sums determined by the Secretary of State. In the past, councils were able to credit the lion's share of interest on capital receipts, but since the 1989 Act, this power has been withdrawn or limited in some years. In the early 1990s, councils were able to credit under this item only interest on mortgages advanced under the Right to Buy – another restriction on the account.

9. Sums directed by the Secretary of State. In the unlikely event of local authorities being given the temporary power to make contributions to the HRA from the General Fund, a determination allowing them to do so, and specifying how much, would be made under Item 9.

10. Credit balances from previous years.

2.2.5.2. Debits to the account (Schedule 4, Part 2)

1. Expenditure on repairs, management and maintenance. Again, housing authorities are free to determine their own policies in these respects, although in practice the subsidy regime makes it increasingly difficult to diverge from official guidelines published annually in the subsidy determination. Authorities are no longer permitted to spend capital sums (raised by loan or right to buy receipts) on these items.

2. Expenditure for capital purposes. This includes loan debt repayments and 'Revenue Contributions to Capital Outlay' (RCCOs). The Secretary of State assumes that authorities will allocate a specified sum from revenue income to undertake capital works, such as improvements to stock, or building. RCCOs were introduced in 1990 under the 1989 Act.

3. Rents, rates and taxes and other charges to which the local authority is liable. For example, if a council rents a property from a private landlord to house homeless people (known as private sector leasing), obviously it is liable for the rent to the landlord. It would be charged under this head. However, since 1992, changes in the subsidy regime have meant that new leases of this sort are financed from the General Fund. Another example: if a council rents an office from the private sector, from which to undertake housing functions, rent would be accounted under this head.

4. Rent rebates granted. A rent rebate is a reduction in council rent (only local authority rents) under the housing benefit scheme. This form of housing benefit is properly termed Housing Benefit (Public Sector), but housing finance personnel and legislation still refer to it under the old name. This used to be allowed for under rent income: net rents were once declared rather than gross rents. Again, the primary reason for this change is the subsidy regime dating from the 1989 Act.

5. Negative HRA subsidy. If a local authority is deemed to be in surplus, on the Secretary of State's reckoning when estimating subsidy, councils have to pay this assumed sum to some other account (normally the General Fund).

6. Contributions to the Housing Repairs Account – if a separate one is kept, and in the event that it runs at a loss.

7. Provision for bad or doubtful debts, i.e. what the council thinks it will lose by way of rent arrears. Again, the Secretary of State has the power to substitute another figure if it is thought to be unrealistically high. It can even be prohibited.

8. Sums calculated by the Secretary of State. Notional HRA deficits can be accounted under this head, as well as any sums payable by the council to another housing organisation if it transfers property from its ownership (for example, under large scale voluntary transfer).

9. Actual debit balances from the previous year. Local authorities are not allowed to carry debits for more than 2 years: that is, they must clear all debts from the year last but one. Prior to the new HRA regime, councils were not allowed to go into deficit on their HRA, and had a duty to make payments from their General Fund if they thought this would happen. Since ring-fencing, this way of providing an internal subsidy has been abolished, and, by way of slight recompense, councils have now only to make 'best endeavours' to balance their HRA, and can therefore carry forward the deficit attributable to the previous year's operations.

Special mention must be made of the funding of sheltered housing services. Most councils with housing departments own and manage either properties which have been specially adapted for elderly people, often with a resident or non-resident warden (sometimes called a 'sheltered scheme manager') on site to deal with management issues, or general-needs properties which have been specifically earmarked for that group. Sometimes, the management of these dwellings is carried out jointly with the social services department, where there is need for specialist management, for example where the residents are frail. This is known as Category Two and a Half provision, as it is provided under Part 2 of the 1985 Housing Act. In these cases, the costs of specialist services are charged to the General Fund.

Category Two accommodation (after the same Act) is where the management is predominantly of a housing nature (collection of rents, provision of maintenance, ensuring that tenancy conditions are adhered to, responding to requests for transfers and exchanges, etc.), and in these cases local authorities charge the costs to the Housing Revenue Account. Where some of the duties of the warden relate to 'caring' – arranging medical attention, lifting, sometimes bathing, giving specialist advice, liaison with social services and the like – many councils charge this element to their General Fund, on the basis that they are not services received by tenants in general, and should not therefore be charged to rents generally. However, some councils charge the entire cost of wardens managing Category Two accommodation to the Housing Revenue Account. This gave rise to a legal challenge by a tenant of the London Borough of Ealing in 1991 on the grounds that part of her rent was wrongly being used to support care services. The upshot of this was legislative clarification, and the current position is that councils have the power to charge warden services, including any care element where provided by the housing department, to the Housing Revenue Account. The difficulties which would have arisen if councils had to apportion caring and housing management costs to the General Fund and Housing Revenue Account respectively are discussed in an article at the end of the chapter: 'Accounting for Sheltered Housing' (p. 72).

2.2.6   Housing Revenue Account Subsidy

The 1989 Act HRA subsidy arrangements were applied to council housing revenue accounts from April 1991. A year's grace was given to allow councils time to get used to the new regulations. Broadly, prior to that, subsidy was based loosely on the actual differences between running costs and income, including an element to help meet loan charges, and a quite separate subsidy from the Department of Health and Social Security to meet the losses incurred by rent rebating. As previously stated, councils were allowed to make good deficits by contributions from the General Rate Fund, and an element in the Rate Support Grant – the E7 Factor – was included to help them do this. This form of subsidy is termed 'deficit subsidy'. From April 1991, HRA subsidy has been based on a notional housing revenue account constructed by the Department of the Environment's civil servants on the basis of ideal expenditure and income figures, which are published in the HRA Subsidy Determination issued each December prior to the council's accounting year. Separate subsidy to help make good losses incurred by rent rebating has been abolished. The result is that some councils no longer receive HRA subsidy, because their accounts are assumed to balance, or achieve a surplus, which means that in those authorities, rent reductions granted under the national housing benefit scheme, notionally part of the fiscally funded income support regime, must be paid for from rents actually paid, or from reductions in service expenditure. Local authorities in question blame the government for unrealism in its accounting assumptions. Government blames the councils for inefficiency.

2.2.6.1 The old subsidy regime

The formula used to determine subsidy prior to 1989, under the 1980 Housing Act, took the following form:

Housing support subsidy = BA + HCD – LCD

where BA = Base Amount (the subsidy received the previous year, starting in 1980/81); HCD = Housing Costs Differential (the amount by which housing 'reckonable expenditure' – i.e. expenditure allowed by statute and eligible for subsidy – in the current subsidy year exceeded 'reckonable expenditure' in the previous year); and LCD = Local Costs Differential (the amount by which reckonable income for the subsidy year exceeded that of the previous year).

It can be seen that where income increases (LCD) exceeded expenditure increases (HCD), subsidy would fall below last year's (i.e. the BA). Assumptions were made by the D.o.E. about rent levels, collection levels, management costs and voids, when the subsidy was worked out. The assumptions were not unrealistic. It was generally assumed that rents would rise faster than expenditure, and so many local authorities fell out of subsidy in the mid-1980s. However, given the large amounts of interest received on Right to Buy receipts and credited to HRAs then, this was not particularly worrying to many councils. When it happened, rent levels could no longer be influenced by central government via the subsidy system, which was one reason for the reform. Additionally, actual deficits could be financed from the rates, and some councils paid for part of their current expenditure from capital resources to avoid putting rents up to what they considered to be unrealistic levels.

Table 2.3 Worked example showing operation of pre-1990 subsidy arrangements

Year	Base amount	HCD	LCD	Subsidy BA + HCD – LCD
1986	£1 000 000	£200 000	£500 000	£700 000
1987	£700 000	£300 000	£600 000	£400 000
1988	£400 000	£400 000	£800 000	£0

It is assumed that the local authority has been selling council homes, and that the LCD has risen because of credits of interest to the HRA. Thus even though costs have risen, subsidy has fallen, as a result of increased income. Therefore this council's rent policy from 1988 need not take account of government rent guidelines, since there is no longer reliance on subsidy.

2.2.6.2   The 1989 Act subsidy regime: HRA subsidy

The government used the 1989 Act to close the loopholes which had arisen under the previous regime. From now on, housing accounts were to be run in a businesslike way, unsubsidised from the General Fund, and subject to strict assumptions about virtually every aspect of income and expenditure, totally unrelated to the previous year's subsidy position. There is no doubt that the new regime is far simpler conceptually than the old one.

A draft determination, showing the principles of the assumptions and guideline income and expenditure figures, is issued every October preceding the subsidy year for discussion with local authorities and their representative bodies. The determination is issued by the end of the December preceding the subsidy year. Payments are made by the D.o.E. in 10 instalments, starting in the March before the start of the financial year.

The D.o.E. constructs a notional HRA for each authority, a simplified version of the real thing. The formula as stated in the 1989 Act is:

Amount of subsidy = (management and maintenance + charges for capital + rent rebates + other items of reckonable expenditure) minus (rent + interest on receipts + other items of reckonable income)

The notional account looks like this:

Credits

1. Rents, i.e. assumed gross rents minus a 2 per cent voids allowance. Rents are assessed on a capital value basis, explained below.

2. Interest on receipts (or whatever is allowable under Item 8 that year).

3. Other reckonable income.

Debits

1. Management and maintenance expenditure – figures are issued in the determination.

2. Charges for rent rebates – assumptions are made about the proportion of tenants eligible for rebates over the year, and a percentage of the assumed losses are put into the calculation. Sometimes it is 100 per cent, sometimes less. This figure is cash-limited, whatever the actual amounts lost through rent rebating might be.

3. Charges for capital – loan charges, subject to the admissible credit allowance, i.e. the amount raised which is eligible for subsidy. This is frequently less than the actual, or even permissible, amount raised in any one year. RCCOs are added to this figure.

Worked example of the post-1989 Act subsidy system: Borough of Notion upon Thames, 1992 settlement

Number of HRA properties	5000
Average capital rent guideline	£40 per week
Management and maintenance guideline	£20 per week
Percentage of tenants claiming benefit	50%
(worked out on 100 per cent eligibility)	
Loan outstanding (at 10 per cent interest rate)	£10 000 000
RCCO assumption	£1 000 000
Voids/arrears allowance	2%
Housing sales receipts assumed	
(reserved portion)	£300 000

NOTION UPON THAMES NOTIONAL HOUSING REVENUE ACCOUNT
Figures are D.o.E. assumptions.

Credits (per annum)

Rent	($£40.00 \times 52 \times 5000) \times 98\%$	£10 192 000
Interest	$£300\,000 \times 10\%$	£30 000
Other reckonable		—
Total notional credits		£10 222 000

Debits

Management/maintenance	$£20.00 \times 52 \times 5000$	£5 200 000
Rent rebates	$50\% \times £10\,400\,000$	£5 200 000
Charges for capital:		
Loan interest	$£10\,000\,000 \times 10\%$	£1 000 000
RCCO	£ 1 000 000	£1 000 000
Total notional debits		£12 400 000

Subsidy = notional debits – notional credits
Subsidy = (£12,400,000 – £10,222,000) = £2,178,000

This amount does not even cover the cost of rent rebates to the authority; thus, even if the D.o.E. assumptions were correct, those on housing benefit (in the public sector) would be part-subsidised by those tenants not in receipt of benefit.

As can be seen, HRA subsidy is the sum of notional debits minus notional credits. It can be positive or negative. Where positive, it is paid in ten instalments throughout the financial year, except the first, which is paid in the March before its start. Negative HRA subsidy is effectively a charge on the HRA, and is entered as such in the account. During the 1990s, expenditure was systematically underestimated, and income overestimated. The resultant low subsidy settlements, paid within an overall cash limit, were regarded as a stimulus to council 'efficiency'. Not surprisingly, local authority rents rose significantly after the introduction of the new regime, which was in line with the government's avowed intention to ensure that council tenants were give realistic price signals in respect of services received.

One aspect of the new regime is the way in which rents are assumed. Mention has been made of 'capital rents'. When the new regime was formulated, one object was to reform the way in which rents were assumed in an attempt to ensure that they bore some relation to the value of the stock, in the way that private rents often do. The principle was that rents in areas with higher property values should be higher than those with lower property values. It should be stressed that there has never been any intention of forcing local authorities to adopt this method of rent setting: it has been used as a way of justifying the D.o.E.'s assumed rents.

Capital rents are based upon the value of a council's stock in relation to the national stock value. Since 1981, Right to Buy has provided evidence of the market value of council homes. To assess the assumed rent roll of a local authority, the following procedure is used (simplified for the purposes of explanation):

1. Work out the value of Council X's stock, using Right to Buy valuations as evidence.

2. Work out the value of the national stock on the same basis.

3. Now work out the share of the national value represented by the local value. For example, if the local value is £1 000 000 and the national value is £100 000 000, then clearly the local stock is worth 1 per cent of the national stock.

4. Now work out the national rent roll, perhaps by using actual figures based on local authority HRA returns.

5. Now work out the local assumed rent roll by multiplying the national rent roll by the factor assessed at step 3. For example, if the national rent roll is £800 000 000, the local rent roll should be £8 000 000 (£800 000 000 × 0.01).

6. Now work out the average 'capital rent' per local property by dividing the assumed local rent roll by the number of council homes owned by the local authority. For example, if there are 5000 properties, the 'capital rent' per property (averaged across all types) is £1600 per annum, i.e. £32 per week (assuming a 50-week rent year).

The crude use of this formula resulted in some rents being assumed to be much higher than was actually the case, and some much lower. The latter was not in line with government intentions to encourage councils to charge higher rents, so a 'damping' formula was applied to the result to ensure that assumed rents did not fall below a given level.

This is a very odd way of assuming rent levels. Most local authorities work out how much they need to raise through rents to run their services, after having applied subsidy and considering all costs. They then apportion the rents in accordance with the relative characteristics of the properties, including size, amenities, height above ground, and the like, ensuring that the global figure will be raised. Newer properties which cost more to build than older ones do not necessarily attract higher rents: loan charges are 'pooled' across the stock to ensure that tenants living in such properties are not penalised. No authority charges rents on the basis of their market value. But there it is.

The method which the D.o.E. uses to estimate subsidy, including the method of assessing guideline rents, is discussed in the third article at the end of the chapter: 'Subsidising council housing' (p. 73). One of the oddities of the system highlighted is the variation in such guideline rents, which bears very little relationship to comparable differences in the private rented sector, and the lack of any firm logic in the assessment of management and maintenance costs.

2.2.6.3 Consequences of the 1989 Act regime

Every year, a new subsidy determination is made, with no reference to the previous year's. The assumptions are fiercely questioned by local authorities. Little attention is paid to this.

Some local authorities receive less subsidy than they need to bridge the gap between income and expenditure. Very rarely do any receive more. Councils are thus forced to raise rents and cut services on an annual basis. Government is then able to argue that the private sector or the housing association sector might provide services more economically, thus paving the way for initiatives such as compulsory competitive tendering of housing management, spurring large-scale voluntary transfers, and causing housing policy analysts to suggest removing council housing from public expenditure rules altogether by forming 'local housing companies'.

Because HRA subsidy has compounded housing support subsidy and housing benefit subsidy, some local authorities have to meet most or all of the losses incurred by rent rebating by reviewing their general rent policy. The effect is that in some areas, the relatively better-off tenants are subsidising their poorer neighbours, a sort of 'Poor Law' benefits system supposedly abolished by the post-war welfare reforms. Thus, in these areas, housing benefit for council tenants is no longer really part of the national income support system, which is funded by tax revenue levied on the national population.

No wonder the system has generated controversy!

2.2.7 Scope for reform

Enough has been said about the local authority housing capital and revenue systems, and the way they are financed and subsidised, to make it clear that councils face stark choices. They can accept a regime of continuously reduced credit approvals, restrictions on re-use of capital receipts, dwindling revenue subsidies and draconian revenue account regulations making it impossible to subsidise accounts from general funds even though council housing is a resource which any household might have to resort to. Or they can give up, and transfer the assets to organisations which are subject to less onerous restrictions and which can use capital raised to invest in new social housing, and in the process lose control of homes managed traditionally by local, democratically accountable institutions.

'Reform' always presupposes assumptions about the value of the organisations which will benefit (or lose out) as a result. Local authority housing has an honourable place in the annals of welfare provision. In 1993, 3 742 000 dwellings were owned by councils in England alone, representing 18.6 per cent of households by tenure (source: *Housing and construction statistics, March quarter 1994 Part 2*). This compares with 768 000 homes owned by housing associations, representing 3.8 per cent of all tenures. There have been losses to council stocks totalling around 1 000 000 since 1983. Thus the council sector was, at the time of writing, still a significant element in the tenure pattern of the nation. Ill-thought-out tinkering with finance regulations and legislation has had the effect of limiting tenure choice, and the availability of housing, for many: witness the doubling of homelessness acceptances over the decade 1983–93 in the face of no significant increase in household formation, virtually zero population growth, and in a decade characterised by both economic boom and slump. The 200 000 or so increase in the number of housing association homes has not matched the falling availability of council housing to those needing it. These facts may or may not convince of the need to sustain a council housing sector, but they do at least point to its significance, and the way in which it has been wounded and prevented from doing its job.

Reform from the point of view of sustaining the sector and allowing it to provide for those who need housing and who cannot compete in the market place would involve the following. First, allow councils to use all the money realised from council house and land sales to supplement borrowing to provide the homes and improvements so desperately required. Second, apply all the savings from a full abolition of mortgage interest tax relief in the form of a grant to local authorities to provide housing. Third, ensure that credit approvals meet the gap between local authority money and expenditure needs. Fourth, ensure that councils are run in a businesslike manner, by regular inspection and audit, to ensure best use of resources to realise this objective. Fifth, bring in a system whereby the losses incurred by rent rebating are met fully by tax revenue, or ensure that the subsidy system provides sufficient finance for councils to run customer-responsive services efficiently and effectively without resort to rent hikes or wages which may fail to attract people of calibre to run services. Capital reform as suggested would increase the production of social housing, make homes available in the quantities needed, and stimulate the house-building industry, thus providing greater tax revenue and tackling unemployment in building and related private sector industries. Revenue reform would ensure that quality homes are provided and managed in a way commensurate with a civilised state. Homelessness and poor housing would eventually be eradicated.

Another approach would be to do away with council housing entirely, albeit at a tremendous democratic cost. All council housing assets could be transferred to the housing association sector and/or housing companies. But if this were done, then in order to maintain standards and a viable building programme, without forcing rents up to unrealistic levels, it would be necessary to subsidise the sector heavily in capital or revenue terms, or both, if it were still intended to meet housing need and eradicate homelessness. It would still be necessary to monitor such organisations to ensure that standards were maintained, and that public money was spent wisely. And if no capital or revenue subsidy were available to the organisations in question, surely there would be a massive commitment to state aid in the form of income support via housing benefit.

There is no clear financial advantage to the state in abandoning council housing. Money to support social housing, however provided, has to come from somewhere, and affordable rents imply either a high-wage economy whereby everybody can afford market rents without recourse to state subsidy, whether personal or bricks-and-mortar, or continued state support to whoever is providing it, or whoever lives in it. The question comes down to the value of democracy, which is beyond the scope of this book.

It is worth now turning to the first article at the end of this chapter, 'The bottom line: the finance of council housing in the 1990s', (p. 70), for its summary of the points made in this section, its highlighting of the problems arising from the 1989 Local Government and Housing Act, and its valuable comments by a practitioner frustrated by these restrictions. In particular, in attempting to answer the questions posed at the end of the article, readers will clarify their understanding of the issues involved.

2.3 Housing association finance

2.3.1 Introduction

Housing associations owned 768 000 homes in England alone in 1993, representing 3.8 per cent of all households by tenure. About 110 000 of these were completed after the commencement, in 1989, of the new financial regime initiated by the 1988 Housing Act. The movement, often known as the voluntary housing sector as housing associations were set up not by statute but by groups and individuals, has thus become an important player in the provision of social housing, and is destined to become the major provider in the future. Housing options include homes for rent and for sale: rented property is let at less than market rents, and for-sale options are provided on a low-cost basis. More will be said about their variety and constitution in a later chapter. This one deals mainly with their financial situation, and cannot give more than an outline of that. It is an area subject to constant changes, and so only the basic principles will be covered.

2.3.2   Capital activities

Housing associations which are registered with the Housing Corporation may receive a capital subsidy to assist them with the capital costs of construction and rehabilitation from the Corporation or from local authorities acting as the Corporation's agents. This is known as Housing Association Grant, or HAG.

Prior to 1989, associations received HAG at a level sufficient to ensure that they need charge no more than a fair rent: that is, a rent registered by the Rent Officer on the basis of size, type, location, amenities and so forth, but not related to scarcity, which determines market rents. Essentially, the following procedure was followed. A fair rent would be set. Estimates of management and maintenance costs would be deducted, plus a voids element. The residue would be assumed to support a small loan at a given rate of interest, obtained from public sources. Any actual allowable development costs, subject to cost limits known as Total Indicative Costs (TICs), not met by the loan would be met through HAG. HAG was payable after development, and included an element to pay for the interest on the loan raised during the development period necessary to pay contractors at various stages of the work. This system was established under the 1974 Housing Associations Act. HAG was typically payable at very high rates – well into the 90 per cent area for some schemes. The costs limits were 'uplifted' if schemes had special design features, but were relatively generous, and permitted good-quality schemes at low rents. HAG was available on for-rent and for-sale schemes.

In April 1989, this old system was abolished under the provisions of the 1988 Housing Act, for all but special needs schemes. The reason was given that the old system was open-ended, and made it difficult to budget for housing association capital expenditure accurately. It was decided to fix grant rates prior to development, and to reduce them on the basis of higher rents. To enable the latter, fair rents were abolished for association developments from 1989/90 onwards. Indeed, fair rents were abolished for private non-resident landlord lettings from then, along with regulated tenancies for new tenants, which were replaced by assured tenancies with unregulated rents.

The new system is relatively straightforward. Every year, the D.o.E., in conjunction with the Housing Corporation and in consultation with interested parties, including the National Federation of Housing Associations and local authority associations, works out an Approved Development Programme (ADP): that is, an amount of cash which it is thought will support a given development programme, in line with national housing priorities. This is the Housing Corporation's capital budget, and the Corporation, now a quango rather than part of the D.o.E., is responsible for its distribution. This exercise is undertaken for Scotland, England, Wales and Northern Ireland. The Housing Corporation's remit covers England. Associations have to bid for their share of the ADP, and are told what they can expect to receive by the start of the financial year in question by their Housing Corporation regional office.

Grant levels are worked out in accordance with a model, as follows. Assumptions are made about affordable rents for given types of units in each of seven regions which exemplify different construction costs – the so-called Total Cost Indicator (TCI) regions. From these are deducted estimated typical management and maintenance costs, and an element for voids. The remainder is held to be able to support a loan raised from the private sector; assumptions are made about interest rates and terms, as well as the nature of the loan, to derive the loan sum via a process known as capitalisation. This sum is then deducted from estimated development costs for types of scheme, known as TCIs, which vary from one region to another. The remainder is expressed as a percentage of TCI, and forms the basis for the typical or 'norm' grant payable on that type of scheme. Scheme TCIs are modified up or down by applying multipliers: special needs schemes often attract significant uplift through this method. Grant rates vary considerably, depending upon the type of scheme proposed, but rates are very much lower than they were under the old regime. A summary of the model used by the Housing Corporation, and the problems which arise from it, is given in an article at the end of Chapter Four, which deals with housing associations ('Grant rates: modelling and manipulation', p. 146).

There is sometimes a lack of realism surrounding building costs assumptions, and always argument with associations when management and maintenance cost assumptions are made, because they crucially affect grant rates (which have fallen in recent years). When the regime started they averaged around 75 per cent: by 1994/95, they had fallen to 63 per cent, and have been falling significantly throughout the 1990s so far. The fall has caused concern about high rents and the so-called 'poverty trap' whereby housing benefit is withdrawn at the rate of 65p for every £1 earned above the 'applicable amount' – the relevant income support level, making it unrealistic to work, as fares and childminding may well reduce earned income below income support levels.

The regime is slightly different for special needs schemes. In 1995, these still received 100 per cent HAG on approved costs, again subject to TCIs, and also revenue subsidies, principally Special Needs Management Allowance, to assist in the very high running costs typical of such schemes.

Worked example of grant rate calculation (simplified for illustrative purposes)

General needs property, three-bedroom house, TCI area A 1998

	Weekly	Annually
1. Affordable rent	£60.00	£3 120
2. Management and maintenance	£30.00	£1 560
3. 1.–2.	£30.00	£1 560
4. Voids assumed	0%	0%
5. Capitalise for loan (10% interest)	—	£15 600
6. TCI for property		£60 000
7. 6.–5.		£44 400
8. 7. as a percentage of TCI, i.e. norm grant		74%

Grant is the appropriate percentage of TCI or approved development costs, whichever is the lower. This is clearly assuming a far more generous regime than the one current in 1996! It can be seen that if the association sets rents lower than those assumed, the grant will be inadequate, and the association will have to consider using its reserves to subsidise the development, or some other method.

Shared ownership and other low-cost home ownership schemes have their own grant regimes. The share of the approved Development Programme taken up by such initiatives has grown steadily to around 25 per cent by the mid-1990s. Grants are made available on the unsold equity of the properties: that is, the part of the value unsold by the association. Assumptions are made about how much leaseholders can afford to pay by way of rent and service charges to arrive at grant levels. As shared owners buy further shares or 'tranches' of the property, the association reimburses the Corporation, until eventually, if the entire property is purchased, the entire HAG amount is repaid. Thus HAG is in this case an interest-free loan. Surpluses are retained by the association.

Worked example of shared ownership grant (simplified)

Three-bedroom house, TCI area A 1998

1. TCI for property	£80 000
2. Equity purchased initially	25%
3. TCI on which grant paid	£60 000
4. Loan-related service charge	£3 000 p.a.

5. Equivalent loan (10% p.a.)*   £30 000

6. Void assumption   0%

7. 3. –5. = norm grant   £30 000

8. Norm grant (%) (7./3.(%)) 50%

In 1999, shared owner purchases remainder of equity

1. Value of property, 1999   £80 000

2. Further equity purchased   £60 000

3. Grant rate (1998)   50%

4. Amount to Housing Corporation
   50% × 60 000   £30 000

5. Amount to association (remainder) £30 000

*Interest-only loan assumed for clarity.

Local authorities can advance HAG to associations. They do so from money borrowed on the basis of credit approvals, or from capital receipts. The rules relating to grant levels are the same as for direct Housing Corporation grant. If a council advances HAG from borrowings, the Corporation will repay the authority. This is known as 'back-to-back' funding. Money recouped in this way has to be offset against debt. If capital receipts are used, the local authority is reimbursed; again, there is a requirement that such money be used to redeem debt. Additionally, councils can make grant funding, even to unregistered associations, available under the 1972 Local Government Act, although levels are generally much lower.

It seems likely that the HAG regime will remain in its present form for the foreseeable future, although equally likely that grant rates will continue to fall, in line with public expenditure restraint. Net capital expenditure on housing associations reduced from a high point of £2 304 000 (1992–93) to stabilise at around £1 450 000 by the mid-1990s, and grant rates have fallen as well.

It is argued that associations are now well known to the private finance markets, and can obtain deferred interest and other low-start products which will offset the real costs of borrowing in early years and allow for the setting of affordable rents. It is also argued that the early 1990s saw real falls in land and construction prices, meaning that associations could make considerable economies, especially if operating in consortia, buying land jointly and dividing it up, to capitalise on the considerable bargaining power of large organisations buying significant chunks of land. However, disappointing completion results in the mid-1990s showed that these attitudes have been rather over-optimistic. As grant rates decline, associations' gearing – the ratio of liabilities to assets, that is, amounts borrowed to prop-

erty owned – increases. Lenders are often reluctant to lend where the gearing is too high – that is, where there is little asset cover to give security
against which a legal charge can be taken, to be activated if the organisation defaults; and if they do, interest rates – the measure of lender risk –
may be high, and terms relatively short. This caused something of a crisis
in the mid-1990s, as many lenders announced their intention to withdraw
from association lending altogether, even though they had been stressing
the importance of examining projected cash-flows and business plans to satisfy themselves of a healthy projected revenue position for some years previously.

Additionally, housing associations have had to plunder reserves to subsidise developments to help ensure affordable rents, or to live with relatively high-rent regimes with consequent risks of high arrears, or the
creation of 'benefit ghettoes'.

Rehabilitation schemes have been hit especially hard as a result of the
structure of the new grant regime. None of this bodes well for the future
of the voluntary housing movement, which is seen as the major provider of
social housing for the future. If greater notice was taken by the Corporation
of the National Federation of Housing Associations when it argues that
management and maintenance assumptions are too low, and that TCIs are
unrealistic, then a more rational grant regime would emerge. Unfortunately,
the production of good-quality, affordable homes for rent and sale to those
unable to compete in the marketplace seems to be secondary to the over-
weening desire to cut public expenditure by any means available, supposedly avoiding inflation. It would be a shame, and to the eternal discredit of
today's policy-makers, if the net result of the application of the 1988 regime
was the production of the slums of tomorrow at high rents.

Attempts have been made to mitigate the negative effects of the 1988
regime, such as cheap or free local authority land to offset development
costs, and land or housing secured from private developers by councils in
return for enhanced planning permission under the 'planning obligation'
mechanism of section 104 of the 1990 Town and Country Planning Act as
modified by the 1991 Planning and Compensation Act, about which more
will be said in Chapter 6. These are essentially cosmetic, and do little to
address the fundamental shortcomings of the grant regime.

2.3.3   Revenue

Prior to the 1989 regime, associations were obliged to charge fair rents. If
they were unable to raise sufficient revenue in any one year to run their
operations, and were able to show that this position was unavoidable, they
could receive revenue subsidy known as Revenue Deficit Grant, via the
Corporation. Special needs housing providers, running hostels and shared
housing projects entailing supported accommodation received Hostel
Deficit Grant, to help with their high running costs. Associations which ran
into surplus, as rents rose and loans were repaid, had to pay some of it back

to the Corporation into the Revenue Surplus Fund. Those associations which developed prior to April 1989 still operate that portion of their portfolios under those rules.

This system was abolished for general needs associations from April 1989. There are no revenue subsidies for properties developed after that date. It is assumed that rents and other charges will ensure that running accounts balance, something made possible since the abolition of fair rents. From 1991, Hostel Deficit Grant on existing special needs properties was replaced by Transitional Special Needs Management Allowance, payable on a similar basis; and for new special needs developments, a cash-limited Special Needs Management Allowance (SNMA) is payable at a fixed rate per unit, without reference to actual deficits. An article at the end of the chapter, 'Funding special needs housing: change on the way' (p. 75), deals with changes in the special needs revenue regime.

At the time of writing (September 1995), the Housing Corporation is considering imposing a limit on housing association rents, popularly known as the X factor. Rents will only be allowed to rise by a factor determined by multiplying the Retail Price Index by X, a figure which has yet to be disclosed. This is a form of rent control, abolished for new private sector tenancies since 1989, and hitherto for association tenancies after that date. There appears to be no suggestion that grant rates will be raised if rent control is adopted. If they are not raised, it is hard to see how associations can possibly continue to develop unless they continue to plunder reserves. Such suggestions follow from the Treasury policy to cap housing benefit. It is generally agreed that association rents should be affordable by those unable to compete in the market without undue reliance upon the housing benefit system, but without increased grant rates it is hard to see how this can be achieved in practice. The debate about personal subsidy versus bricks and mortar subsidy is highlighted in an article at the end of Chapter 1: 'Welfare housing and the Minister' (p. 30).

Associations are required to keep revenue accounts in a 'PLC' (public limited company) format, under the 1992 Registered Housing Association (Accounting Requirements) Order. These changes were made in 1993 to ensure that accounts were readily understandable by private financiers: previously, the accounts had been designed for civil service consumption, and were non-standard. The two main accounts are the Balance Sheet and the Income and Expenditure Account. The Balance Sheet is a list of assets and liabilities, of use to lenders when considering what security to take when making loans; the Income and Expenditure Account shows all the association's revenue operations, and contains a Property Revenue Account, the management account which relates to income from and expenditure on homes run and/or owned by the association rather than more general operational income and expenditure. This is of great interest to potential lenders in assessing how prudently the organisation is being run; and lenders will often, as a matter of course, demand to see past revenue accounts and projections before committing money. The Housing Corporation receives these accounts annually for audit purposes, to ensure that public money is being spent wisely, and in accordance with the law. It also undertakes inspections on site for the same purposes.

The format of housing association accounts – theoretical case

CENTRAL HOUSING ASSOCIATION (OWNERSHIP) LTD, ANNUAL ACCOUNTS TO YEAR ENDED 31 MARCH 1995

1. INCOME AND EXPENDITURE ACCOUNT

ITEM	1995	1994
	(£'000)	(£'000)
Turnover (1)	497	505
Operating Costs	(301)	(289)
OPERATING SURPLUS	196	216
Result of property sales	—	—
Interest receivable and similar income	11	4
Interest payable and similar charges (2)	(187)	(110)
SURPLUS ON ORDINARY ACTIVITIES BEFORE TAX	20	110
Tax on surplus on ordinary activities (3)	(24)	(18)
Grant receivable against taxation	24	18
SURPLUS FOR THE YEAR	20	110
Balance brought forward	184	74
BALANCE AT 31 MARCH 1995	204	184

Notes:

(1) *Turnover.* This is the total (gross) income from lettings – in this case, from rents and service charges.
(2) *Interest payable*, i.e. on loans raised by the association.
(3) *Tax.* Payable at 25 per cent (1995) on surpluses. However, this is covered by grants received from the Secretary of State for the Environment under section 54 of the Housing Act 1988.

2. BALANCE SHEET

ITEM	1995 (£'000)	1994 (£'000)
TANGIBLE FIXED ASSETS (1)		
Housing Properties at Cost	10 000	8 000
Less Housing Association Grant	(7 000)	(5 000)
	3 000	3 000
CURRENT ASSETS (2)		
Debtors	150	300
Cash at bank and at hand	300	400
	450	700
CREDITORS: amounts falling due within 1 year	100	500
NET CURRENT ASSETS	350	200 TOTAL
ASSETS LESS TOTAL LIABILITIES	3 350	3 200
(*i.e. tangible fixed assets plus net current assets*)		
CREDITORS: amounts falling due after more than 1 year	3 000	2 800
PROVISION FOR LIABILITIES AND CHARGES	146	216
CAPITAL AND RESERVES:		
Called-up share capital	—	—
Income and Expenditure Account	204	184
	3 350	3 200

Notes:

(1) *Tangible fixed assets* are accounted as the capital cost of providing housing, from which is deducted any grants received from the Housing Corporation (in the form of HAG).

(2) *Current assets* includes any cash in the bank, and debts owed to the association. From this is taken any sums which must be paid to the association's creditors within the year, to give *net current assets*.

To balance the books, the value of amounts due from the association after one year, any provisions made for liabilities and charges, and capital and reserves which the association has must be set against assets minus liabilities.

A Cash Flow Statement to the end of the accounting year is also required. This shows the operating surplus over the year, any changes in financing during the year (that is, the extent to which loans have increased), and changes in cash held by the association over the year.

More will be said about housing association finance in the Housing Associations Chapter.

2.4   Personal subsidies

As previously stated, social housing tenants are increasingly reliant upon personal subsidy: income support, family credit and housing benefit. Housing benefit comes in two forms: Housing Benefit (Public Sector) – rebates deducted from council tenants' rents prior to payment; and Housing Benefit (Private Sector) – cash payments made to qualifying private and housing association tenants to help with rent payments. The present system, whereby local housing authorities are responsible for its assessment and payment, was instituted fully in 1988 under the 1986 Social Security Act, although subsequent regulations and primary legislation have significantly affected it.

The concept is relatively straightforward. Claimants, whether on income support or not, are assessed for their 'applicable amount'. This is the amount the state deems that a household can live on, and is broadly the same as what they would receive from Income Support if eligible. Those on Income Support receive full housing benefit, covering their entire eligible rent (some things, like heating charges, are not eligibles). Those earning at their 'applicable amount' also receive full housing benefit. Having capital above £16 000 disqualifies people from claiming housing benefit; lower amounts are assumed to earn a notional rate of interest, which is added to the income calculation and thus reduces benefit. Barring a small allowance, which is varied annually, (for 1995) 65p is withdrawn from the benefit for every £1 earned above that applicable amount. This gradual withdrawal of benefit is known as the taper. In 1995, limits were placed on rent eligible for housing benefit to try to encourage renters to bargain with their landlords more effectively when taking up accommodation, and to be realistic about what they can afford; but the real objective was to save public money and reduce the need to increase indirect taxation excessively.

The systems of subsidy to local authorities have already been described. Whilst the majority of Housing Benefit (Private Sector) claims are reim bursed up to 100 per cent with penalties for inefficient processing and other delays, the same is not true for public sector claims.

Housing benefit is supposed to form part of the national income support system, but in some authorities the public sector part is in reality a throwback to the local Poor Law system of parish relief beloved of the Victorians, with poorer tenants' rebates being paid for from the rents of those who can afford to pay them without reduction. Its most controversial aspect is the poverty trap, whereby the steepness of the taper means that, when childcare and fares are taken into account, it is often more expensive to work at a given wage level, even one considerably over Income Support levels, than to continue to rely upon state support. This cannot be right if it is desired to encourage people back to work: it cannot be correct to condemn people to a life on benefit and in dependency just because they cannot afford to take on work, and it must be a powerful stimulus to a burgeoning informal, or 'black' economy, at tremendous loss to the Exchequer. Unfortunately, the effects of local authority and housing association subsidy 'reforms' have been to raise social housing rents, and effectively deepen the poverty trap, with worrying social consequences.

2.5 Conclusion

Since the early 1980s, the subsidy emphasis has shifted from 'bricks and mortar' to personal subsidy. Local authorities and associations have been subjected to capital and revenue restraint, entailing higher rents. Councils have been reduced to the role of enabler, supplying cheap municipal land or private land through planning negotiations to housing associations. Associations have, in turn, seen their programmes cut by a reduction in the number of Approved Development Programmes, with a greater emphasis on low-cost home ownership. What it all amounts to is that housing need has manifestly not been met sufficiently. The existence of homelessness and appalling housing conditions for some is witness to this, and it is an indictment of the values of today's society. The final article at the end of this chapter, 'The Budget, social housing and homelessness', (p. 77), seeks to summarise the effects of financial stringency in the social housing sector, and argues that the resultant increases in homelessness will inevitably increase the social security bill. It is difficult to escape the conclusion that macro-economic decision-making fails to account adequately for the social consequences of a declining social housing programme; and it is to the subject of homelessness, the most pressing manifestation of housing need, that we now turn.

Articles

1. 'The bottom line: the finance of council housing in the 1990s'

2. 'Accounting for sheltered housing'

3. 'Subsidising council housing'

4. 'Funding special needs housing: change on the way'

5. 'The Budget, social housing and homelessness'

The bottom line: the finance of council housing in the 1990s

The community charge controversy has overshadowed other local government issues recently, but the financial aspects of the 1989 Local Government and Housing Act, effective from 1 April 1990, will have equally significant consequences. It will change the ways in which relatively low-cost housing is provided to meet increasing levels of need.

The government is tightening its control on housing expenditure. Local authorities still need the Secretary of State for the Environment's permission to finance their capital programmes, and will receive this as a 'Basic Credit Approval': permission to borrow up to a certain limit, plus 'Supplementary Credit Approvals' for projects in line with government priorities. But for the first time, central estimates of cash from the sale of council land and housing are taken into account when setting borrowing limits. It is likely that these will be tight, in line with the government's stated intention to limit public sector borrowing in attacking inflation. Councils will, more than ever before, be reliant on council house sales to bolster their capital programmes, but what if sales do not meet expectations.

The ability to spend capital receipts is further restricted, with an emphasis on paying off debts incurred through the mass housing programmes of earlier decades. Seventy-five per cent of such receipts have to be used for this, leaving only 25 per cent for major improvement and new-build programmes. The old cascade system, where most of the cash could be spent over a number of years, has been swept away with the 1980 Local Government Planning and Land Act – prescribed expenditure rules. Several options used by councils to supplement programmes faced with declining Housing Investment Programme allocations have been halted, and capitalised repair schemes have been restricted. Increasingly, councils will have to work as enablers to the voluntary and private sectors to try to meet housing need in their areas.

New subsidy arrangements for Housing Revenue Accounts (HRAs) will have equally dramatic effects. Most authorities outside London, and several within it, had become ineligible for 1980 Housing Act subsidy, owing both to rent increases and to large amounts of interest credited to HRAs from unspent cash realised through house-sales. This reflected the government's desire that council housing should be self-financing. Some generated a revenue surplus, and transferred it to the general rate fund. But many found that the costs of running a housing service could not be met through rents and interest alone, and passed rates money to the HRA to avoid big rent rises or cutting services. The government recognised these transfers' value, including a related element in the rate support grant. The new Act removes the power to subsidise the HRA from rates, the so-called 'ring-fence'. This will inflate rents in councils which made such payments, although in the first year such withdrawals will be roughly covered by an element in the new subsidy. However, surpluses will have to be paid into a non-housing account: it is a one-way route.

Controversy has been stirred by the novel treatment of rent rebates. Councils received 97 per cent of the cost of providing such reductions from the Exchequer's Department of Social Security budget. Traditionally, rent rebates have been regarded as a national welfare benefit in the same way as Income Support. Now this separate support has been abolished, and integrated into the new HRA subsidy. What will happen when a council loses subsidy eligibility? It is clear that the rebates of poorer tenants will then be supported by the rents of the better-off. The principle of treating rent rebates as a national income support measure has been been abandoned. Studies show that council tenants are drawn increasingly from lower-income groups, those unable to secure housing elsewhere. How then will increasing demand for rent rebates be financed?

The 'bottom line' – balancing the books – depends on the relationship between the Government's income and expenditure assumptions used to calculate subsidy, linked to its directive that rents should increase, and the actual figures in accounts. Likely overestimates of income and underestimations of expenditure will mean less subsidy than required, entailing tough decisions on both rents and service-levels in attempts to keep accounts out of the red.

The comments of Richard Darlington, Cambridge's Assistant City Housing Manager, express common concerns. He said,

The new rules mean rents go up by 20 per cent from April; higher levels have been avoided only by cutting costs on essential services. Due to cash constraints, there won't be any council housebuilding next year. We're increasingly reliant on housing associations – and this at a time when we're facing a growing homelessness crisis. We provided a good but economic service before; the new Act will make this very difficult. It's quite a challenge.

A challenge indeed. Future articles [in *PSLG*] will examine the prospects for meeting housing need under the new financial regime.

PSLG, April 1990

Addendum (October 1995)

The subsidy system has been in place virtually unchanged since its introduction. The community charge has been replaced by the council tax. There is no sign of councils being allowed to use all their receipts from housing sales to build new houses or improve older ones.

Questions

1. In what ways did the government tighten its control over council capital and revenue finance in 1990?
2. What were the new rules on the use of capital receipts?
3. What is the ring-fence, and why is it unwelcome to local authorities?

Accounting for sheltered housing

A central tenet in Care in the Community initiatives is that those requiring specialist care and services by virtue of mental or physical disability or age should be able to live as independently as possible. There has been a wholesale move away from institutionalisation over the past 2 decades, and Category Two sheltered housing for the elderly provided by the public sector exemplifies this desirable aim. Local housing authorities have a pivotal role, as strategic planners, providers and enablers, in ensuring that the residential and care needs of elderly people are met. Their warden services help ensure that clients receive the care they are entitled to within the familiar community of friends and relations. Recently, questions raised about the funding source for this service have led to a re-evaluation of the role of the warden.

Warden services have traditionally been accounted within the Housing Revenue Account (HRA), the council fund into which rents and subsidies are paid, and to which housing management services are charged. The 1989 Local Government and Housing Act entails that this account should reflect the purely housing functions of local authorities. In 1992, the Court of Appeal ruled that certain activities performed by wardens in Ealing were akin to social services 'care' functions, and that therefore the cost of such services is not properly chargeable to the HRA, but should be charged to the general fund.

This arose from a tenant of Ealing Council taking that authority to court over an average £28.48 weekly rent rise in 1991, on the grounds that rent money was being used to pay for non-housing management tasks. Since the Ealing judgment, the government has consulted with councils and other interested parties as to the accounting arrangements for the service. The Housing and Urban Development Bill contains a clause allowing housing authorities to provide 'welfare services' and charge them to the HRA on a temporary basis, until arrangements are eventually decided by regulation, which may withdraw such powers. It is expected that the welfare element of the warden service will be excluded from the HRA from April 1994, or following local government reorganisation.

The implications of these changes go beyond accounting conventions, and serious definitional questions are raised. It is undeniable that, because of the nature of their client group, wardens of elderly schemes' activities go beyond enforcing tenancy conditions and other traditional housing management duties. Wardens may, but do not invariably, counsel on health and personal matters, liaise with medical and social services, and administer first aid; and they may, unusually, provide basic nursing. These are some of the 'welfare tasks' recognised in the government consultation paper *Housing welfare services and the Housing Revenue Account* (September 1992).

They certainly provide 'housing management' services as well: collecting rents, assisting with allocations, overseeing contractors, tenant consultation, attending meetings, and so forth, although, just as with welfare services, the extent to which this is true varies with organisation and scheme. But this over-simple attempt at categorisation raises the question as to where housing services end and welfare services begin. For example, suppose the warden advises a client about housing benefit and income support. The content of such advice relates both to housing management (such information is vital to ensure maximal rent collection) and client welfare (underclaiming may result in poverty, with resultant health implications). How is it possible to cost out each element without bureaucratic absurdity? The same applies to liaising with social and medical services about health needs. Such discussions are rarely confined to medical matters: the issues of aids, adaptations and possibly transfer to other accommodation frequently arise. What looks at first to be a straightforward categorisation matter turns out to be a labyrinth of uncertainty.

Even supposing it were possible to devise a clear list of 'housing' and 'care' functions, how would local authorities decide how to apportion the costs? In such a complex area, generalisations are not possible, and unless they are, it would be impossible to account the activities accurately unless wardens were continually monitored, or their duties unreasonably restricted. Assuming that this issue is resolved, or more likely ignored, the quality of warden services would become vulnerable to General Fund constraints. And the thought of two funds paying for such a diverse service, unless the apportionment problem is simplified to the point of absurdity, is enough to make any rational council treasurer quit for offshore fund management!

The central objection to these proposed changes is that any tenant may eventually require warden services. Housing management duties in this area imply caring duties (they are inseparable); therefore there is every reason why tenants should continue to pay for the package of warden services, with appropriate central subsidy, as hitherto. Best practice would be to allow councils to charge these costs to the HRA on a permanent basis.

PSLG, June 1993

Addendum (October 1995)

The position at the time of writing is that councils are allowed to pay for warden services, including care, from the Housing Revenue Account, but are encouraged to recharge other budgets where appropriate. This power may be revoked at any time by the Secretary of State for the Environment.

Questions

1. Why is warden-controlled sheltered accommodation an essential part of Care in the Community?
2. What were the objections raised by the Ealing tenant to that council's method of financing warden services?
3. What problems would be involved in budgeting separately for the care and housing management aspects of warden costs?

Subsidising council housing

In December 1993, the Department of the Environment issued its housing revenue account subsidy determinations for the coming year. The year 1994/95 will be the fourth to be governed by the provisions of Part 6 of the 1989 Local Government and Housing Act, supplying further evidence that government wishes to progressively withdraw central financial help until it can be phased out altogether.

Four proposals in relation to the determination were made by the Department, for consultation. They were: to increase rent guidelines by around 7.5 per cent (£1.50–£2.90 per week) for individual councils; to increase the management and maintenance allowance by 4 per cent, but adjusted to reflect performance; to simplify the rules on disproportionate rent increases; and to change the method of calculating consolidated loan fund interest rates for subsidy purposes. Following discussion, the first three proposals were carried, with the fourth deferred until 1995/96. Tables indicating guideline rents and management and maintenance allowances for each authority have now been published.

The first two issues are of great importance to the level of financial assistance which councils can expect to receive towards running their housing stock, and have significant knock-on effects for funding losses through rebates. The 1989 Act system pays subsidy – known as Housing Revenue Account (HRA) subsidy, on the basis of 'notional' HRAs – what the government believes council housing accounts should look like. The level of subsidy which authorities receive is therefore based on notional deficits. Accounts in deficit can thus be treated as if they were in balance, or even in surplus. In the latter case, the authority is required to pay the notional surplus into its General Fund. Additionally, there is no longer a separate, ring-fenced housing benefit subsidy; a low estimate of rebates granted is included in a general calculation, which simply weighs notional income against expenditure. A consequence is that some councils must finance losses through rebating from internal resources – by raising rents, or cutting services. Commentators have pointed out that this reduces what was conceived as part of a national social security system to local Poor Law provision!

Rent guidelines and management and maintenance figures issued by the D.o.E. are not binding on councils: rent policy and management and maintenance expenditure are local policy issues. These figures form the basis of the notional calculation. But the consequence of failing to approximate to these guidelines is often unacceptable subsidy losses, with consequences for rent levels and service provision. It is arguable therefore that local policy has in this case been usurped by central diktat.

The rent guidelines have been increased by a figure in excess of inflation trends, whereas management and maintenance allowances, though increased by a slightly higher factor than inflation, are assumed to rise less steeply. This looks like an attempt to deliberately overestimate rent yields and underestimate expenditure in order to justify shaving subsidy further: it is hard to find any other explanation for these assumptions. Otherwise why not assume a similar increase factor for both income and expenditure?

The guideline rents are based on capital values: the assumption is made that the local rent yield will be proportional to the Right to Buy value of councils' stock in relation to the national portfolio. This odd formulation purported to ensure that rents reflect property values, as they sometimes do in the private sector, although the formula had to be subtly adjusted to try to avoid the glaring absurdities which resulted. But the figures make strange reading. It is hard to understand why rents in Kensington and Chelsea, assumed for 1994/95 to average £55.67, should be so much higher than those in Westminster (£49.11). And residents of St Albans will be surprised to learn that their average rent, based on capital value, is assumed to be around £1 less than that in Southwark! What is clear is that this method of estimating rents bears little or no relation to either the historic costs or the revenue costs of running housing stock.

The management and maintenance guidelines are based upon a national figure, weighted by eight factors ranging from 'sparsity' – presumably the distance officers have to travel between dwellings – to the amount of basic credit approval received, having little to do with running costs. The results are so obscure that the department might as well have divided the actual costs by a number selected by a counting horse.

The upshot is a wholly unsatisfactory settlement, which will do nothing to assist with the running of a national asset, and which underlines the need to reform the subsidy system. It is necessary, in the interests of credibility and equity, to devise a system which takes account of the actual costs of running social housing rather than relying upon an increasingly arcane conjuring trick, which is what the 1989 Act system has patently become.

PSLG, April 1994

Questions

1. Why are rent guidelines and assumptions made about management and maintenance expenditure so important in determining the ability of local authorities to provide housing services?
2. What is the notional housing revenue account?
3. What are the main criticisms of the subsidy system made in the article? What changes might be made to rectify some of the problems which result from it?

CORNWALL COLLEGE
L R C

Funding special needs housing: change on the way

Councils and others working with special needs housing providers need to be aware of the financial constraints within which they operate. Care in the Community implies the closure of institutions and their replacement by housing and care schemes, but councils are unable to make new provision for vulnerable client groups to any great extent. They must therefore enable other organisations – principally housing associations – to do so. The Housing Corporation has recently published a consultation paper which, if accepted, will force further economies on to associations, affecting the quality and affordability of special needs provision.

There is no generally accepted definition of special needs groups, but the Housing Corporation classification, not intended to be exhaustive, suggests that they are those requiring intensively managed housing. This includes those with learning difficulties, physical disability, mental health-related problems, drug or alcohol-related problems, ex-offenders, women at risk of domestic violence, single homeless people in need of intensive housing management, frail elderly people, young people at risk or leaving care, and HIV and AIDS sufferers.

Prior to the passage of the 1988 Housing Act, special needs housing schemes, mainly hostels or shared housing, received housing association grant (HAG) on a residual basis: fair rents would be set first, and grants would be assessed to cover any capital costs which could not be met via a loan raised from rents, management and maintenance expenses having been deducted. The latter were often so high that grants were around 100 per cent of approved costs. In addition, in recognition of the extremely high management costs of such schemes, the Housing Corporation paid additional revenue subsidy known as Hostel Deficit Grant, based on actual shortfalls between rent yield and expenses. Additionally, 10–15 per cent of void costs were met, as well as furniture replacement cost. Generous staff to client ratios were assumed in the calculation of subsidy.

This all changed as a result of the new financial regime introduced under the 1988 Housing Act, which, initially just for general needs schemes, replaced residual Housing Association Grant (HAG) with grant fixed on assumed costs subject to strict value-for-money limits known as Total Cost Indicators (TCI), with associations having to make up the shortfall with private loans. The new system was introduced for special needs providers later, from April 1991, with adjustments to ensure unbroken provision, a reflection of the importance attached to Care in the Community. For special needs schemes, 100 per cent HAG on anticipated costs, subject to TCI, was guaranteed, but with the risk of overrun being met by associations, although the Corporation still shares the risk 50:50 with 'non-programme' smaller associations. Hostel Deficit Grant (HDG) was replaced by Special Needs Management Allowance (SNMA) for new schemes, based on ideal rather than actual management costs, and thus tighter. For existing schemes, HDG was replaced by Transitional Special Needs Management Allowance (TSNMA) based on prior HDG levels, to allow a smooth transition to the new system.

A consequence of these changes was that new rents were significantly higher than rents had been previously, leading to charges of creating or deepening a poverty trap for tenants reliant on housing benefit.

The 1994 Consultation Paper, The Housing Corporation's proposals for introducing a system of three year contractual review of special needs housing revenue funding, is a further step on the road to cost control. There is suspicion in the Housing Corporation that, owing to the multiplicity of revenue support avenues available, TSNMA is being paid at over-generous rates. This, combined with impetus given by remarks made by former Housing Minister Sir George Young that special needs revenue funding must secure better value for money and reflect national priorities (presumably greater targeting), means that a cash limit of £128 million may be imposed on special needs revenue subsidies, whatever the actual costs. The Housing Corporation has admitted that this may drive up rents, and so increase the depth of the poverty trap. Understandably, the Department of Social Security has questioned the value of the proposal.

It is likely that every scheme will be subject to a three-year annual review of costs which will be used to assess subsidy levels, a keystone of which will be whether the scheme offers 'good' value for money. This could be used as an excuse for further cuts in subsidy. Such economies could lead associations to decrease space standards, go for shared accommodation, reduce management support, and other cost-cutting exercises to keep rents affordable in the light of declining central help.

If they do so, the most vulnerable clients will suffer. The report is out for consultation with a variety of bodies ranging from the NFHA to local authority housing and social services departments. It is vitally important that all players consider the proposals carefully, and argue against a somewhat arbitrary cash limit which may worsen the lot of the most vulnerable members of society.

PSLG, January 1995

The Budget, social housing and homelessness

The December 1994 Budget was significant for housing: its effects will become apparent later this year [1995]. Councils' credit approvals are reduced by £88 million for 1995/96: last year, excluding Estate Action Approvals, the figure stood at £3977 million. The only capital boost will be a £25 million increase to the earmarked Single Regeneration Budget, encompassing Housing Action Trusts and Estate Action. This provides further evidence of greater targeting of resources on centrally directed priorities, taking control away from local democratic bodies. Prior to the Budget, net capital expenditure supported by credit approvals was to be £1235 million; reducing Right to Buy receipts, expected to fall from the 1994/95 yield of £245 million, compound the inability of councils to invest in their housing.

Credit approvals have been static in real terms since 1988, as has local authority capital expenditure. Clearly, councils will increasingly have to take on the enabling role, supporting housing associations and other providers via grants and through planning, to ensure continued social housing provision.

The Budget paved the way for housing benefit changes. October 1995 will see restrictions on benefit levels payable in the private sector, although it will not affect existing claimants – until they wish, or have, to move. Peter Lilley, the Secretary of State for Social Security, believes in re-erecting the sort of benefit caps which were tried, but abandoned, in the late 1980s. Lilley and the Chancellor think that relatively generous housing benefit payment levels led to landlords increasing rents to those on social security in the firm knowledge that the state would ensure payment, and that capping reduces the incentive to push rents upwards. The cap will supposedly give prospective tenants more incentive to negotiate a reasonable rent with landlords, and consider choosing cheaper accommodation. Councils will generally be restricted to benefit payments up to the average rent for similar properties in the area, and only 50 per cent of the rent above that, although there will be some discretion to pay more in exceptional cases. There will be subsidy restrictions to reinforce this policy.

This did not work in the 1980s. Then, with property prices rising, the policy led many landlords to sell their assets rather than renting them. Now the property market is flat, it is unlikely that this strategy will be pursued. Instead, private landlords will charge market rents to those who can afford them, and ignore 'negotiations' from those dependent upon benefit. This strategy will increase homelessness and the plight of the badly housed.

It is likely that councils will have to deal with the consequences of more repossession in the owner-occupied sector from October 1995: those taking out mortgages after that date will not be eligible for income support to cover interest payments until nine months after losing employment. It is expected that borrowers will arrange mortgage protection insurance to cover this eventuality; but this is not readily available for many, including those who are self-employed or whose income is seasonal.

Mortgage insurance adds considerably to outgoings; and if interest rates continue to rise, the net effects of this may be to put such strain on some household incomes that default and homelessness will rise. Will lenders really accept much-reduced payments during the period of ineligibility for income support help? With reductions in council capital budgets, it will be difficult to provide substitute homes for those who are driven to default.

Housing associations have also suffered from public expenditure cutbacks, with almost £300 million being lost from the projected Approved Development Programme, entailing a loss of 17 000 new homes from the 1995/96 development programme. Shared ownership will suffer, with an estimated 12 500 homes as opposed to the projected 20 000 being made available through traditional and Do It Yourself Shared Ownership channels. Approvals for new homes will be down to around 27 500 homes for 1995/96, lower than any informed estimate of need, ranging from 50 000 to 100 000 every year for the foreseeable future. If housing associations are to be the main providers of new social housing, and their ability to do so is savaged in this way, who will house the homeless in the future? If associations try to do more with less, given that interest rates may well rise, the results can only be higher rents. Will they be caught by the housing benefit cap?

One thing is certain: increased homelessness, which must surely result from the above, will increase social security expenditure, as councils are forced to increase use of bed and breakfast, private sector leasing and housing association as management agents schemes, all relatively expensive. The homeless and those lacking decent accommodation will be the main casualties of ill-thought-out public expenditure control measures, until the problem is defined away by redrafting housing legislation.

PSLG, February 1995

Questions

1. What evidence is there for increasing central government control over local authority housing and housing-related finance?

2. Is it reasonable to expect that imposing caps on housing benefit subsidy and payments will reduce private sector rents? Summarise the arguments for and against.
3. What are the likely long-term effects of continued public sector spending restraint on social housing provision and management?

3 Homelessness

3.1 Introduction

Homelessness is the housing problem which will not go away. In 1990, almost 170 000 people were accepted as homeless in Britain by local authorities, a figure which rose from 63 000 in 1978, when the legislation changed. There is no sign of these figures diminishing significantly, although there were slight falls in the mid-1990s. In 1990, in England alone there were over 45 000 households in temporary accommodation, nearly one quarter of whom were in bed and breakfast. This figure rose from just over 4 000 in 1980. Each one of these figures represents a human tragedy, dashed dreams, and often months or even years in squalid short-term accommodation before a permanent home can be secured, if ever.

Nobody who has visited central London, or any major city, can fail to notice the street-sleeping and begging there: railway stations, bridges and arches have their cardboard cities, and the doorways of famous stores become refuges from the cold and rain at night, despite the availability of limited hostel places. Behind the impressive facades of Bayswater hotels, in Central West London, families are crowded together in tiny rooms, sometimes sharing basic cooking and sanitary facilities with ten others. Seaside towns like Morecambe and Scarborough are now known more for housing homeless families in their faded guest-houses than for offering holiday pleasures. And Brighton, symbol of Regency opulence, with its pavilion and famous pier, is the undisputed homelessness capital of the South-East: in the 1990s it had the highest percentage of homeless persons per population of any city in the United Kingdom.

The mismanagement of Care in the Community has added to the tide of human misery: all too often, those in care or who have lived most of their lives in institutions which at least offered some semblance of security, if precious little dignity, have been ejected on to the streets with a threadbare care package, to find their own solutions. It took a succession of documentaries and sad news stories to force new legislation – the 1989 Children Act – to take the plight of young, vulnerable care-leavers seriously and guarantee at least limited accommodation to those deemed at risk.

It has already been argued that there is serious underproduction of social housing – the facts speak for themselves – and this trend seems set to continue. The rate of homelessness increases coincides almost exactly with the reduction in social housing starts between 1980 and 1990. Homelessness acceptances increased by more than 100 per cent. Whereas 30 000 new social homes were built in 1979, this figure fell to around 2000 in 1989, a reduction of almost 90 per cent. The rate of household formation has not increased markedly. The private rented sector has continued to decline. Owner-occupation remains relatively expensive. There has been a reduction in re-lets, largely due to Right to Buy sales, and failure to replenish losses. It is unnecessary to blame social change or a growth in 'irresponsibility' to explain the growth in homelessness. Homelessness is the housing nightmare which will not go away, even though attempts are made from time to time to massage the figures, or redefine it away by attempted legislative change. The tragedy of *Cathy Come Home* will haunt us for many years to come, unless a co-ordinated approach is taken to invest in much-needed social housing.

3.2   Evolution of duties towards homeless people

In the nineteenth century, homeless families had to rely upon the goodwill of their parish for rudimentary workhouse accommodation, if anything was provided at all, under the Poor Law regime. Although the problem was recognised, precious little was done about it until after the Second World War, when the 1948 National Assistance Act imposed a rudimentary duty on local authorities to provide some sort of temporary accommodation for limited categories of homeless persons. At the end of the war, many homeless persons, including those displaced by enemy action, took the law into their own hands in the face of a quite inadequate official response, and squatted ex-service camps, holiday lets and even fashionable central London apartments, which helped to force legislative response.

The 1948 Act gave local authorities a duty to secure temporary accommodation for those made homeless 'in circumstances which could not reasonably be foreseen, or in other circumstances they may in any particular case determine'. This was generally interpreted to mean homelessness as a result of fire, flood or eviction – it was far easier to evict than now. Additionally, the duty was applied largely to families with children, and it did not extend to the able-bodied, pregnant women, split families or single people. At the time, it was thought that mass municipal housing programmes would sweep the problem away, and that it would be possible to repeal the legislation in the foreseeable future. Homelessness was seen as a social problem rather than as a function of a shortage of affordable housing. Initially, welfare departments of local authorities had the responsibility to find temporary housing for those affected. The regimes were often harsh, with much use being made of hostel accommodation which often only housed women and children, forcing families to split.

In 1966, the television play *Cathy Come Home* was screened. It follows the imaginary, but all too familiar, plight of a young family that had recently moved into a privately rented flat in London, where the husband loses his job as a lorry driver through a road accident. This causes financial difficulties, leading to eviction, and ultimately forced separation, after the family has endured worsening accommodation. Cathy is eventually rehoused in a hostel run by the then welfare department of a council, which excludes the husband, who eventually disappears. When Cathy is evicted for what is deemed to be unruly behaviour in response to the patronising behaviour of the warder-nurses in charge, she makes for the railway station, only to have her children taken from her and into care. The film, made in a documentary style, is accompanied by opinions of a range of observers on housing issues. It is ironic that the film was made at the height of the municipal housing boom, when received opinion indicated that homelessness would soon be a thing of the past. Partly as a result of the film, SHELTER, the national campaign for the homeless and badly housed, was founded, and began to lobby for improved legislation to prevent the situation so graphically depicted from arising.

There is no doubt that the film heightened public awareness of the problem: but it was followed by no official response whatever. However, in 1968, the Seebohm Committee, whose prime responsibility was related to pioneering the creation of distinct social services departments, suggested that homelessness should be dealt with by housing authorities, thus confirming the problem as a housing rather than primarily a social issue, although it was not until 1974 that a joint Department of the Environment/Department of Health and Social Security circular (Circular 18/74) recommended that housing authorities should have primary responsibility for homelessness. The same circular recommended that all who found themselves homeless should be assisted, even if only through advice, and that priority for rehousing should be given to specific groups, including those with children.

However well-meaning the circular was, it was not legislation: and the 1972 Local Government Act had weakened the 1948 duty to a power. It was only after long campaigning by SHELTER and other concerned bodies that at last, in 1977, what started out as a private member's bill became the Housing (Homeless Persons Act) 1977, albeit considerably watered down from the form desired by its originators. It is to the eternal discredit of the then government that it was taken over as a government bill only when it seemed inevitable that it would go through. It received royal assent on 29 July, and came into force on 1 December 1977. It has remained substantially unchanged since that date, although threatened on occasions, especially in 1994, when an ill-fated government Homelessness Review sought to reduce local authority rehousing duties. In the mid-1980s, it was consolidated as Part 3 of the 1985 Housing Act. In 1977, a Code of Guidance was attached to the Act, to which local authorities must have regard. It was modified in 1991 as the result of much case law, and suggestions from bodies such as SHELTER and SHAC.

3.3 Local authority duties towards homeless persons

In essence, local housing authorities have a duty to find somewhere to live for homeless persons who fall into a priority category, although this means temporary accommodation in cases where they are deemed to have made themselves homeless. Additionally, authorities can refer homeless people to areas with which they have a connection if they have none in the area they apply to. For those with no priority designation, only advice and limited assistance need be offered.

The main relevant sections of Part 3 of the 1985 Housing Act are outlined in more detail in what follows.

Section 58 defines *homelessness*. Essentially, this is where the applicant, or anyone who might reasonably be expected to live with the applicant, has no accommodation that they might reasonably be expected to occupy, or no rights to occupy anywhere, or is unable to live in that accommodation (for example, for reason of anticipated violence), in England, Wales and Scotland. Thus homelessness does not mean rooflessness. Someone could be homeless in a bed and breakfast hotel, where they have at best a licence to occupy, which can be terminated on very short notice; or on a friend's floor.

Section 59 defines priority need. This is principally where the applicant, or person who might reasonably be expected to reside with them, has dependent children, is pregnant, or is vulnerable through mental or physical illness, disability, or old age. Those made homeless in emergency – through fire, flood or other disaster – are deemed to be in a priority category regardless of any other considerations. Priority need has a wide definition, and is open to interpretation by local authorities, although much case law has interpreted its meaning. If illness or disability is the issue, the extent to which it impinges on the housing situation is relevant to whether that person is considered to be in a priority category. If, for example, that illness would be made markedly worse by the person being homeless, then the person would certainly be regarded as being in priority need.

Section 60 defines *intentional homelessness*. Someone is intentionally homeless where they have deliberately done something or failed to do something in consequence of which they lose their home. For example, cases where someone refuses to pay their rent, or has been evicted for anti-social behaviour, or failed to take advice from a reasonably qualified person and finds themselves in such financial difficulties that they default on their mortgage with the consequence of repossession would all constitute intentional homelessness. The Code of Guidance does say that loss of a home through repossession following mortgage arrears should not automatically entail the judgement of intentional homelessness, since the financial difficulties might have been insuperable – so discretion is needed in coming to a decision here.

Section 61 defines local connection. A local connection may arise through residence on a continuous or discontinuous basis (6 months and 3 out of the last 5 years respectively) where residence was of the person's choice; through employment; because of family association, or for special circumstances which the authority may determine, such as its being an area with family associations, or an area in which the person was brought up. The criteria for determining local connection were devised by agreement between local authorities in 1977, amended in 1979 and approved by the House of Lords in 1983. If authorities cannot agree as to local connection, adjudication machinery exists, usually involving referral to a solicitor mutually agreed upon or other authority.

Section 62 defines the initial duties of the authority. If the local authority has reason to believe that the applicant is homeless or threatened with homelessness, it has a duty to make enquiries to establish the fact of the matter, then to establish whether there is priority need, then to discover whether homelessness is intentional. Only then may it enquire as to local connection – although it may find somewhere for the person to live without doing so. In these days of housing shortage, this is highly unlikely.

Section 63 states that if a local authority has reason to believe that the applicant is homeless and in priority need, it has a duty to secure accommodation pending outcome of those enquiries. This is usually of a temporary nature, and can include bed and breakfast, assured shorthold tenancies, short-life property, privately leased accommodation, hostels and the like.

Section 64 deals with the authority's duties of notifying its decision. This must be done in writing. Many councils use a standard form. This gives concrete information on which an appeal may be based. The notification must give information on the authority's investigation results – and will tell the applicant if the council thinks they are homeless, in priority need, or intentionally homeless, and their local connection status, if relevant. Reasons must be given for negative decisions.

Section 65 gives the local authority duties. Section 65(2) states that if the finding is that the applicant is homeless, in priority need, and not intentionally homeless, there is a duty on that local authority to secure permanent accommodation, even if some interim temporary accommodation has to be found first. It must be suitable both for the applicant and for anyone who might reasonably live with them.

Section 65(3) states that if the finding is that the applicant is homeless, in priority need, but is intentionally homeless, the duty is to find temporary accommodation for a reasonable period to allow the applicant to find a place to live. There is a duty to give them appropriate advice and assistance to help them do so. Twenty-eight days is deemed to be the minimum period by most authorities, but the period is supposed to relate to the difficulty of finding suitable accommodation in the area concerned.

Section 65(4) states that if the applicant is found to be homeless, but not in priority need, then the duty is to furnish appropriate advice and assistance: perhaps a list of accommodation agencies, or referral to a housing association or another provider, or advice on house purchase.

Section 66 states that where someone is found to be threatened with homelessness, in priority need, but not threatened 'intentionally', there is a duty to ensure that accommodation does not cease to become available, perhaps through ensuring that illegal eviction does not take place, or making sure that, when homelessness does result, there is somewhere secure for that person to go. If a person is threatened with homelessness, but not in a priority need category, or is in a priority need category but has become threatened with homelessness because of something they did or failed to do (i.e. 'intentionally'), the duty is to offer appropriate advice and assistance only.

Section 67 makes it clear that a local authority may refer someone to another authority's area only if that person has no connection with the referring council. If someone has no connection anywhere, they are deemed to be the responsibility of the authority to which they first apply.

Section 68 imposes a duty on the referring authority to find accommodation for the person referred until they are accepted and offered somewhere by the other council. There is no question of such people being left 'in the lurch'.

Section 69 deals with the provision of accommodation. There is nothing in the Act which states that councils need provide their own accommodation, although s. 22 of the same Act does state that reasonable preference must be given to homeless persons in the allocation of council property. Certainly, duties can be fulfilled by letting the authority's own accommodation under part II of the 1985 Act, but it can also be achieved by securing it through someone else, such as a housing association, or by giving appropriate advice and assistance which actually leads to the person finding somewhere reasonably permanent, perhaps an assured tenancy in the private rented sector.

These are the main provisions but others include section 70 (duty to protect belongings of those found to be homeless and in priority need); section 72 (duty of other authorities and bodies to co-operate); section 73(1) (the Secretary of State for the Environment may give public money to organisations concerned with the prevention of homelessness); section 73(2) (local authorities have analogous powers): and finally section 74, which makes it an offence to give false information in connection with a homelessness application, punishable by a fine.

The 1989 Children Act improved the situation somewhat for young care leavers. Section 20 requires that every local authority shall provide accommodation for any child in need within its area who appears to require accommodation as a result of:

- there being no person who has parental responsibility;

- being lost or abandoned;

- the person who has been caring for the child being prevented from providing the child with suitable accommodation or care.

The Act came into force in October 1991. The definition of child extends
from 16 to 21. Although social services departments are the lead agency,
there is need for close co-operation with housing departments and housing
associations to ensure that the duty is fulfilled.

The legislation is extremely complex, taken together with the Code of
Guidance and case law, and is usually administered by Homeless Persons
Officers who are specialists in that field. It is possible for aggrieved applicants to obtain a judicial review of decisions, and to obtain an order of man-
damus to force local authorities to discharge their duties. The Local
Authority Ombudsman can hear and decide on cases involving maladmin-
istration in this as in other council operations.

The legislation amounts to a method of rationing scarce resources, of sep-
arating the 'deserving' from the 'undeserving'. Those who have fouled up
through what is considered to be their own fault are penalised, ending up
in temporary accommodation and possibly eventually on the streets unless
they are lucky enough to sort their problems themselves. Those who have
no children and are in good health can expect very little help, unless they
are young and vulnerable; for them, the streets unless they are able to
secure a rare housing association offer or can buy their way out of the crisis. No wonder squatting is still a phenomenon: is it any wonder that many
have abandoned all hope of permanent housing and have become 'New
Age' travellers? And if it is the case that some become pregnant and engi-
neer parental eviction to obtain council housing, it is not surprising, given
the exclusive nature of the legislation and the near impossibility of obtaining such housing through more conventional methods.

It should also be said that at the time of writing, in 1995, the legislation
was subject to review, and proposals were contained in the White Paper of
that year to change the duties of local authorities in this respect. It was suggested, without much evidence, that homeless persons stand at an advantage in the allocation of council housing in comparison to other groups in
need. Essentially what was suggested was that homeless persons would be
placed in temporary accommodation, and their housing circumstances
weighed with others on housing registers to decide on who gets housed
first. There was considerable opposition to the proposals from local authority associations and professional and advisory bodies on the grounds that
most authorities have allocations systems which already weigh most housing need factors in this fashion: and that homelessness does not necessarily imply that a council need find permanent accommodation. An article at the end of the chapter, 'Reviewing homelessness: changing the legislation' (p. 105), addresses this issue, and concludes that if such proposals

lead to an increase in the use of temporary accommodation, not only will the suffering of homeless people increase, but so will the bill to the tax-payer, as councils are forced to resort to bed and breakfast once more.

3.4 How do people become homeless?

Every quarter, local authorities are obliged to send returns to the D.o.E. informing them as to how those accepted for rehousing as homeless reached that situation. This gives some evidence as to the reasons for homelessness, but it does not tell the whole story, because it reflects only those who actually applied. Many may not do so, believing that it is hopeless. Not every homeless person feels able to approach a council; some try instead to solve their own problem, believing that to approach officialdom is a mark of failure, a stigma which they will live with for ever.

None the less, the categories – and statistics – bear examination. The principal categories include homelessness by reason of:

1. parents, friends and relatives no longer willing or able to accommodate;

2. breakdown of relationship with partner;

3. mortgage arrears;

4. rent arrears;
   (a) local authority dwelling;
   (b) private dwelling;

5. loss of private rented dwelling (other reasons);

6. loss of service tenancy;

7. other.

Almost one-half of homelessness acceptances result from the first category. This reveals a number of things: family tension resulting from overcrowding leading to eviction; a shortage of affordable accommodation which would enable concealed households to find somewhere independent to live; personal incompatibilities; conflicts due to different stages of the family life cycle (for example, older parents not wanting to be bothered by the sound of crying infants of their children); or other lifestyle incompatibilities. The underlying reasons are endless, and it is too simplistic to apportion blame on 'the family'. It is a myth that in Victorian times families chose to stay together whatever the circumstances. There was precious little alternative then: families often needed to stay together for good economic reasons, as the entire family might have to work to generate enough for collective necessities. Those who level these criticisms usually come from well-heeled families which have been able to launch offspring into the world with sufficient cash to meet housing needs, or those who have been fortunate enough to acquire an education allowing them to compete in the jobs market, secure well-paid employment and therefore satisfy their housing needs without recourse to the state. It is the riposte of the smug and self-assured; and this dogma should be avoided by thinking people, especially those interested in the housing profession. Unfortunately, this smugness and prejudice helped generate the Homelessness Review, referred to later and in an article at the end of this chapter, 'justifying' suggestions to drastically reduce help for homeless people, enforcing the mass use of unsatisfactory temporary accommodation.

Between 1989 and 1991, the three other most significant reasons were breakdown of relationships, mortgage arrears, and 'loss of private dwelling (other reasons)'. Increases in interest rates – up to 15.4 per cent in 1990 – helped to put intolerable strain on the finances of many homeowners who found themselves homeless as a result of repossession; there is evidence in the mid-1990s that this cause is diminishing. One initiative which gave some respite to these unfortunate people was the mortgage rescue scheme, involving building societies buying the house and renting it back to the occupier, having paid them any equity after settlement of debt. Losses of private dwellings have become easier since the 1988 Housing Act. Assured tenants – tenants of non-resident landlords, where the tenancy was created after the 15 January 1989 – have far fewer rights than regulated or secure tenants, and can be evicted more easily for being in arrears. The assured shorthold tenancy is now (1995) the preferred letting vehicle for private landlords, and comes with guaranteed repossession at the expiry of 2 months' notice, with a 6 months' minimum term. The 1990s private rental regime has homelessness built into it.

Relationship breakdown may effectively create two households where there was one before. In many cases, violence or threats of such behaviour is involved, and it is possible to be homeless whilst having rights to accommodation if it is impossible to exercise that right owing to threat of violence. Much good interim work is done by a network of Women's Aid hostels, offering relatively confidential and secure temporary housing in a shared context for female victims of relationship violence, and their children. It is often the woman who has to seek assistance from the local state, because she is often weaker economically and therefore cannot find a solution through the marketplace; and because the woman often obtains interim or full custody on relationship breakdown, these households fall into a priority category, thus entailing a duty on the council to secure accommodation. Some local authorities have arrangements whereby they will agree to rehouse someone fleeing violence from another authority on a reciprocal basis.

It is arguable that relationship breakdown may often have a housing root cause. If concealed households have to live cheek by jowl with friends or relatives because they cannot afford market accommodation and have not obtained sufficient points to be rehoused in the standard manner, it is no wonder that strain and tension develops, which may cause the relationship to falter. Financial worries about mortgage or rental payments, and the

other paraphernalia associated with maintaining a home, may have a deleterious effect on partnerships. Overcrowding, especially when children
come along, may occasion problems.

Whatever the reason, it behoves homeless persons officers to behave with
courtesy and sensitivity when dealing with all cases of homelessness,
although this part of the profession is recognised as one of high stress.

3.5 Temporary accommodation

If a local authority believes that someone may be homeless and in the priority need category, it must make investigations to establish the fact of the
matter, but must also make temporary accommodation available until it has
completed its inquiries. Similarly, if it finds someone intentionally homeless
and in priority need, it must find somewhere temporarily for a reasonable
time to allow them to secure somewhere themselves. If a council does not
have any suitable accommodation itself available at that time, and cannot
find anywhere permanent through a housing association or in the private
sector, it may have little option other than to find temporary housing, even
though there are no further inquiries to be made.

The Code of Guidance (Part III of the 1985 Housing Act) discusses temporary accommodation, and when it is appropriate. The following are considered, although there are many variations on a theme:

- short-life housing
- hostels
- womens' refuges
- homeless at home
- private sector leasing
- empty government property
- mobile homes
- lodgings
- bed and breakfast.

To these could be added:

- housing associations as managing agents (HAMA)
- homes over shops (HOTS OR LOTS)
- assured shorthold tenancy schemes.

Before the early 1980s, it would have been rare to find any council using
as temporary housing anything other than bed and breakfast, its own hostels or possibly licences on permanent property. The growth in homeless-

ness since then has forced councils to seek for ever more creative, cost-effective and humane stop-gap solutions to the problem.

3.5.1 Short-life

A 'short-life' property is broadly one which has a life of less than 30 years, if a conversion or rehabilitated property, or 60 years if new-build. Local authorities used to be able to obtain public loans of a maximum of 30 years and 60 years for rehab and new-build projects respectively, corresponding with an estimate of the building's useful life. Few generalisations can be made about such places, as conditions of acquisition vary so greatly. Some councils have acquired private housing through compulsory purchase: they may have been in the path of a municipal development which has not yet happened. Some properties were acquired under slum-clearance powers, but never demolished. From 1986, many London boroughs found themselves the lucky recipients of thousands of Greater London Council properties, granted them via the London Residuary Body, which was appointed to wind up the GLC's affairs. Many of these had been acquired under road-widening schemes, or under slum-clearance or other environmental powers, and were unfit to live in, sometimes squatted. Many had been forgotten about, and quietly decayed behind wooden shuttering and corrugated iron, disfiguring their neighbourhoods. Some houses and flats had been decanted prior to development schemes, and never reallocated. Most councils have some housing which is substandard in some way, as do many housing associations. To their eternal discredit, some councils filled toilets with concrete, ripped out services and destroyed roofing to stop desperate people squatting their substandard properties, but the housing crisis is now so acute that thankfully very few do so now.

Instead, many authorities work with housing associations to maximise use of short-life properties. Mindful of the capital constraint they labour under, they grant a lease to a housing association, which then undertakes renovation work on the property to 'wind and watertight' standard. Housing Association Grant, once known as Mini-HAG, now Short Life HAG, is available from the Housing Corporation to back the cost of part of this work, and councils have the power to top up these resources to a certain extent from their own funds to ensure that a reasonable job is done, in order to guarantee the property's useful life for anything up to 10 years. Any loan finance raised to cover the difference between grant and capital costs, and management and maintenance expenditure plus losses through voids, are covered through appropriate rents, which are eligible for Housing Benefit (Private Sector). The council then nominates homeless persons who have been found to be intentionally homeless, or who are still under investigation, or for whom no suitable permanent accommodation is yet available, to the association, which may grant a form of assured shorthold tenancy giving limited security. Some still use 'licences' which purport to guarantee rapid repossession, but there is doubt over the legality and status of such agreements. Successful schemes have been devised in Southwark, Greenwich, Lewisham, Camden (all in London) and many other metropolitan and non-metropolitan boroughs. Some boroughs use such housing for groups of single people or childless couples, non-priority homeless people who would otherwise receive no assistance whatever, or who might be forced to squat the very same buildings, and encourage the formation of management co-operatives, with housing associations acting as advisers and development agents. Others use the accommodation only for priority homeless cases: some do both.

The short-life housing scheme as developed in Southwark is typical of several, and is discussed in an article at the end of Chapter 6 (p. 222). Entitled 'Short-life: the logic of necessity', it presents an ideal opportunity for housing associations and local authorities to work together to address the need for self-contained short-term accommodation and the scandal of empty, decaying council homes where there is a shortage of municipal cash to refurbish to permanent standards. The scheme has now changed: associations are now granted a lease on such properties, renovate to short-life standard using Short Life HAG, and accept nominations from the council exclusively of homeless persons. The part of the scheme by which single persons forming co-operatives can be granted a licence in such property is being run down owing to increased homelessness demands.

The advantages of such a strategy are several. It secures self-contained accommodation of a reasonable standard at affordable rents, and therefore some dignity to those who might otherwise have been condemned to bed and breakfast. It utilises assets which would otherwise have deteriorated, especially if unsaleable. It generates rent for a social housing organisation. It is subsidy efficient in that housing benefit subsidy can be used to back the housing benefit paid to those living in such accommodation who are dependent upon it. It is much cheaper to the nation as a whole than bed and breakfast, which in the mid-1990s in London averaged around £15 000 per year for a family of three or four. It provides another avenue for councils and housing associations to work together, and therefore to understand each other's constraints and possibilities. These outweigh the disadvantages, which include the legal and operational complexity of setting up and managing such schemes, the displacement of non-priority homeless persons in many cases (eviction of squatters), the emergence of often quite serious defects, and the fact that short-life accommodation may be perceived as many times better than that ultimately made available. None of these is sufficiently serious to stop responsible authorities trying out schemes of this kind.

3.5.2 Hostels

Hostels may be owned by local authorities or housing associations, targeted at specific groups (such as, young people or lone-parent families) or generalist, and are usually managed by a warden or supervisor, resident or off-site. Often, cooking and laundry facilities are shared, although it is impossible to generalise about this form of accommodation, except to say that it is somewhat institutionalised. It is obvious to the world that someone is homeless if they are housed temporarily in a hostel, and this may stigmatise that person. The lack of privacy, the necessity of sharing, and the presence of a manager can do little to foster independence and a sense of worth amongst those unfortunate enough to live in such places, although the segregation of the sexes has long gone.

Some forms of hostel accommodation may be worthwhile, especially where the person or household needs some form of support: for example, where they are elderly and frail, or mentally disabled, or perhaps are young and the institution can offer some form of work training and counselling, as is the case with 'Foyer' projects. But they cannot be regarded as a panacea for the relief of homelessness, even temporarily, because they can dehumanise and alienate. Local authority developments' capital aspects are funded through a combination of loans and capital receipts, and running costs are funded through the HRA, unless there is some special needs management, in which case there may be a recharge to the Social Services budget. Housing association schemes' capital works are funded through the local authority or Housing Corporation via the HAG regime, plus, in some cases, public or private loan finance, and running costs may in some cases be met partially through Special Needs Management Allowances, plus top-up funding from other bodies, including social services, housing authorities, sometimes departments of state, depending upon whom the provision is targeted. Advantages include availability of advice and assistance on the premises, security, heating and lighting provided, perhaps some companionship; and licences or non-secure tenancies (in council hostels) give local authorities maximum scope to evict or remove if required, for example to force acceptance of suitable alternative accommodation. Disadvantages have already been referred to, but principally are the stigma and lack of independence entailed.

Hostels are also provided by the voluntary sector, and an article at the end of this chapter, 'Local authorities, voluntary hostels and the homeless' (p. 104), discusses a number of such initiatives. Some such organisations serve specific client groups: for example, Centrepoint attempts to offer first-call accommodation and advice to young people arriving in London, although it also provides advice on a national basis. Such organisations are vulnerable not only to withdrawal of central government grant but also to changes in voluntary donation levels, and the article also identifies the problem of 'silting up': there simply is not enough room to meet demand.

3.5.3   Women's refuges

Women's refuges were first set up by Erin Pizzey in the late 1960s, the first one being in Chiswick, West London. Women's Aid has a nationwide network of such places, and strives to provide a supportive, confidential, secure environment to which women fleeing actual or threatened domestic violence may resort, with their children if applicable. It is customary, and there is some case law to support this, to regard the residents of such hostels as truly homeless: the fact that they are accommodated there should not be taken to imply that this is their settled residence. One of the excellent features of such establishments is that the women residents there are encouraged to form committees and workers' groups to run the houses themselves, thus removing much of the institutional feel that would otherwise inevitably result. Some ethnic groups have established hostels to cater for women of colour fleeing domestic violence: witness the successful refuge set up by Asian women, Southall Black Sisters, in that part of London. Organisations dealing with women fleeing violence are sometimes developers in their own right, as registered housing associations, or may use associations as development agents.

3.5.4 Homeless at home

'Homeless at home' may sound like something of a contradiction, but has been practice in several authorities since at least the early 1980s. Essentially, it involves the local authority accepting that a household is homeless, but negotiating with the host family or landlord to let them stay until somewhere more permanent can be found. It is a rather shabby and dangerous practice. Shabby, because it entails diminishing the significance of the homelessness situation, implying that it is right that people 'hang on' in often the most appalling conditions of tension or physical squalor until somewhere more suitable is found; and dangerous because it may lead to the allegation that individuals are not homeless at all, and could almost always hang on where they were until housed in the 'normal' way, justifying the dilution of the legislation, or the redefinition of homelessness as rooflessness, which it isn't (or isn't only).

However, it can be understood why some authorities do this. Faced with a chronic shortage of temporary accommodation or permanent relets, it may be the only way to discharge the duty. It may be preferable to bed and breakfast: for example, if the parents of a young concealed household know that they will be rehoused in measurable time, perhaps the tension will be diminished and the temporary stay made more bearable. But equally, the prolonged presence of an unwanted household may provoke yet more tension, with potentially serious consequences.

3.5.5 Private sector leasing

Private sector leasing (PSL) involves a council taking a lease on a privately owned property for up to 3 years, and then subletting to a homeless household. Sometimes the properties are managed by the authority, sometimes by a housing association; and sometimes the council uses an association as a procurement agent. In most cases, the occupant becomes a subtenant of the council, but sometimes an association takes on the lease, in which case the household becomes an association tenant. The majority of these schemes started in the late 1980s, and were commenced in order to replace or to avoid the use of bed and breakfast. Indeed, by the early 1990s, the use of PSL had outstripped that of bed and breakfast in London.

For the scheme to be viable, there must be a ready supply of private sector property in the area, although it has been known for associations to purchase property and let it on a PSL basis to local authorities. The danger is that private landlords will let to the council rather than to individuals because of the obvious advantages, which include a guarantee of rental income, no voids, return of property in good condition, and no hassle involved in collecting rent or in management, as well as there being no agency fees. This may well reduce the supply of private rented accommodation in an area, and thus lead to a housing shortage, perhaps causing some non-priority homelessness: single people and childless couples in the early stages of household formation often look to this sector for housing. It is very difficult to measure the extent to which this happens, because there are no reliable statistics to show the extent of such homelessness, since no housing solution is officially demanded, but that does not mean it can be ignored.

However, such a strategy can produce good-quality, well-managed self-contained accommodation. If it is let through the council, the form of tenancy is a Non-Secure Tenancy, which gives the council the right to repossess relatively easily purely on the grounds that it is that sort of tenancy, thereby preventing the 'silting up' of this form of temporary housing, which might occur where occupants prefer their temporary arrangements to the permanent solution offered.

The legal aspects of PSL can be complex. Essentially, the local authority draws up a business tenancy agreement with a private landlord based on the 1954 Landlord and Tenant Act terms. A council cannot be an assured tenant because it is not a person. The occupant generally takes on a Non-Secure Tenancy, a variant of the Secure Tenancy granted to council tenants under the Tenant's Charter provisions of the 1985 Housing Act. Responsibility for major maintenance matters rests with the head landlord, although an agreement can be reached such that the council (or its agent) acts as agent in this respect, in consideration of a reduction in the lease payments or payment by the landlord. If a local authority uses a housing association or other organisation as a management agent, then care must be taken in specifying the duties to ensure both that there is no undue duplication, for example in the matter of selecting properties or inspections, and that there is the opportunity for the council to inspect the work of the agent to ensure that quality standards are maintained. If the council wishes the managing agent to take court action to remove a tenant, then there must be excellent liaison between the bodies, as ultimate responsibility for the subtenant rests with the local authority. It is necessary to think through all the aspects which constitute good management, including liaison with the head landlord, giving welfare benefit and other advice and assistance, conducting viewings, co-ordinating moves in and out, explaining and facilitating the signing of tenancy documentation, as well as the more usual management responsibilities. Such schemes rarely work well unless there is a dedicated team or individual responsible for the project in the local authority, and where there is a similar facility in the managing organisation. Also, the task of co-ordinating the work of various parts of a housing department – homeless persons, staff procuring dwellings or liaising with associations, policy sections responsible for setting up and monitoring the scheme – should not be underestimated. No wonder that many authorities have used consultants to help formulate their strategy, or have farmed the entire operation out to other organisations.

Advantages include the fact that the provision is usually of good quality and is self-contained. It implies no stigma, since the property could be anywhere. PSL may reduce private sector voids and underuse in an area, and can be at least as cost-effective as bed and breakfast, although, since such schemes have been funded from the General Fund since the early 1990s, it is less cost-effective than it used to be. Disadvantages include the often very high rents: some authorities recharge the full cost of the landlord rent to the subtenant, and some even add to this the charge levied by the managing agent (if any). Such rents may well be over the housing benefit threshold, becoming effectively a cost to the local authority. Additionally, high rent or recharge strategies can give rise to an almost inescapable housing benefit poverty trap. Yet the decision to use General Fund resources to subsidise the rent, especially to working households, may impact on the council tax. This may be a price well worth paying to secure decent accommodation for homeless people, and avoid bed and breakfast.

An article at the end of this chapter, 'Private property, public need' (p. 109), highlights the PSL initiative as it was developed in the London Borough of Southwark, although it should be noted that the funding regime has changed since its publication, as mentioned above. One key criticism of such schemes is that they may remove much-needed private rented accommodation from the market, penalising non-priority homeless persons by creating a shortage, or by driving up rents. It may also lead to unscrupulous landlords harassing existing tenants to force them out in order to take advantage of the good deal offered under the scheme.

3.5.6 Housing associations as managing agents

In a type of arrangement similar to PSL, and in some cases its successor, a housing association may enter into a management agreement with a private landlord, and accept nominations of homeless households from a local authority. The association may undertake running repairs, and will manage the property, perhaps in consideration of a reduced landlord rent or a fee from the landlord. Typically the form of letting is the assured shorthold tenancy. Landlord's notice cannot be given before 4 months have expired, and

Fig. 3.1 Squatted house, West London

the notice period is 2 months, although the tenant can determine (that is, end the tenancy) prior to this. In some ways this is more legally straightforward than PSL, since it does not involve entering into a lease, neither is there any need to enter into a management (rather than a nominations) agreement with the association, and the association can use quite standard terms when securing a property to manage. However, to ensure goodquality properties, the council must make periodic visits with the association when considering properties to manage. The advantages are similar to those of PSL, in so far as occupants could be granted assured tenancies on expiry of the assured shorthold if they like where they are living, and can afford to continue to do so. This would certainly constitute a rehousing under the terms of the 1985 Housing Act.

Homes over the Shop (HOTS) initiatives are essentially similar: the association may enter into a management agreement with the owner, or indeed take on a lease, and perhaps repairing obligations, to make a home available. HOTS schemes have been around since the late 1980s: sadly, the sight

Fig. 3.2 Flats above shops used for temporary accommodation

of vacant, boarded up or curtainless attic rooms or substantial flats over shops is common in most high streets, and such flats represent one of the nation's great underused housing assets, although they are not suitable for all client-groups. Access is often difficult; however, there is no reason why they could not be used for fit single people or childless couples.

3.5.7 Foyers

Foyers are an innovation from France: the first British foyers were developed in 1993. They are hostels, developed and run by housing associations, which offer young people the chance to live in supervised but essentially self-contained accommodation, and also offer training in vocational skills. Many have a commercial aspect – perhaps a cafe or restaurant or bar – which is open to the general public, can offer limited work experience, and earn money for the establishment to subsidise running costs.

One of the articles at the end of the chapter 'Foyers, work and housing' (p. 112), gives an example of this form of provision in North Kensington, London, where a local housing association has joined forces with a further education college and the local authority to provide a foyer-type scheme providing homes for young people and valuable craft training. London and Quadrant Housing Trust established a foyer in 1994 in Camberwell, South-East London, which provides training in catering as part of its package.

3.5.8   Bed and breakfast

The final form of temporary housing, bed and breakfast, deserves to be discussed last, because it is in most cases the worst possible option. It is relatively expensive, usually unpleasant, unhealthy, cramped and definitely stigmatising. Most readers may have stayed in a guest-house or a small hotel by the sea, or in a beautiful location such as the Lake District, the west of Scotland, Cornwall or some other idyllic spot. Renting a family room can be a very convenient, comparatively cheap and pleasant way for a household to spend a few days or even a week, especially if the budget is tight; but imagine having to spend a year in the same room, having to share essential facilities with five or more other families, being unable to invite friends and relations round because of the shame of having to resort to this form of existence, and attempting to exclude cockroaches, ants and other vermin. It is expensive: in 1989, the London Research Centre estimated that it cost around £14 000 on average to house a family in bed and breakfast in London for a year. Often, bed and breakfast establishments are far away from family and friend networks, and sometimes miles away from the home area: some London authorities have placed victims as far out as Brighton. The proprietors often know they are on to a good thing, and charge up to the benefit ceiling, knowing there is a ready market from local councils for what amounts to very poor value for money, and for accommodation which often constitutes a health risk, as the many fires in such establishments reported throughout the 1990s testify. Thankfully, evidence suggests that use of this form of temporary respite is dropping as more cost-effective and humane 'solutions' are sought.

At its best, however, bed and breakfast can be useful, provided the room is clean, meets basic health and safety requirements (which demands regular inspection), and has adequate facilities, ideally self-contained. It can be used in cases where there is real doubt as to the authenticity of the homelessness claim, or where someone's accommodation can be repaired within a short time, or where the applicant has no furniture or effects, and would benefit from furnished, supervised accommodation until somewhere suitable can be found. But in my own work experience, most such establishments are totally unsuitable for stays of any more than a few weeks.

3.6 Prevention of homelessness

Timely advice and assistance can prevent homelessness in some cases. Most housing authorities, and some associations, either provide housing aid and advice within their central offices or have separate housing aid and/or advice centres. Local authorities have a duty to ensure that those threatened with homelessness are given appropriate advice and assistance, along with non-priority cases and those found to be intentionally homeless. In addition to, or sometimes instead of, having their own housing aid and advice function or centre, councils support independent centres, perhaps run by SHELTER, SHAC or local organisations. They have the power to make grants to them under Section 73 of the 1985 Housing Act.

SHELTER was founded in 1967 following the outcry over the television play *Cathy Come Home*. It was instrumental in sponsoring the bill which led to the 1977 Housing (Homeless Persons) Act. It has two functions represented by its constituent parts: SHELTER, the campaign for the homeless and badly housed; and SNHAT, the Shelter National Housing Aid Trust. The former part is basically a campaigning organisation, lobbying for legislational changes in favour of its interest groups, conducting publicity campaigns by media and posters and occasionally by organising demonstrations. It has branches in England, Wales, Scotland and Northern Ireland. In 1994 and 1995, it conducted a major campaign against the government's Homelessness Review, set to limit local authority duties towards homeless people and in particular to restrict the duty to one of securing temporary accommodation with such cases being considered against all others within the context of a common 'points' prioritisation system. The latter is concerned with the provision of over 20 SHELTER housing aid centres, and the funding or part-funding of other independent facilities. These centres often receive financial assistance from local authorities under s. 73 of the 1985 Housing Act.

SHAC is a London-based advisory organisation which merged with SHELTER in 1995, but which still has a distinct identity within that organisation. Although its core work is housing aid and advice, it also offers training courses to housing and related workers, and is a major publisher of housing books, as is SHELTER. It has also worked with the government in setting up and monitoring the Rough Sleeper's Initiative, which was initiated in 1990 to attempt to provide basic advice, hostel and move-on accommodation to those who would otherwise resort to the streets.

The role of SHAC in promoting this initiative, which received additional central government funding in 1995, is discussed in an Article at the end of this chapter, Streetwise Solutions. SHAC worked with SHELTER and the National Association of Citizens' Advice Bureaux to increase the provision of advice to London's homeless. The initiative has since been diffused throughout major urban centres, although it does depend upon partnerships with local authorities, who may make cash available through their powers under s. 73 of the 1985 Housing Act, if they have the resources to do so.

The SHELTER group's advisory arm is concerned primarily with the giving of housing aid and advice; but mention should also be made of more generalist organisations. The Citizens' Advice Bureau network, co-ordinated by the National Association of Citizens' Advice Bureaux (NACAB), offers a valuable resource in this area. Some organisations, for example CHAR, the Campaign for the Homeless and Rootless, offer mainly secondary advice, to housing advice workers, especially concerning 'non-priority' homelessness. Other organisations, such as Centrepoint, offer both accommodation and advice. Taken as a whole, generalist and specialist agencies are broadly complementary, and reflect the need for good preventive work and the complexity of housing legislation.

A distinction should be made between 'primary' and 'secondary' advice: the former involves direct advice and/or counselling of clients/customers, the latter the training of (or giving advice and information to) housing aid workers or organisations concerned with these matters.

Some local authorities prefer not to provide their own housing aid centres or functions, but to support the independent sector. Sometimes this is done on cost-effectiveness grounds, but a good case can be made for this policy in non-financial terms. There are bound to be occasions when local authority tenants are in dispute with their landlord; for example, where they are threatened with eviction because of alleged non-payment of rent or other alleged breach of tenancy conditions. Would it be reasonable, in these cases, for the tenant to seek advice from the landlord, and would the tenant have much faith in its impartiality? Of course, the advice may be impartial, but a council has a dual responsibility: to give appropriate advice and also to protect its financial position and to maintain its standing with other tenants by enforcing tenancy agreements. In such cases it would seem more reasonable for the tenant to seek independent advice. Indeed, many tenants might feel unable to approach the council for advice, even if this was suggested, through suspicions of partiality, even if this was not the case: and such hesitation might well cost their tenancy, and create a problem for the council.

Second, private tenants or homeowners might not wish to approach the council's housing department for advice, even if it were presented in a discreet office away from the town hall, because they do not wish to be associated with council tenure. This may be somewhat wrong-headed, but it is understandable, and the point is to ensure that people do not miss out on advice rather than to criticise their motivations. Some potential clients may have been so alienated or upset by the bureaucracy of obtaining, for example, housing benefit or other services from the council that their views on the organisation are tainted, with the result that they do not seek advice there.

Whether or not a local authority chooses to use the independent sector wholly or partially to deliver advice, it is essential not to underestimate the complex nature of the field. A housing adviser of the 1990s even if 'only' dealing with landlord and tenant, would have to have a thorough grounding in not only the 1988 Housing Act (as amended) which covers Assured and Assured Shorthold tenancies, but also preceding legislation such as the 1977 Rent Act (as amended) covering regulated 'fair rent' tenancies, as well as the 1985 Housing Act which specifies the Secure Tenancy conditions. This complexity precludes the use of generic (generalist) housing officers for the job. If councils cannot provide a separate advice service, or officers dedicated to just that task, it would be better if they relied upon a highly trained independent sector.

3.7   Conclusion

Homelessness will not go away. The Homelessness Review of the mid-1990s suggests that those found to be homeless be placed in temporary accommodation as a matter of course, then processed through the points system to determine their access to local authority housing. This amounts to temporarily alleviating homelessness, only to subject those unlucky enough to be in the system to unnecessary waits. It will not solve homelessness; it will entail rising costs to the state of temporary housing, and shore up the unacceptable, exploitative practices of some of Britain's worst landlords.

The early 1990s Street Sleeping Initiative may have temporarily reduced the number of those finding refuge in shop doorways, but failed to address the significant issue of housing for non-priority cases.

It is clear that much more needs to be done to address this issue, and that cosmetic legislative change is the wrong way to do it. Much revolves around the problem of providing sufficient affordable housing. An article at the end of this chapter, 'Housing, the economy and homelessness' (p. 107), sets the problem in the more general context, and suggests that homelessness is a tangible result of high rents, a lack of housing investment, and of suitable housing in the right place, and can only be tackled fundamentally by addressing these issues, rather than tampering with the rationing legislation.

Articles

1. 'Streetwise solutions: tackling homelessness the D.o.E. way'

2. 'Local authorities, voluntary hostels and the homeless'

3. 'Reviewing homelessness: changing the legislation'

4. 'Housing, the economy and homelessness'

5. 'Private property, public need: Private Sector Leasing for the homeless'

6. 'Foyers, work and housing'

Streetwise solutions: tackling homelessness the D.o.E. way

So official concern for the homeless wasn't dead, just resting! Alarm at the very visible growth of street-sleeping in London has prompted a government package of £15 million to provide basic shelter; and a less well known initiative to increase the availability of housing advice, first mooted in 1989's Homelessness Review, has begun.

The latter initiative, known as the Homelessness Advice Service, aims to increase the effectiveness of existing resources such as Citizens' Advice Bureaux, supported by specialist knowledge and training from SHELTER, the National Campaign for the Homeless, and SHAC, the London Housing Aid Centre, and will initially be confined to London and the South-East. The greater availability of guidance on housing rights and accommodation sources, combined with salutary words to those contemplating leaving home on the perils of doing so, will supposedly reduce more obvious and newsworthy forms of homelessness, whilst the spartan nature of the basic accommodation to be provided from the £15 million will offer temporary respite to those who fall through the net.

Bob Widdowson, Director of SHAC, was positive about his organisation's involvement in the Homelessness Advice Service.

SHAC's support of independent advice agencies is nothing new — we've been giving such support for 20 years, and we were surprised but pleased by the government's resolve to develop a secondary advice service on a more formal footing. We'll be offering assistance to independent advice centres as well as Citizens' Advice Bureaux, notably to local community initiatives, including those aimed at the ethnic communities, within London. This year, SHELTER, SHAC and the National Association of Citizens' Advice Bureaux have been given just £1 million to develop the project, with any funding next year dependent on the government's assessment of our performance. With the average annual cost of family bed and breakfast in London at between £17 000 and 320 000, it won't take much preventive work to save £1m in temporary accommodation costs.

To date, SHAC's progress has been impressive, with May 1990 seeing the establishment of an emergency advice line to help independent advice centres, July bringing a training programme for generalist advisers in east London, with similar plans for west London in September, and a similar initiative for south London by the end of the year. Bob saw a link with the £15 million homelessness initiative. 'Those having to be housed temporarily in that way will need good specialist guidance in finding a permanent solution to their difficulties: but more to the point, decent advice may help people from reaching those desperate straits in the first place.'

There's nothing new in central and local government financial support for, and significant help from, the independent housing advice sector; there are powers to make such grants under s. 73 of the 1985 Housing Act specifically to organisations providing 'appropriate advice' to those needing it, which has deflected homelessness to an extent, with savings in human misery, and public money.

Reasons for entering into such a relationship are legion: it's often cheaper than developing an in-house service: council tenants may prefer to take their grievances to an independent centre; and others may be put off seeking advice from the council through wariness of bureaucracy. Jill Saunders, SHELTER Casework Co-ordinator for the South-East of England, said:

Independent centres have an important role to play in giving good advice, especially to the non-priority homeless, and on the whole, councils value their help. What support councils do give to the independent advice sector is more than repaid. We in turn have assisted in offering training to such centres, as well as providing a service through our own network. We'll be working with NACAB in providing extra housing training to CAB workers from October 1st as part of the Homelessness Advice Service, which underlines our commitment to preventive work.

Sadly, with new financial constraints on councils as a result of the 1989 legislation and tight community charge budgets worsened in some cases by capping, many councils have been forced to cut cash help, or may have to consider this unwelcome path. If so, it is clear that the undisputed benefits of the new Homelessness Advice Service and the excellent work of SHELTER and SHAC will be seriously undermined. Accepting for the moment that good advice can prevent many ending up on the streets, will the £15 million initiative be able to provide enough basic shelter? If not, as seems likely, then further work to co-ordinate government policy is needed to address the problems of homelessness.

The well-meaning policies outlined hardly get to the root of the problem: SHELTER and SHAC deserve applause for responding to the challenge, but it has to be said that 'preventive' advice alone can have only a marginal impact only on homelessness whilst investment in affordable social housing remains at its present abysmal level.

PSLG, August 1990

Addendum (October 1995)

Since the article was written, the initiative has gone national, with renewed government support. There are fewer visible signs of street sleeping, but the planned review of homelessness legislation will entail greater use of temporary accommodation, and does not address the needs of non-priority homeless persons, who often end up on the streets or in hostels.

Questions

1. What are the links between good advice and homelessness prevention?
2. Which agencies played what part in the Homelessness Advice Service?
3. What is Section 73 assistance, and how is it used by local authorities to help homeless people?

Local authorities, voluntary hostels and the homeless

Hostels loom large in the public perception of homelessness, as the place of last resort before the street for those falling through society's net. Such voluntary and statutory establishments highlight the difficulties some face in finding permanent housing, especially the young, old and otherwise vulnerable. With changing attitudes and legislation towards the mentally distressed, those who run voluntary hostels are having to learn new skills: and with youth homelessness at an all-time high, some organisations seek to provide basic accommodation to prevent the growth of cardboard cities. Councils have increasingly to work with voluntary providers to fulfil their duties towards the homeless, and will have to do so for the foreseeable future.

Centrepoint and St Mungo's are bodies providing hostels to meet desperate need in London, and exemplify many of the sector's problems. Shaks Ghosh is the Team Leader of Centrepoint's National Development Unit. Describing the service offered, she pointed to two shelters for the homeless, one for young people who have just left home, the other for those literally sleeping on the streets, together with four hostels for clients including homeless 16-year-olds and young women, and 50 self-contained flats and bedsits. Although it has been around for 17 years, there has recently been considerable growth in demand, with poverty and shortage of affordable housing, together with the de-institutionalisation of the care system, identified as root causes rather than a misplaced sense of independence amongst the young.

Last year, 75 per cent of those housed by Centrepoint arrived from outside London, although the decision to move there is often taken when homelessness has occurred; thus Centrepoint sees itself as dealing with a national rather than purely a London-based problem. Hence its National Development Unit has been set up to do preventive work outside the capital, involving discussion with councils about policies towards the young homeless – many do not recognise teenagers as a priority category for rehousing – and to encourage the provision of counselling services for those leaving care to help them find accommodation. A consultancy service is available to councils, in liaison with other agencies concerned with youth homelessness. There is little point in developing new hostels without attempting to address the source of the problem.

Although some funding comes from central and local government, public fundraising is an increasing source of finance. In recognition of this, Centrepoint is constantly trying to raise the profile of youth homelessness. As if it were needed: any visitor to central London cannot fail to notice the Dickensian spectacle of begging on the streets.

'Our hostels are silting up,' said Shaks. 'We need to develop move-on accommodation, and have a projected programme of 50 flats in London over the next three years.' She had no illusions that this response fits the scale of the problem – but at least the will is there: let's hope that cash materialises to back these projects.

Another high-profile organisation in the London hostel world is St Mungo's. Its existence reflects serious underprovision for special needs groups, including the elderly, chronically sick, and mentally distressed. A recent development has been a hostel for emotionally disturbed and mentally ill 16 to 26-year-olds. Most of St Mungo's 530 clients have come directly from the streets, or have been located by St Mungo's outreach service. There are 31 hostels, ranging in size from 10 to 110 bedspaces.

Sixteen per cent of all clients housed by St Mungo's are local authority referrals, and pressure from this quarter is growing. 'Some of our clients are those who councils literally can't house,' said a spokesperson for St Mungo's.

There was one guy from north-east England placed in our Harrow Road hostel because our establishment was apparently the only suitable place in the country. This points up the dire lack of special needs housing provision – and we're increasingly having to cover for this inadequacy.

Like Centrepoint, St Mungo's hostels are silting up, and its staff are worried that, with an increased emphasis of expensive private funding, their accommodation will become less affordable than hitherto, although there is no evidence that this will reduce pressure on their establishments.

Although these organisations are doing a sterling job in scratching the surface of street homelessness through basic provision and preventive initiatives, they are under severe strain due both to demand and to impending changes in the system of hostel finance.

Hostels were initially conceived as temporary accommodation, a stopgap between literal homelessness and permanent housing, but they have often become a long-term resort of those who do not have the resources to meet their housing needs. This is no solution to homelessness, and to rely unduly on this sector is simply papering over the cracks. Their very existence cries out for large-scale investment in affordable housing, the only rational way forward.

PSLG, September 1990

Questions

1. Who are the main clients for hostels, and why?
2. Why are mentally ill people particularly vulnerable to homelessness?
3. What is 'silting up', and what might the solutions be?

Reviewing homelessness: changing the legislation

In January 1994, the Department of the Environment issued a consultation paper, *Access to local authority and housing association tenancies*, along with *routes into local authority housing: a study of local authority waiting lists and new tenancies*. The former states that homelessness legislation passed in 1977, now Part 3 of the 1985 Housing Act, is to be significantly amended. The latter implies that homeless persons have an unfair advantage over those on council waiting lists in tenancy allocation.

The present legislation gives local housing authorities a duty to secure permanent accommodation for certain categories of persons found to be homeless, namely those in priority need, and not intentionally homeless. Priority includes disability, pregnancy, having dependent children, and being over pensionable age. Those with a local connection through work, family associations or past residence, have a right to accommodation in the district applied to; others may be referred elsewhere. The Act is accompanied by a Code of Guidance revised in 1991, reflecting case law developed since the original legislation.

There has been a significant growth in households accepted as homeless and entitled to permanent accommodation since 1980: the figure for that year, recorded by the D.o.E., was 60 400; 1986: 100 490; 1988: 113 770; 1991: 144 530. (source: *PI(E) returns*, D.o.E.). Whereas lettings of council secure tenancies to waiting list applicants fell from 173 000 (1982/83) steadily to 126 000 (1990/91), equivalent lettings to homeless persons have risen over that period from 44 000 to 74 000, following the trend of acceptances shown above (source: Housing Investment Programme Returns, D.o.E.). The government believes this shows that the homeless have an unfair advantage over those living in unsatisfactory accommodation, but willing to 'wait their turn', thus justifying legislative amendment.

The proposals are that councils should have a duty to secure only temporary accommodation for homeless people in priority need whose situation has arisen through no fault of their own, and who have nowhere else to go. Waiting lists will be the sole route by which people are allocated a secure council tenancy, or nominated to a housing association, to ensure fairness in allocation across groups. Finally, councils will be encouraged to help lower-income households find suitable accommodation by greater use of housing advice centres, meaning housing in public and private sectors, including shared ownership.

In late 1993, there was much criticism in Parliament of single parents, who many think receive advantageous treatment in terms of social housing access and welfare benefits. Some MPs asserted that many single mothers may have become pregnant to obtain council housing, and the media predicted the exclusion of this group from homelessness duties, in line with 'Back to Basics' policy. Policy changes suggested do not single this group out, but it is clear that much of the momentum for the proposals has its origin in the moral hysteria over single mothers.

The need for a degree of equity in allocation of council tenancies is already provided under s. 22 of the 1985 Housing Act, stating that reasonable preference must be given to those occupying insanitary or overcrowded housing; persons having large families; those living in unsatisfactory housing conditions; and those accepted as statutorily homeless. However, the government proposes to change this to require allocations to be made, with limited exceptions, to those on waiting lists.

There is consensus amongst housing pressure groups and professional bodies that the premises on which the proposals are based are misguided. The Chartered Institute of Housing's Director of Policy, John Perry, told *PSLG* that a recent survey of local authority housing managers revealed little evidence of 'queue jumping' for tenancies by the homeless: many were already on council waiting lists. He identified the loss of 1.6 million rented homes across tenures over the past decade, and a two-thirds fall in the level of social housing output over that time, as the main reasons for rising homelessness. Bob Widdowson, Director of SHAC, the London Housing Advice Centre, supported the notion of equity across demand groups for council housing, but warned that many homeless households would be stigmatised by the new temporary duty, regardless of their circumstances, though he welcomed the increased emphasis on preventive advice.

The upshot of this is that simply redefining homelessness will not do: simply stigmatising groups as undeserving and banishing them into temporary accommodation will not address the central problem of social housing supply.

The bill to taxpayers will be increased: it costs over £15 000 annually per family housed in bed and breakfast in London. And if some do seek to jump the queue, it is only because other channels are made unavailable by unrealistically low provision. Instead of moral posturing, and tinkering with the law, it is necessary to rethink the supply issue, to ensure the availability of a decent home for all who need one.

PSLG, March 1994

Questions

1. Outline the duties of councils towards homeless persons in 1994.
2. On what grounds was it suggested that some homeless people have an unfair advantage in obtaining council housing over others?
3. What are the cost and social implications of the proposed reforms?

Housing, the economy and homelessness

There was an air of *déjà vu* at 1994's Chartered Institute of Housing Conference in June. The economy, and the riddle of expanding the supply of affordable housing whilst cutting capital subsidies were major issues once again. The debates were heightened by four impending events: compulsory competitive tendering (CCT); local government reorganisation; imminent social security changes; and the Homelessness Review – issues clearly interlinked.

CCT will be extended to council housing management from 1996. The ostensible aim is to enhance quality in housing management by forcing housing authorities to tender their work to those who can meet quality standards at lowest cost, with possible savings to the Exchequer. Recently, tenants have been given a greater say in the specification and monitoring of contracts, surely correctly when most housing revenue accounts are unsubsidised and financed largely from tenant rents.

Local government reorganisation will delay the implementation of CCT for shire districts, because of the disruption following the formation of new authorities. The conference saw the launch of the Chartered Institute of Housing's contribution to the debate, 'Out of the Shadows', broadly supportive of reorganisation. There is a good case for bringing together county and district functions as long as the resultant organisations are of a scale to which customers can relate. CCT means that many functions will be performed at arm's length, entailing fewer staff except in legal departments, which supports the idea of amalgamation; also, as council housing moves inexorably towards welfare housing, there is a greater commonality of clients between housing (a district function) and social services (a county function), which might support merger. This will increase as community care policies continue to grow. The paper suggests seven models for the housing service within the new unitary authorities, of which the following four have been considered by some authorities: a stand-alone comprehensive service; a technically oriented service combining housing and environmental services and/or property services; a socially oriented department combining housing and social services; and a strategically oriented department combining housing and planning functions. There has been some resistance to assuming that housing and social services should be co-terminous, if only because tenants might be stigmatised as just another case on a social worker's list, and because tenants might be seen collectively as a social problem. Whatever the combination, resultant departments should not dominate council structures, and should result in good-quality service delivery to customers. An important issue is how and whether different district rent and management policies would be harmonised within a new, perhaps larger, unitary authority, and the challenge of combining revenue accounts and capital expenditure strategies.

Whether an authority remains as a provider or becomes an enabler, through stock transfer or via loss of management functions, the issue of affordability dominates. Although no firm conclusions have yet been reached from the social security review, it is clear that higher rents in the voluntary sector are a direct result of grant cuts, and that increased private rents follow from deregulation; and so it is government policy which has heightened the problem, and increased the benefit bill. Neither the Social Security nor the Housing Minister gave any hints of reversing capital subsidy withdrawal policy accompanying shifts towards personal subsidies, so it must be assumed that the housing benefit bill will continue to rise, especially if, as widely predicted, interest rates increase, inflating association rents through the increased cost of borrowing. With no hint of any adjustment to the housing benefit withdrawal taper, it seems that the poverty trap, where those finding work can find themselves subject to a marginal tax rate of over 90 pence in the pound through the loss of a number of benefits, will continue to force many to remain on social security rather than taking low-paid work. The dire effect on the economy and the social security bill was highlighted, although ironically the effect of keeping large numbers out of the labour market might be to force wages up in some sectors as the number of vacancies in that market rises on the pathway from recession, thus helping at least some out of the trap, though this is a perverse way of encouraging recovery!

Homelessness is a tangible result of high rents, a lack of housing investment, and a lack of suitable housing in the right place, and can only be tackled fundamentally by addressing these issues; but despite around 10 000 responses largely critical of the proposed legislative changes, it seems that the government response will be to attempt to massage the numbers by making the rules for obtaining a secure home tougher.

If, despite the radical changes to housing reviewed above, there are still people sleeping through no fault of their own in appalling temporary accommodation in the coming years, the policy initiatives so carefully debated at the conference will have been a waste of time.

PSLG, August 1994

Questions

1. How would merging housing and social services departments in unitary authorities help the homeless?
2. What does the article claim to be the major cause of homelessness?

Private property, public need: Private Sector Leasing for the homeless

Homelessness is growing fast: many in this predicament have to endure spells in temporary accommodation before being housed permanently by councils or, increasingly, by housing associations or other agencies. Until recently, options for emergency housing were limited to hostels, bed and breakfast and other unsatisfactory remedies, but since the mid-1980s, many local authorities have turned to the private sector to help alleviate the crisis. Private sector leasing (PSL) is one such approach.

This involves a council renting a privately owned property for up to three years, then letting it to a homeless household pending permanent housing, as an alternative or supplement to other measures. Such schemes may be run completely in-house from initial inquiry to handover, or with the help of other bodies, typically housing associations or specialist companies engaged to acquire properties or manage and maintain them, or both, an example of the new enabling role of councils. Terms vary, but are generally advantageous to landlords: internal repairs are usually performed throughout the term; the rent, often highly competitive, is not only guaranteed, but often increased annually in line with inflation; the management responsibilities are taken over; and vacant possession can more or less be guaranteed at the end of the let, when properties will be handed back in the same state as let. No wonder such arrangements remain popular with owners, to the extent that many authorities are finding it hard to keep up with the volume offered!

It may be objected that this is an expensive way of providing housing: rents are often at a level with those found in the market, and can exceed the mortgage payment on equivalent properties, with levels of £150 per week and much more being common in parts of London. How, then, can such schemes be afforded? The cost of PSL has to be viewed in relation to the alternatives, not just in itself. Hal Pawson, a researcher at the London Research Centre, which has completed a major study of the subject, told me that even in local authorities not currently eligible for housing subsidy, such arrangements cost between one-half and two-thirds as much as comparable bed and breakfast, where only about one-fifth of expenditure can be recovered; but it must be recognised that living conditions in privately leased accommodation are far superior to that offered by the lower end of the hotel market, if only because the properties are generally self-contained. This makes straight cost comparisons invidious.

Indeed, considerations of quality and not only economy have helped reduce London's reliance on bed and breakfast considerably. Hal says:

In 1988, it was thought that there would be at least 15 000 households in bed and breakfast by now – but private leasing programmes have effectively halved this; the encouraging thing is that councils outside London are now beginning to take the initiative and reducing their use of hotels for the homeless.

The economic aspect is, however, a major point in PSL's favour. Hitherto, councils eligible for subsidy could claim from the government up to 75 per cent of the rent paid to landlords, provided a small up-front payment or 'premium' was paid, to conform with rules drawn up in the D.o.E.'s *Housing Subsidy and Accounting Manual*. Many authorities charged occupants the difference between subsidy and rent paid to the landlord, thus keeping costs to the tenant down. Since the properties were included in housing revenue accounts, management and maintenance costs attracted subsidy; thus schemes could be run in a cost-effective manner. Some authorities even charged tenants rents equal or approaching those paid to landlords, thus theoretically running schemes at no cost or at a surplus, even taking management and maintenance fees to housing associations into account. Typically, only tenants on income support, and therefore eligible for full rebates, were chosen for this form of housing to ensure affordability. Most of the cost of such reductions was defrayed by housing benefit subsidy from central government, although the introduction of what amounted to high council rents into the system could entail subsidy penalties. Housing subsidy rules have recently changed, in that the lower of the entire rent paid out, or what would have been the annual loan charge paid if the property had been purchased, subject to cost limits, will be received. In practice, it is believed that rents will be lower, and therefore subsidy will be maximised.

However, it should be remembered that because of the way Housing Revenue Account subsidy will be assessed under the new Local Government and Housing Act, some councils may end up getting little or no subsidy anyway, which could mean standard council tenants picking up the bill, thereby perhaps causing controversy. This also goes for councils electing to recharge the cost of paying the landlord to occupants on full housing benefit, which may in the future be paid from the rents of non-rebated tenants. Great care will be needed to skirt these pitfalls, if indeed this is possible.

What then are the prospects for PSL? 'Before the decision was taken to go for PSL, there were well over 1000 families in B & B,' said Hilary Wright of Hammersmith and Fulham, manager of the country's largest scheme.

Now we've managed to cut down hotel usage to around 2000. With a growing homelessness crisis, we're out to maximise our programme. I've found working with housing associations, who help to acquire and manage properties for us, a very positive experience, showing that public and voluntary agencies can work together well to solve common problems.

The same positive message came from Brendan Sarsfield, London and Quadrant Trust's Head of Temporary Lettings. 'Associations like London and Quadrant have played a major role developing PSL schemes in London, both in acquiring and managing temporary homes,' he said.

We have a good track record of co-operation with boroughs, and offer an excellent deal from the perspective of value for money. The key to success is liaison, and getting to know the problems faced by councils: once a clear brief is established, and good working relationships set up, as long as targets are mutually agreed and realistic, we can deliver the goods.

What of financial constraints? 'The problems of homelessness are increasing; the resources to tackle the problem must be found. I can't see our work diminishing in the foreseeable future.'

London boroughs in particular have set ambitious targets for their schemes, with one borough in particular having aimed to bring 1700 properties into lease by the end of the 1989/90 financial year; but there is cause for concern. Present rules limit leases to 3 years; beyond that, councils have to find capital equivalent to the market value to cover the arrangements, quite impractical in today's financial environment, although leases signed after February 1988 and before 23 November 1989 can be extended for a further 3 years. In most cases, a gap of 10 years must elapse before properties can be re-leased by any authority, thus reducing the useful life of such schemes, and creating a rehousing problem at the end of leases. Although there appear to be no supply problems at present, who knows what the situation will look like in 3 years? The government hopes that the problems of homelessness will be solved by the revival of the private rented sector following the 1988 Housing Act's deregulation of rents; let's hope so, or, if not, that concessions are made to allow private leasing to make a continued contribution to resolving the misery of homelessness, whilst the green light to invest in much-needed permanent housing is awaited.

PSLG, April 1990

Addendum (October 1995)

Since the article was written, there have been amendments to the way in which PSL is subsidised. Housing Revenue Account Subsidy is no longer available for this scheme. PSL rents to landlords are paid through the General Fund, and recouped through charges to occupants. They are treated as private sector tenants for housing benefit purposes, and the local authority receives subsidy towards the cost of granting benefit in the usual manner. Private sector leasing is no longer as cost-effective as it once was. Many authorities have abandoned their schemes and entered into nomination agreements with housing associations, which run Housing Association as Management Agents schemes, whereby an association manages a property on behalf of a private owner and accepts nominations of homeless persons. Authorities also nominate to Housing Association Leasing Schemes, whereby an association leases a property for a mutually agreed term from a private owner, and accepts nominations from councils of homeless persons, creating a subtenancy.

Questions

1. What is private sector leasing, and what are the benefits for residents and owners?
2. Why did some schemes entail high rents in 1990?
3. How do housing associations work together with local authorities in providing private sector leasing?

Foyers, work and housing

In France, 450 hostels known as 'foyers' offer housing and a package of work and training to young people, and receive substantial central government subsidy. They are developed and managed by housing associations, and represent an important strategy in addressing youth unemployment and alienation. Sadly, in Britain, too many young people are caught in the 'no home, no job' syndrome, exacerbating high crime rates. The idea of providing homes with work training to assist self development is worth examining, and some social housing providers here have started doing so.

The YMCA already has seven pilot foyers, and London and Quadrant Housing Trust, together with Essex-based Countryside in Partnership, is set to produce one each later this year. There is already a body representing interested organisations: the Foyer Federation, which takes the view that rents should lie between £30 and £50 per week to avoid the housing benefit 'poverty trap' arising when those paying relatively high rents get employment, owing to steep withdrawal of housing and other income support benefits. Although it has proved difficult to guarantee rents within this band, they are generally no higher than in other hostel schemes.

A conference in March 1994 of housing professionals providing housing with care and support criticised foyers. Government has provided some funding under the Employment Training Initiative, but on a cash-limited year-by-year basis, thereby constraining the number of trainees who can be taken on, as well as length of stay. There was concern that packages would entail people leaving with insufficient skills and entering the 'revolving door' of no home, no job once more.

Despite these criticisms, there are a number of ways forward. Foyers should be regarded as a form of special needs housing for funding purposes. If that were the case, registered associations could receive 100 per cent Housing Association Grant (HAG) on approved costs, plus Special Needs Management Allowance, a revenue subsidy payable by the Housing Corporation to bodies providing and managing such schemes. Such subsidies help guarantee affordable rents and reduce development risk. It would have to be established that intensive and supportive housing management is required, and that the young people in question include those 'at risk' or care leavers perhaps, although the Corporation's criteria are intended to be flexible. It is likely that many residents would fall under the necessary categories. Top-up revenue funding (and in some cases additional capital grants) could come from a range of sources, including the DSS and social services authorities. It is unfortunate to have to label young people seeking work skills as 'special needs' as this stigmatises, but if it secures much-needed public finance, so be it.

Even if general needs HAG is used to support such schemes, associations could charge lower rents to those finding employment, pooling any surpluses from rents charged to full housing benefit clients, thus avoiding the poverty trap. Local authorities should prioritise these work-and-housing initiatives when deciding their capital programmes, in the interests not only of young people, but of society as a whole. Councils can also help through land deals, property disposals and planning powers.

Training is central to the foyer concept, which gives educational providers opportunities for involvement. Two years ago, *PSLG* reported on a project in North Kensington involving City Challenge, on a Kensington Housing Trust estate, Wornington Green, involving craft skills training for unemployed residents. The partners in that initiative – principally the Trust and Hammersmith and West London College – are planning a foyer, Bridge House, in the same area, to address the urgent socio-economic problems of youth unemployment there. It is a model which, if successful, should be widely noted.

The development comprises a training centre and three residential blocks, funded by the Housing Corporation, City Challenge and the Royal Borough of Kensington and Chelsea and managed by Kensington Housing Trust, St Mungo's Association and the St Christopher Fellowship. Due for completion in July, 60 training places will be available, with priority given to homeless people living in the scheme area, including young people of 16 years and over, although unemployed residents in the area will be offered training if places are unfilled. Training opportunities include carpentry, joinery and a variety of building skills, as well as access to other courses. A club for residents and past trainees will ensure continued support. Chris Mounsey, Assistant Principal of Hammersmith and West London College, told *PSLG* that it had not been difficult to allocate places, and cited childcare and resident involvement, provided by CATCH, a secondary housing co-operative, as evidence of the inclusive nature of the package.

PSLG will report on the progress of this scheme. It is a positive step to intervene constructively in providing a way out of unemployment, and an example of partnership between diverse agencies to help solve problems which go to the heart of the malaise of today's society.

PSLG, June 1994

Questions

1. Why are foyers important in resolving the economic plight of some homeless young people?
2. What criticisms have been levelled at this initiative? Are they reasonable?
3. How did the various agencies co-operate to create the North Kensington scheme?

4 Housing associations

4.1 Introduction

In 1995, there were 1525 housing associations in the National Federation of Housing Associations' yearbook. Between them, they owned some 1 109 906 properties, and 115 120 homes were planned for completion that year, or were in the development pipeline. Twenty-two of these associations had over 10 000 homes in management – the size of a medium-rank district authority – and four had over 20 000. The movement employed over 60 000 staff, around one-third of whom were part-timers. By any standards, associations are major players in the social housing field.

Housing associations own property for rent and for sale. They come in all shapes and sizes, from small, local co-operatives to vast, national organisations owning up to 30 000 properties. The movement is diverse and growing, and will play an even larger part in providing affordable housing in the future, despite the financial and other challenges they face.

4.2 What are housing associations?

Housing associations are voluntary social housing organisations. They are controlled by shareholders with no financial interest in them, are independent of external bodies (although they work with them), and are run by volunteer committees and paid professional staff.

The first associations were the philanthropic housing trusts and charities of the nineteenth century, for example the Guinness Trust and Shaftesbury Housing, set up to house working people in the absence of official provision and against the background of appalling private rented accommodation, crowding and sheer shortage. Many of these early associations have survived, and the majority of associations are charities for historical reasons.

To paraphrase section 1 of the 1985 Housing Associations Act, all housing associations are societies, bodies of trustees or companies established to provide, construct, improve, manage, facilitate or encourage the construction or improvement of housing accommodation. They do not trade for profit, and their rules prohibit the issue of capital with interest or dividends exceeding a rate prescribed by the Treasury.

Associations are commonly incorporated as Industrial and Provident Societies under Part 4 of the 1965 Industrial and Provident Societies Act; such associations are known as '1965 Act associations'. Many such bodies are also registered charities. In order to be eligible for registration with the Housing Corporation, companies must also register with the Charities Commission, although this does not apply to Industrial and Provident Societies.

Housing associations that are charities have to have something in their constitution to the effect that they house those in necessitous circumstances, usually taken to imply selecting those who cannot compete in the marketplace, through poverty or for some other reason, for example because there is no suitable accommodation available. There are advantages to being a housing charity: they include relief from Corporation Tax, business rates, stamp duty on land and property purchased, and special status in the eyes of the public, who can make donations. However, they are limited to housing (in the words of the 1960 Charities Act) 'impotent, aged or poor people'; although it seems that they may construct homes for low-cost home ownership, many have set up non-charitable subsidiaries to do this form of work, and other more commercial activities.

Most housing associations are members of the National Federation of Housing Associations, (NFHA), which was formed in 1935 as a central agency for associations. Its role is to provide its members with information, research and services, and plays a valuable role in representing the movement's interests to the Housing Corporation, local authorities and central government, as well as to the public at large, financiers and other important co-players. It publishes *Housing Associations Weekly*, and the monthly *Voluntary Housing*, which should be read by all who are seriously interested in social housing.

A key division between associations is those that are and those that are not registered with the Housing Corporation. Registration gives access, at least potentially, to Housing Association Grant (HAG) and sometimes revenue subsidy, but carries with it duties to submit returns, monitoring visits, and abidance by a vast number of bureaucratic rules and regulations, ostensibly to safeguard the public purse. The Housing Corporation is a quango run by an unelected board and a chair appointed by government, and has the task of dispensing an annual budget voted by Parliament to almost 2500 registered associations to assist them in creating new homes through conversion and new-build.

Both Corporation and local authorities can give HAG. Even unregistered associations can receive public finance via section 24 of the 1988 Local Government Act, although the amounts are relatively restrictive.

The principal legislation affecting housing associations is the following:

- 1985 Housing Act – details secure tenancy (*see* p. 113–4) terms, and Right to Buy, which affects some associations.

- 1985 Housing Associations Act – replaced and updated parts of the 1974 Housing Act. It has itself been extensively amended, and contains most of the powers and duties applying to associations.

- 1986 Housing and Planning Act – voluntary transfers, and gave associations the power to undertake some local authority housing management functions.

- 1988 Housing Act – introduced a new financial regime for capital and revenue functions, as well as assured tenancies for lettings after January 1989.

- 1989 Local Government and Housing Act – amended Right to Buy, and defined 'controlled and influenced' companies, affecting the status of some voluntary transfer associations.

Housing associations are subject to all the legislation affecting private landlords. They can take over many local authority housing powers, both by management agreement and under compulsory competitive tendering, but cannot make decisions on their behalf relating to housing benefit or homeless persons.

Finally, housing co-operatives are also a form of housing association, and many are registered with the Housing Corporation. Some co-ops are ownership co-ops, in that the members collectively own a stake in the properties, and some are management co-ops, where the properties are owned by another body, perhaps a local authority or housing association, and where the resident members manage their homes collectively. There are primary co-ops, which are direct providers of housing, and secondary co-ops, which, as well as sometimes engaging in direct provision, also advise other co-ops on management and development issues.

The idea of housing co-ops is further explored in an article at the end of this chapter – 'A tenant management co-operative in London' (p. 147), which discusses the Alexandra Road Tenants' Co-operative. This took over the management of the estate, which is in Camden, North London, in 1991, and has since provided management services to tenants living there, as well as having involvement in repair and improvement programmes. It has proved an effective way to involve local residents in the running of their estate, and is generally popular: a large majority of tenants – 80 per cent – voted for the co-op in 1989, in a preliminary ballot. The co-op is granted a budget by the London Borough of Camden annually, and staff and residents have received training from CATCH, an arm of the secondary co-op SOLON Co-operative Services. The co-op employs its own staff, and its committee meets regularly to determine management policy, although some functions, for example, allocation, are dealt with by Camden.

As seen above, associations and co-ops are important partners with councils in providing and managing social housing. More will be said about the legal framework later.

4.3   Housing association committees

As was said before, associations are run by committees, which legally constitute these bodies. Housing associations which are not trusts have members, but trusts are run by trustees appointed in accordance with a private Act of Parliament or the relevant instrument or deed of trust which set it up.

Housing association committees which abide by the Model Rules issued by the NFHA have at least seven and generally not more than 15 members. Under the 1989 Local Government and Housing Act, no more than 20 per cent of board members may be 'local authority people' without the association becoming a controlled or influenced company, thus threatening their independence. Prior to registration, the Housing Corporation will need to be satisfied that the committee has the requisite skills and experience required to run such a body and manage private and public finance. Members are wholly unelected, and may be selected from a number of fields, including local government, finance, business, academia, architecture, or any number of other professions: there is no closed shop. Each committee must have a chair whose role it is to ensure that meetings run smoothly, and to give a degree of leadership. The main functions of committees are to:

- ensure the duties imposed by statute and the corporation are carried out;
- make sure the association acts according to its own constitution;
- make decisions on policy and practice; and
- appoint and dismiss staff, and supervise their activities.

Many larger associations have subcommittees which consider aspects of their operation, for example allocations subcommittee, finance subcommittee, development sub committee, and so on. This is similar to local authority practice. Having subcomittees is useful, if they are properly co-ordinated, in that it allows the detailed consideration of matters which may be complex and rather long-winded by those who may have a specific interest or expertise in these matters, and makes general meetings rather shorter.

The NFHA publishes a *Committee members' handbook* for guidance. Committees often have tenants' representatives on them, and such practices were encouraged in the early 1990s by the Housing Corporation, perhaps in response to the oft-levied charge that such committees often have the appearance of unaccountable closed shops. Tenant representation is very important, as tenants are customers, and their rents have been rising rapidly recently owing to reduced grant rates; but a balance must be struck between due influence and the risk of self-interest. As is the case for all members, adequate training must be made available to ensure that members understand legislation, practice and the challenges and opportunities available to the association. Good committees take full account of equal opportunities issue in selection and training, to ensure that as many aspects of the local community served are represented as possible; indeed, the Corporation looks for this when considering registration.

There is debate as to whether committee members should be paid. Most can claim expenses, but payment, as in wages, is a different matter. There is a strong tradition of voluntary service in Britain, exemplified by local authority councillors, trustees of charities and other benevolent organisations, persons running clubs and societies for no financial gain, and so forth; and membership of a housing association committee is in a similar vein. It could be argued that the level of technical knowledge and importance of the decisions made – these may relate to the expenditure of many thousands of pounds – justifies the payment of committee members rather than simply relying upon goodwill. But the following questions arise. Why should the quality of decision-making be any better if there is payment: is it deficient at present, and, if so, is it because people comprising committees are not paid? There is no evidence of this. Do associations find it difficult to recruit suitable members of committees because they are unable to make payments to them ? Again, there is very little evidence of this. Would members be more committed to the organisation if they were paid? Again, to measure commitment in relation to remuneration is to isolate only one factor which motivates people to serve on committees of this sort; the desire to advance housing opportunity is not treated by this argument at all. On the other hand, it could be argued that if such committees demand much time commitment, but no payment is made, then this restricts the sort of people who can reasonably be expected to serve. Those with children who have to find child-minding fees, those who cannot attend because it would mean losing money from other employment, and those who would be able and dedicated members if there was some remuneration may be excluded. Additionally, one may question the ethics of demanding hard work from somebody for no monetary consideration: is voluntarism just another word for exploitation? At present, committee members do not receive wages, but the argument continues, although finding a ready source to pay them would present new problems, and perhaps affect rents.

The Housing Corporation, in its stewardship role, monitors the activities of associations, and from time to time reviews the structure and membership of committees. If it believes that an association is deficient in this respect, it can appoint its own nominees. But if a committee contains the appropriate range of skills and experience, there is no reason why this should happen. It is impossible to define adequately the sort of people required, but, in view of the development, finance and management roles of associations, consideration might be given to architects, town planners, finance specialists, ex- or current housing managers, builders (although conflicts of interest should be avoided, and have in any case to be declared under s. 15 of the Housing Associations Act), employees of housing pressure groups, lawyers and, of course, tenants. With respect to the latter, although there are restrictions as to the number of tenants who can serve, the Corporation expects every association to have a tenant involvement strategy which at the very least entails having some tenant representation on the board. It is essential, as with other members, that proper training be given in the roles of associations, so that there is a level playing field for debate and decision. The danger of not doing so is the emergence of cliques of 'experts' who dominate meetings and alienate other members, resulting in an imbalance in policy and practice; the views of non-experts are just as valid as others. The issues relating to the provision and management of social housing are not in themselves complex: it should be left to trained staff to deal with the legal and operational complexities. The job of the committee is to determine policy and give direction, without forever getting bogged down in details, although committee members must be mindful of the legal consequences of their actions.

4.4   What do housing associations do?

Housing associations are a diverse bunch. They do a number of things, including:

- providing rented accommodation by new-build, renovation or conversion;
- providing low-cost homes for purchase;
- buying property for the above purposes;
- helping people to buy homes for low cost ownership;
- managing the above;
- managing local authority accommodation, including temporary lettings;
- managing private rented accommodation;
- acting as development agents for other associations and co-operatives;
- providing housing aid and advice;
- owning and running charity shops;
- and a range of other housing and related activities.

Some co-operatives are also housing associations.

4.4.1   Provision of rented accommodation

Much has already been said about the grant regime, but it is worthwhile to recap. Registered housing associations bid each year for their share of the

Housing Corporation's Approved Development Programme (ADP) budget, voted annually by Parliament. So-called *programme* associations bid for resources over three years, promising to provide a given number of units for a given amount of subsidy. *Non-programme* associations bid on a scheme-by-scheme basis annually and receive grant to cover a percentage of anticipated costs per scheme at three stages during the development process: at exchange of contracts; start on site; and practical completion. The assumptions underlying the Corporation's grant model are designed to ensure the production of affordable rented homes. The majority of associations have to raise private finance to meet the difference between Housing Association Grant (HAG) and total development costs; this loan is charged to rents on a scheme-by-scheme basis, or pooled across rents in the general portfolio, sometimes a bit of both. These are known as 'mixed finance' schemes, because some of the money comes from the public purse and some comes from private sources. Some associations (or schemes) still have access to public loans – those providing special needs accommodation, or others targeted by government. These are 'public funded' as all the resources come from public finance. Only association schemes developed before March 1989 or special needs schemes can receive public revenue subsidy from the Corporation. In the case of pre-1989 fair rent schemes, this is known as Revenue Deficit Grant, although there is also a liability to pay back a portion of surpluses into a pot known as the Revenue Surplus Fund which is distributed through the annual programme. In the case of special needs schemes, the subsidy is known as Special Needs Management Allowance, and is paid at a predetermined rate based on expected deficits on running costs, and reviewed annually.

The rented aspect of the total housing association programme is still dominant: in 1996/97 it is planned to spend £1134.3 million on capital support for rental projects compared to £316.6 million on for sale schemes (source: D.o.E. *Annual report 1994*), although there has been a shift in favour of for-sale schemes in recent years. Grants have been reduced as a percentage of costs, so rents have increased, and several associations have decided not to develop unless or until grant rates rise to the extent that they can guarantee to provide affordable homes once more.

Properties are rented on an assured tenancy basis, subject to the Tenant's Guarantee, a document published by the Corporation and revised from time to time, requiring registered associations to write standard clauses into their agreements to increase the security rights of their tenants. Generally, assured tenants have fewer rights than 'fair rent' secure tenants (those granted prior to January 1989), including no Right to Buy, except where the tenant and property have been transferred from a local authority. The key feature of the assured tenancy is that it is not possible for the tenant to fix the rent as it is for fair rent tenancies. This is a clear consequence of the new financial regime: associations need to set rents to cover their running costs and loan repayments, and cannot therefore be saddled with 'fair rent' determinations which are independent of these considerations. It is also easier to evict an assured tenant, even if covered by the guarantee, than a secure tenant; for example, mandatory possession is granted on 3 months' arrears if existing at the date of service of notice and court hearing. This gives private lenders greater comfort, as it gives associations greater powers to remove poor payers and replace them with better ones, thus serving to increase the reliability of cash flow projections, but it surely also entails associations being prepared to offer a range of debt and benefit counselling facilities to ensure that tenants do not fall into this position, especially given that rents are higher than they were.

Depending on their income, tenants may be eligible for Housing Benefit (Private Sector). Application is usually directly to the authority, and tenants will receive a cheque on a periodic basis. However, tenants may agree to the association receiving the benefit directly; this cannot be insisted upon, except in arrears cases, but the certainty of receipt, especially where the tenant is entitled to full housing benefit, can assist cash flow projection and minimise arrears. Heating and lighting bills, along with care charges, are generally ineligible for benefit.

The role of housing associations which provide housing for rent, and the challenges faced by them, is explored in an article at the end of this chapter, 'Interview with Mike Cohen, Chief Executive, Guinness Trust Group' (p. 142). By the mid 1990s, many associations were beginning to question whether they could continue to develop affordable homes, given falling grant rates and the necessity to raise relatively expensive private finance, and were becoming concerned about the poverty trap in which many tenants on income support found themselves in. Cohen wonders whether the Guinness Trust, an old-established association which has developed over a hundred-year time period, would better serve its customers by managing its existing stock rather than jeopardising rent levels by continuing to develop.

4.4.2   Low-cost housing initiatives

Since the early 1980s, associations have been providing low-cost housing for sale. Sometimes this is done through a non-charitable subsidiary specifically set up for that purpose, so that there are no conflicts between the charitable objectives of the association and its operations, although it is now generally understood that charities can provide low-cost homes as long as they target them on those who cannot afford to compete in the market. Many of these non-charitable subsidiaries have other functions, including running temporary accommodation schemes, managing commercial properties and providing services to other associations.

Housing for sale has received greater priority than hitherto for public financial support. In 1996/97, it is planned that £316.6 million should be spent by way of HAG support to these initiatives, out of a total Approved Development Programme (ADP) of around £1503 million – that is, 21 per cent of available resources, compared to just over 5 per cent in 1991/92 (source: D.o.E. *Annual report 1994*).

The principal elements of low-cost home ownership are traditional shared ownership and Do It Yourself Shared Ownership (DIYSO).

Traditional shared ownership schemes entail an association building or purchasing a property, backed by HAG, and selling a percentage of the value on to a purchaser selected from its or a nominee's waiting list, on a leasehold basis, generally for a 99-year term. The purchaser arranges a mortgage to cover the percentage they have acquired, usually 25 per cent minimum, and pays rent to cover the loan charges and other expenditure (management and maintenance) incurred by the association. The leases are generally 'full repairing leases' which means that the occupier is liable to do all repairs, there is minimum management, and the occupier has responsibility for the usual items which any owner-occupier is liable for, such as insurance and any incidental costs. Under the majority of schemes, it is possible for the purchaser to acquire further shares, often in multiples of 12.5 per cent of the valuation at the time they wish to do this, until they buy the whole value. This is known as 'staircasing'. The occupier will then become either a freeholder (if the property is a house owned by the association on a freehold basis) or a leaseholder (which is the general case with flats, where the association retains the freehold and is entitled to charge ground rent and service charges, which are reviewed periodically in accordance with the lease). In 1993, over 2500 homes were sold on a shared ownership basis in England alone – larger than any other category (source: *Housing Associations in England 1993*).

The case of one housing association – Garden City Homes Housing Association – is discussed in two articles at the end of this chapter (pp. 138 and 140). Garden City Homes Housing Association started as a vehicle enabled by Welwyn Hatfield District Council to take over ownership of properties sold under lease through the shared ownership provisions of the 1985 Housing Act. The motivation for this was primarily financial, as housing associations are free to reinvest 100 per cent of capital receipts from sales of properties (including the remaining equity purchased by householders in shared ownership homes), in comparison to the restrictions suffered by councils, as already discussed. It was advised, and its properties managed by, Sanctuary Housing Association, a body experienced in the development and management of social rented and ownership accommodation. Garden City Homes Housing Association has now grown to the extent that not only does it manage the leasehold properties transferred by Welwyn Hatfield District Council, but it has developed properties for rent. It was registered with the Housing Corporation in 1992, and receives local authority and Housing Corporation Housing Association Grant (HAG).

The method of public subsidy is similar to that for rented housing, in that HAG is advanced to cover a proportion of the acquisition and development costs incurred by the association. It is payable as a percentage of these costs, subject to cost limits (Total Cost Indicators) minus the amount paid by the purchaser. If and when further shares are acquired, the association

has to reimburse the Housing Corporation; thus HAG on shared ownership can be seen as an interest-free loan to the association.

The rental element is, in appropriate cases, eligible for Housing Benefit
(Private Sector). In some cases, associations may buy back the property,
and it is possible for the association to exercise first refusal when a
share of the property is sold on by the purchaser, as it has a legal interest
in it. Associations will want to ensure, as far as possible, that the new
purchaser is someone who cannot afford to pay the market price, or perhaps a nominee of an organisation they work with (such as a local authority).

Shared ownership schemes are seen in two ways by central government.
First, they increase the scope for house purchase – which is regarded as a
'natural' form of tenure (even where there is negative equity and purchase
is seen as a rather poor investment!), and second, they are seen as a way
of releasing social rented housing for those unable to purchase on any
terms. This is why existing social tenants have been prioritised under such
schemes. There may be a danger of stigmatisation here: if, in the future,
most tenants who can afford to do so buy shared ownership properties,
those left will be easily identified as 'the poor', with social consequences
for them, especially if they are contained in specific areas. On the other
hand, this ascription need not necessarily follow: it seems reasonable to
expect that a typical housing career might involve being housed in social
rented accommodation until the household has sufficient money to buy into
shared ownership. This need not be seen as a reflection of absolute poverty,
rather as an indication of being at a certain stage in the income life cycle,
just as being a teenager or young person and relatively poor does not indicate one's position a few years further on.

Similar 'filtering' arguments may be applied to those on social housing
waiting lists. For every household which is removed on purchasing a shared
ownership home, presumably some other case is advanced further up the
list (if this is the way the authority operates) and thereby has a better
chance of getting social housing. Additionally, there is no reason why homeless households should not be offered shared ownership if their income and
other circumstances justify this.

There is also a case to be made for seeing rented and shared ownership
housing as forming a reverse–move type system. Supposing a shared owner
falls into financial difficulty to the extent that repossession seems inevitable.
At this stage or earlier, would it not be rational for the association to allocate that person a social rented home, and simultaneously sell the share to
a tenant who wishes to purchase, where the household needs are similar?
If housing associations pooled their resources in this respect – a kind of
national rental–shared ownership exchange scheme – it is conceivable that
many households could be assisted. Additionally, the notion of converting
shared ownership tenure to rented tenure *in the same property*, and vice
versa, should not be beyond the wit of policy-makers; indeed, the former
alternative is already done in some cases.

Thus shared ownership schemes can play a vital part in the social housing system of the country. Whilst it should not be assumed that ownership is a 'natural' form of tenure, or is inherently superior to renting, neither should the reverse. Tenure neutrality, especially where owner-occupation is no longer a credible investment and where mobility of labour is an issue, is a sensible viewpoint, and the treatment of shared ownership in the fashion described supports this view.

4.4.3 Do It Yourself Shared Ownership

Do It Yourself Shared Ownership (DIYSO) is a variant of shared ownership. Initiated in 1983, it lay dormant after a relatively unsuccessful pilot period until being revived nine years later. The key difference is that the prospective purchaser chooses a suitable property on the open market, subject to cost and size limits, which is then acquired by the association. The remaining details are identical to traditional shared ownership. Certain associations have been earmarked as DIYSO agents, and can deal in property anywhere in the country. In the mid-1990s, social housing tenants were prioritised, to increase the supply of re-lets. In the first year of operation (1992/93), just over 2000 DIYSO sales were made. The advantage over traditional shared ownership is that purchasers can search for properties that meet their specifications in a larger field, although second-hand properties – the majority of DIYSO purchases – may have greater repair needs. It has been seen as a way of reducing the surplus of homes on the market.

4.4.4 Managing of temporary accommodation by housing associations

Much has already been said about the variety of accommodation available on this basis (see Chapter 3). Many councils work closely with associations in this area. Examples include:

- Using associations as acquisition agents for private sector leasing schemes; using them as managing agents for PSL; or getting them to take on both roles.

- Nominating homeless applicants to HAMA (housing associations as managing agents) schemes, whereby an association rents a property from a private landlord, and houses the applicant on an assured tenancy basis.

- Nominating people to hostels run by associations, often of a specialist nature. For example, the St Mungo Association houses those with drink or related problems in supervised hostel accommodation, and works with a number of authorities in London, including Westminster City Council and the Royal Borough of Kensington and Chelsea.

- Appointing associations as development and managing agents for short-life schemes, whereby associations are granted a lease on a property owned by a council, apply a mixture of Short Life Housing Association Grant and council 'top-up' funding to renovate the property to at least wind-and-watertight standard, and accept nominations of homeless households from the council, housing them on a licence or assured short-hold basis.

- Nominating young single homeless people to foyers. Foyers are essentially hostels built, converted and managed by associations (the YMCA was a pioneer) which offer work or training as part of a package to enable residents to secure their own permanent housing. The idea came from France in the early 1990s.

Many housing associations have their own Short Term Housing Units (an example is the London and Quadrant Housing Trust), which operate the above initiatives. Such associations have built up much expertise in this area, and it would be foolish to reinvent the wheel. Savings can be made on development and running costs; and the field is sufficiently competitive to allow for keen fee negotiations.

4.4.5   Housing associations acting as development agents for other associations

A small, unregistered association may not have access to public funds, or the expertise to work up developments; this is where a larger, more experienced association can play a role. This is commonly found in respect of associations developing for co-operatives. In some cases, they also undertake management for these organisations.

4.5   Financial and other assistance from bodies excluding the Housing Corporation

At their best, associations are partners in social housing development and management. Indeed, given HAG restrictions, it is hard to see how the movement could expand without some form of co-operative working. Financial assistance is forthcoming for registered housing associations, in the main, from the Housing Corporation in the form of HAG and sometimes revenue subsidy, but there are other routes.

4.5.1   Local authority HAG and Section 24 payments

Councils have to bid annually to the D.o.E. for permission to 'incur credit' – that is, to borrow towards capital programmes – and receive Credit Approvals in this respect every year. They can use the bit they borrow under the Basic Credit Approval element to support housing association activity. HAG granted via a local authority does not come from the ADP of the Housing Corporation, and therefore represents true additional capital funding, although it is ultimately resourced via the Corporation. The percentage and other rules are identical to Housing Corporation HAG. Basically, the council borrows money and immediately advances local authority HAG (LA HAG): simultaneously the Housing Corporation reimburses the council, which repays the loan. Another way of financing LA HAG is via the usable portion of capital receipts. In this case, money paid out as HAG is reimbursed by the Corporation, but this money must be used to redeem debt. Councils may also advance HAG from RCCOs (already discussed in Chapter 2 on p. 50).

A council pursuing this partnership gains in a number of ways. First, because the grant rate is always less than development costs, it can produce more social housing than it could if it used that money itself. Second, it is possible to obtain high nominations (often exceeding 50 per cent) to such schemes; thus pressure on waiting lists can be eased, although households are typically on housing association and local authority registers. Third, such an operation costs only the arrangement fees for the loan, and any staff time used working up the deal.

However, credit approvals can be used only once, and the council must take a view as to how to divide its capital budget. Much will depend upon the state of repair of its own stock. However, the advantages appear to outweigh the disadvantages.

Local authorities can use LA HAG to fund projects which would not otherwise receive Housing Corporation support, or which may be low down on that organisation's list of priorities. It can be used to top up low HAG, where that grant is below the standard amount, provided that it does not take subsidy beyond that level.

Local authorities are also able to advance smaller capital sums via their powers under s. 24 of the Local Government Act. This enables them to grant financial or other assistance to providers of private rented accommodation, which includes associations. Generally, the council has to clear this with the D.o.E. first, but there is a general consent allowing councils to grant annually an amount equivalent to the number of inhabitants in their area times one pound for these purposes. Such funding can be advanced to non-registered as well as registered associations.

4.5.2 Revenue subsidy

Local authorities can make revenue payments to associations to help them run their schemes. A common form of this is funding advanced from social services budgets to assist in the running of special needs schemes, where there is a care element. Payments can also come from other sources, for example, associated charities, health authorities, and, in some cases, the probation service or Home Office. Generally, however, association rents have to take the strain of meeting running costs, although housing benefit, whether paid to tenants or received directly, is obviously a very important source of revenue subsidy.

4.5.3   Other assistance

The sale of land or property at less than market value by a council is a valuable source of subsidy to the association, although again 'total public subsidy' rules apply. The discount is treated as a financial payment, and HAG is reduced accordingly; but with land costs often amounting to one third of total costs, such assistance is extremely valuable none the less. Local authorities are subject to penalties under s. 61 of the Local Government and Housing Act if they grant cheap or free land: essentially they lose the ability to incur credit to the tune of the discount – but can avoid this by securing nomination rights to the scheme, and such penalties do not apply if the development is for low-cost home ownership. This issue will be discussed at further length in Chapter 6. Additionally, associations can benefit from deals made under s. 104 of the 1990 Town and Country Planning Act, whereby a council can secure land or housing from a developer on the back of a planning application at no or low cost under certain circumstances, and pass the benefit on to a third party. This is known as planning obligation (*see* Chapter 6).

Given the continued restrictions on council finance and development powers, the above forms of co-operative working will become much more important in the future.

4.6   What is the Housing Corporation?

The Housing Corporation's publication *The next three years – The Housing Corporation's plans and priorities 1994–1997* summarised its key aims as follows:

* regulating the activities of associations;

* safeguarding the investment of public funds and ensuring that associations manage their affairs efficiently and effectively;

* making new capital and revenue investment;

* maximising the value obtained from resources available to meet priority housing needs;

* improving the delivery of its services; and

* ensuring that it provides an economic, efficient range of services to meet the needs of its customers.

The Corporation is a quango – a quasi autonomous non-governmental organisation – which regulates and funds housing association activity. It has regulated the movement since 1974. Since 1989 it has had its own budget, voted annually by Parliament, and is the grant-making body – a role it took over from the D.o.E. in the same year, under powers granted within the 1988 Housing Act.

Quangos are a peculiarly British institution. At present, in the mid-1990s, there are about 500 such organisations. They may be defined as 'organisations which have been set up or adopted by Departments and provided with public funds to perform some functions which the government wishes to see performed, but which it does not wish to be the direct responsibility of a Minister or Department' (source: G. Bowen, *Survey of Fringe Bodies*, 1978). Examples include the British Library, the Equal Opportunities Commission, the Commission for Racial Equality, the Gaming Board, the White Fish Authority and English Heritage.

Common characteristics include the fact that they derive their existence from ministerial decisions; they are answerable to Ministers; they are created by legislation; most produce annual reports for parliamentary scrutiny; their chairs and boards are appointed by Ministers for a fixed term; and their accounts are audited annually by the National Audit Commission, or privately.

Advantages include the following: their activities can be conducted relatively freely from parliamentary interference, although in 1992 the Corporation was the subject of inquiry by Select Committee. They allow administrative solutions to problems created by legislation: for example, the 1988 Housing Act was complex to interpret, especially in translating its terms into tenancy conditions for housing associations, and the Corporation came up with the Tenant's Guarantee. They relieve much of the administrative burden of the Civil Service – as when the Corporation took over grant administration from the D.o.E. Regional Offices in 1989.

Disadvantages include institutional proliferation, with all the expense that this entails, as well as the difficulties associated with controlling their activities. They allow for ministerial patronage – one sometimes wonders how the prominent builders and finance mandarins who end up on some of these boards are selected. Additionally, they are definitely not part of government as controlled and regulated by Parliament: they are unelected and not particularly accountable, and yet they have considerable power.

The Housing Corporation is a statutory body reporting to the Secretary of State for the Environment, who appoints its chair, deputy chair and its 15 board members. It was founded in 1964 to promote cost rent and co-ownership housing, but has changed its functions considerably since then, to include the role of grant aid financier to the housing association movement and acting as a provider of limited revenue subsidies, and supervisor of the activities of associations it has registered.

Cost rent housing was rented housing where the charge covered the cost of borrowing to develop or acquire property, and management and maintenance costs. Under the 1961 Housing Act, the Corporation made loans as

Fig. 4.1 Housing association new-build terraced housing for rent and for sale, Notting Hill Housing Trust, 1994. Lime Grove, London W12

Fig. 4.2 Housing association new-build flats. Notting Hill Housing Trust, 1994. Lime Grove, London W12

Fig. 4.3 Offices of Shepherd's Bush Housing Group

an agent of central government to bodies that did this. They were superseded by co-ownership societies, where members paid rent towards repaying the loan raised to build the development, and received a premium or cash sum on leaving. This form of development was largely abandoned in the mid-1970s.

The 1974 Housing Act enlarged the Corporation's powers, giving it the power to authorise government grants to assist housing associations develop fair rent housing, as an agent for the Department of the Environment, itself formed in 1973, and to register housing associations. It was given new supervisory powers, including the power to conduct inquiries into the running of registered associations, to wind them up or to freeze their assets. The 1980 Housing Act gave the Corporation the role of overseeing the provisions of the Tenant's Charter, which defined new rights for association tenants, who became Secure Tenants, with rights analogous to those with local authority landlords. It also conferred on certain tenants the Right to Buy, which the Corporation was charged with implementing.

Fig. 4.4 Terraced housing built to less than Parker Morris standards. Gwalia Housing Association, Swansea

Additionally, it had to implement the grant redemption fund, a mechanism to claw back revenue surpluses made by associations as rents exceeded out-goings under the high grant regime, and ensure that associations produced accounts in the required form.

The 1988 Housing Act, which came into force in January 1989, gave the Housing Corporation new budgetary responsibilities; a budget voted annually by Parliament from which to make grants; powers to decide which areas of the country (England in this case) and which associations received grant at given levels; the duty to oversee and administer the new financial regime, as already discussed; and responsibility for the development of the Tenant's Guarantee. It has also devised a system of performance indicators to measure the strengths and weaknesses of associations, and has produced numerous circulars and advisory documents exhorting associations to design in specific ways and to involve tenants in their operations, amongst many other topics. In addition, it oversees the 'change of landlord' provisions of the 1988 Housing Act, whereby local authority tenants can vote to choose another landlord to take over ownership of their homes (*see* Chapter 5). In this context, it is the body charged with 'approving' landlords or other-wise. It is also responsible for implementing and monitoring s. 71 of the Race Relations Act: it must eliminate racial discrimination, and promote equality of opportunity in housing practices in associations.

The Corporation has its counterparts in Scotland, Wales and Northern Ireland, although they have slightly different powers. The Scottish body is known as Scottish Homes. In addition to providing grant funding for associations, it also provides so-called GRO-GRANTS to aid private sector developers build for rent and low-cost home ownership. The Housing Corporation's work is divided into regions, which administer the details of grant applications and payments. Its headquarters is in London; its regions are London and Home Counties (NE); London and Home Counties (NW); London and Home Counties (S); West; East Midlands; West Midlands; North East; North West; and Merseyside.

The Housing Corporation is responsible for setting grant rates annually, and uses a model to do so. For further details, read the article 'Grant rates: modelling and manipulation' at the end of this chapter (p. 146).

There is undoubtedly a need for some sort of regulator to oversee the financing and operation of the burgeoning voluntary housing movement: it spends too much public money to be allowed the luxury of self-regulation, and the Corporation has proved itself to be an effective if somewhat bureaucratic big brother in this respect. But is it necessary to have an independent body acting as major public financier, when there are many local authorities that understand the housing need in their areas intimately, and which may be better judges of where the money should be applied than the Corporation? Councils understand the grant system, and have been administering LA HAG for years. They are subject to considerable legislative and other controls which help prevent the abuse of power; and they are definitely democratically accountable. A very good case could be made for devolving the finance aspects of the Corporation to local authorities, or even regional associations. This would save much public money, whilst reinforcing the enabling role which councils are asked to adopt. Associations and councils have worked fruitfully together for many years: why not as principal funder and beneficiary? The Corporation could be retained as a central regulator and monitor of the movement. It would not be a mammoth task to rejig the Credit Approval system to allow for councils to pay out grant, to be reimbursed from D.o.E. funds in the way that the Corporation does at present.

The fourth article at the end of this chapter, 'The future of the Housing Corporation' (p. 144), examines possible future roles for this body, in light of criticisms levelled by the National Federation of Housing Associations and others, and highlights some of the issues referred to above.

4.7 Secure tenants, assured tenants and the Tenant's Guarantee

As stated earlier, from 15 January 1989 association tenants have had the status of *assured tenants*. Those whose tenancies were granted before that date are mostly *secure tenants*. The basic differences are stated below, and modifications created under the 1994 version of the Tenant's Guarantee are discussed further on:

- *Exchange.* Secure tenants have the right to exchange their tenancy with another secure tenant; assured tenants do not have this by right.

- *Succession.* A secure tenant's spouse, or resident member of the family, can succeed on the death of tenant; for assured tenants, there is a right only for the spouse to succeed.

- *Lodgers.* Secure tenants have the right to take in lodgers; assured tenants do not.

- *Subletting.* Secure tenants have the right to sublet part of their home; assured landlords may prohibit this.

- *Improvements.* A secure tenant has the right to undertake certain improvements; an assured tenant does not.

- *Repairs.* A secure tenant has a right to repair, and can recharge the landlord. The assured tenant has no such right, and might have to take court action to force a recalcitrant landlord to make repairs under the terms of the contract.

- *Information.* A secure tenant has the right to information about the tenancy: an assured tenant has no specific right.

- *Consultation on management changes.* A secure tenant has this right; not so the assured tenant.

- *Right to buy at discount.* Secure tenants have this right; assured tenants do not in general, although those who have transferred to a housing association from a local authority under voluntary transfer conditions (*see* Chapter 5) have the 'preserved' right to buy.

- *Security differences.* In both cases, the tenancy can be ended only by order of court on grounds specified by the 1985 Housing Act (Secure Tenancy) or 1988 Housing Act (Assured Tenancy). However, whilst there is only one mandatory repossession ground for secure tenancies (the so-called redevelopment ground), there are eight for assured tenancies, notably where rent is three months in arrears, for whatever reason; where the property is to be demolished or reconstructed, or where repairs are to be carried out and this cannot be done with the tenant in residence; and where the mortgagee has obtained repossession.

- *Rent terms.* Non-local authority secure tenants have the right to register a fair rent with the rent officer under the provisions of the 1977 Rent Act. For assured tenants, there is no such right, although after a year of tenancy either party may apply to the Rent Assessment Committee (RAC) for an RAC rent to be set (based on market levels). The landlord cannot charge more than this, unless the tenant agrees.

The Tenant's Guarantee modifies the above considerably. The primary reason for the introduction of assured tenancies for new association lettings after January 1989 was to allow associations to set rents to cover management, maintenance and private loan costs, and to allow them to vary these in relation to increases in the above. Had fair rents been continued, the Corporation would have been committed to continue to pay subsidy on deficits. It was not intended to create a second class of tenants with far fewer rights: so the Tenant's Guarantee was formulated after the Act to give new-style association tenants similar rights to those of secure tenants. It has been revised several times.

The 1994 edition was, at the time of writing, the latest revision. It was revised because of changes in tenancy law as a result of the 1993 Leasehold Reform, Housing and Urban Development Act. It falls into eight sections, namely:

A meeting housing need;

B allocating accommodation on assured periodic tenancies;

C terms of periodic assured tenancies;

D principles upon which rent (and other charges) for assured tenancies are to be determined;

E maintenance and repair;

F consultation and tenant involvement;

G information to tenants;

H equal opportunities.

4.7.1 Summary of the Tenant's Guarantee

4.7.1.1 A. Meeting housing need

Associations must have housing access policies which address the needs of homeless and badly housed people, and those who cannot compete on the market, and should co-operate with local authorities and other bodies such as social services and health authorities. At least 50 per cent of nominations should be granted to public authorities, where there has been public subsidy (e.g. HAG).

4.7.1.2 B. Allocating accommodation on assured periodic tenancies

Associations must be open about how they allocate tenancies; it is suggested that those on management committees, employees and close relatives should be excluded from access. The Housing Corporation and local authorities with which they work should be sent a copy. In such policies, special attention should be paid to groups who may experience particular difficulty in finding somewhere suitable to live, for example those from ethnic minorities, and people with disabilities.

4.7.1.3   C. Terms of assured periodic tenancies

This applies to tenancies granted after 15 January 1989. The main form of tenancy should be the assured periodic type, although assured shortholds can be granted in exceptional circumstances, as for example in connection with temporary accommodation. Prospective tenants, whether new, or existing tenants who may take on an assured tenancy, have the right to full information on the terms.

The rights which the corporation requires associations to write in are as follows:

1. Right to exchange with other association or local authority tenants.

2. Right to take in lodgers or sublet part of the accommodation, subject to agreement of the association, which is not to be unreasonably withheld.

3. Right to carry out improvements with the association's permission.

4. Right to be compensated for expenditure on certain improvements at the end of the tenancy.

5. Compensation if the association fails to carry out certain repairs within a certain time.

6. Right to be consulted on management changes.

7. Provided the tenant is not a successor, the right of succession to a spouse (whether or not married) who, immediately before the tenant's death, occupied the property as his or her only or principal home. It is suggested that this right be extended to a person of the same sex who lived as a partner for at least a year before death of the tenant. Offers of alternative accommodation are contemplated as an alternative.

8. The agreement should state the initial rent payable, and any procedure for altering it; also the complaint procedures, and the right to refer complaints to the Housing Association Tenants Ombudsman Service.

9. Eviction should be contemplated only as a last resort.

10. There should be clear policies responding to harassment or nuisance by tenants.

4.7.1.4   D. Principles on which rents determined

It is intended that properties should be accessible to those on low incomes, whether or not in paid employment or on housing benefit. This usually means rent setting below market level. However, the guidance makes it clear that rents also have to cover management, maintenance and loan charge liabilities. In practice, such rents are likely to be below market levels – but the only appeal is to the Rent Assessment Committee, which only has the power to set a market rent. High rents are an inevitable consequence of grant reductions.

4.7.1.5   E. Maintenance and repair

Properties should be fit for human habitation. Future maintenance should be planned. Tenants are entitled to clear information about the association's and their repair responsibilities, what to do if need for repair arises, and how to complain if it is not done properly. Associations should have a repair prioritisation system which classifies repairs as emergency (24-hour response); urgent (5 working days' response); and routine (at association's discretion).

4.7.1.6   F. Consultation and tenant involvement

This is taken to mean not only consultation on management changes, but real involvement in management by facilitating, taking on board the views of tenants' associations and allowing involvement in design issues.

4.7.1.7   G. Information to tenants

Tenants are entitled to information on the performance of the association with respect to such matters as:

1. rents charged for different sizes of home;

2. how quickly repairs are carried out;

3. association's success in collecting rent due;

4. the association's empty properties;

5. speed of letting and re-letting and to what categories of people.

This should be made available in plain English, in other languages where appropriate, and in Braille or on tape; and it should be explained at the start of the tenancy and/or in meetings with tenants.

4.7.1.8   H. Equal opportunities

Associations are reminded of the Corporation's duties to attempt to eliminate unlawful racial discrimination and promote equality of opportunity; and the Guarantee states that associations must have written equal opportunities policies which should be made widely available. Their lettings should also be monitored to demonstrate equality of access.

All in all, the Guarantee represents a sensible set of guidelines for associations. If followed, it should ensure that in many important respects there is little difference between the rights of council tenants and housing association tenants, except in the matter of rents, and right to buy. The latter point is dealt with by the Tenants Incentive Scheme, which is Housing Corporation funded, and cash limited. It provides a lump sum to qualifying association tenants who are unable to buy because they are tenants of charitable associations, to assist them in buying property on the open market. But not all associations are charitable; and assured tenants do not automatically qualify.

4.8   Conclusion: the future of housing associations

Housing associations are the main developers of social housing, although not yet the main social landlord. A number of challenges face the movement.

- Given that grant rates are set to reduce further, how can associations sustain a new-build programme to produce truly affordable accommodation, at rents which do not need to be supported by housing benefit?
- Will they repeat the same mistakes as often made by local authorities in managing large estates?
- Will they compete for local authority contracts under compulsory competitive tender, and how will this affect the working relationships with councils?
- To what degree will tenant involvement and management be extended?

Associations live, and will continue to live, in interesting and challenging times.

Articles

1. 'In partnership for housing'
2. 'Enabling social housing: Garden City Homes Housing Association'
3. 'Interview with Mike Cohen, Chief Executive, Guinness Trust Group'
4. 'The future of the Housing Corporation'
5. 'Grant rates: modelling and manipulation'
6. 'A tenant management co-operative in London'

In partnership for housing

Council house-building has declined over the last decade through councils' reduced ability to borrow and to spend capital realised from property sales. Local authorities have had to strike deals with housing associations and companies in order to meet their responsibilities, consistent with governmental desire that councils should become 'enablers' rather than direct housing providers. 'Partnership' deals, involving land being sold at discounted prices, or transferred freely to associations or companies to produce lower-cost housing for sale or rent, follow this approach. Paradoxically, recent legislation potentially makes such options more difficult.

Transfers of council land effectively in return for nomination rights to properties built on it have been threatened by s. 61 of the 1989 Local Government and Housing Act. This bizarre section treats benefits received by councils as capital receipts, in that if land is given to another party, an authority has to offset the equivalent of 50 per cent of the market value of the discounted land against its capital resources – the element that it would have had to find to repay debt if it had received cash. This could make 'nomination rights' on such schemes prohibitively expensive. This would seem to be an own goal for a government wishing to encourage the enabling function! Only lobbying by concerned councils led to a late amendment to the Bill enabling the Secretary of State to exempt selected schemes: but how often will this power be used?

The risk that it won't has not deterred Welwyn Hatfield Council from working up a scheme potentially involving the free transfer of land to a local housing association to help provide affordable rented homes. 'We're planning to transfer 14 acres of land in three parcels to Sanctuary Spiral Housing Association for development as homes for rent and shared ownership, to be aimed at households on our waiting-list. This will produce around 200 dwellings,' said Neil Dutton, Housing Development Officer.

The rents would be significantly less than anything in the private rented sector, directly as a result of the land subsidy. It's understood that we can give the land freely without adverse consequences for housing association funding. However, everything depends upon whether the D.o.E. will exempt the deal from its capital controls, and on the HAG level available for the association. It's the only way we can see of getting any new build in the district.

Another partnership scheme developed in the district to provide lower-cost homes involved the formation of a housing company, with the status of a housing association, to provide shared ownership homes to local residents. Last year, the council bought 180 houses in the district on the open market, for leasehold sale on a part-rent, part-buy basis to families on the housing waiting list, using capital receipts. The council realised it could spend only a proportion of money from the sale of equity, and that, following the 1989 legislation, much of that would have to be used to repay debt; therefore Garden City Homes Ltd was created, to which the freehold of the properties has been transferred.

The company can use all the money realised through sales of remaining shares towards further purchases. Care was taken to ensure that the company board contained no more than one councillor, the Housing chair, in order to avoid falling foul of legislation restricting council influence over companies set up for such purposes; but it contains local citizens who have a clear interest in local housing issues: for example, a representative of a leading building society and a caseworker from the charity SHELTER, which has its regional office in Welwyn Garden City.

Garden City Homes contracted Sanctuary Spiral as a management agent, to collect the rent on the unsold portions, to act as accountants, and to advise on future developments – a good example of the partnership the government wants to see develop. The council will assist the company with a grant, under its general powers to aid housing associations, from its capital resources, to enable more purchases, but it is anticipated that up to 14 properties will be bought merely from the proceeds of equity sales to occupiers in 1990.

The initial share can cost as little as 20 per cent of the full value, which can be acquired at any time. Even when rents are added to monthly mortgages, total payments undercut private rents for similar property to be found locally. Thirty-one homeless families have been able to buy these homes, which shows that the scheme meets housing need as well as demand.

These schemes show that councils have the expertise to produce lower-cost housing indirectly, even under a tight financial regime: but such gymnastics would surely be obviated by a more liberal approach to housing finance allowing councils to build good-quality affordable rented accommodation themselves, in the quantities so desperately needed.

PSLG, July 1990

Questions

1. Why were partnership deals involving sale of council land at discount to housing associations jeopardised by section 61 of the 1989 Local Government and Housing Act?
2. How did Welwyn Hatfield District Council facilitate low-cost home ownership by using a housing association as a vehicle?
3. What are the advantages of this strategy (a) to councils and (b) to associations?

Enabling social housing: Garden City Homes Housing Association

Readers of *PSLG* will be aware of the constrained financial environment within which local authorities operate, and particularly the problems of providing affordable homes. Attempts to retain social housing and ensure further production have recently suffered setbacks – witness the failure of the Hillingdon transfer, limitations on large-scale voluntary transfer, and doubt over housing companies, combined with a tight public spending round. It is good therefore to report on a venture exhibiting pragmatism, partnership and potential.

Garden City Homes Housing Association was registered by the Housing Corporation on 21 July 1992, a feat in itself. It was established as an Industrial and Provident Society in 1989, at the behest of Welwyn Hatfield Council, but is now independent of the council. The main objective was the transfer of 182 equity share properties from the council to the association, to enable the maximal reuse of capital receipts from staircasing. Following valuation and registration, this is pending: but the association has also become involved in further enabling projects, such as purchasing the homes of people in mortgage difficulties and selling them back on a shared ownership basis. It has renovated properties purchased from the council for shared ownership, and is managing the properties shortly to be transferred. Site acquisition and development for rent and part sale will follow.

The association was developed with help from Sanctuary Housing Association. One of its senior staff sat on the management committee, providing expertise vital to ensuring success, and is now an adviser. Sanctuary acts as management agent for the homes owned by Garden City Homes Housing Association, but only until the organisation can do so itself. This typifies the enabling function of more experienced associations encouraged by the Housing Corporation. Garden City Homes Housing Association employs an operations manager and administrator, and has plans to expand its establishment to enable further development.

The committee profile ensures independence and expertise, as well as maintaining the political links vital in managing partnership, without becoming a 'controlled or influenced company' under the 1989 Local Government and Housing Act. A local councillor holds the chairmanship, and the council has been invited to nominate another member to the committee, but such representation will not exceed 20 per cent, thus ensuring independence. The presence of local politicians with an electoral mandate goes a long way to countering the view that such committees are closed shops of self-selecting like-minded if benevolent people and therefore helps ensure wider accountability. It also enhances credibility with the council, with which the association must work in partnership.

Other members come from commerce and professions; and representation is being sought amongst shared owners. Housing availability and employment are interdependent, so it is right that local business interests are represented.

The Housing Corporation insists that committees should be capable of exercising management control. The secretary is a senior financial executive with London Underground, and the treasurer an academic with a background in housing finance and policy; another member is a senior manager with Northern Rock, and yet another manages a special needs housing association. The range of skills therefore reflects the possibilities and challenges inherent in providing and managing social housing today.

Access to public finance through Housing Association Grant (HAG) is a major reason why associations seek registration. However, no guarantee is given that associations will ever receive Housing Corporation funding: that depends on the Corporation's view of the extent to which needs can be met by existing associations and other agencies. Councils are not tied to any particular associations when dispensing local authority HAG, although unregistered associations cannot receive it. For all that, registration does imply the possibility of HAG, and without it, it is very hard to produce social housing for rent or sale at affordable levels, even with grants made under s. 25 of the Local Government Act, cheap or free land, or via planning agreements.

Registration has in this case unlocked substantial local authority HAG, enabling the acquisition and development of further properties for rent, as well as for shared ownership. Credibility with potential lenders may be improved by registration, although the association managed to negotiate a loan in excess of £3m to acquire the council's shared ownership stock without its benefit. But the advantages of respectability and recognition are also important, and should not be overlooked.

This is undoubtedly a repeatable model: there are better prospects for this type of association, essentially small-scale at the outset without comprehensive transfer aims, than for prospective large council-sponsored associations. A greater diversity of social housing providers may well inject the competition in social housing provision that ministers are looking for without entailing monopolies: private, quasi-public or public. It is, however, essential that this is accompanied by the sound strategic planning which only councils, or bodies very similar to them, can provide, to avoid the fragmentation and dissipation of effort that would otherwise ensue.

PSLG, October 1992

Questions

1. Why was registration with the Housing Corporation so important to ensure the success of Garden City Homes Housing Association?
2. What committee strengths do the Corporation look for when considering registration?
3. What financial support is available to registered housing associations?

Interview with Mike Cohen, Chief Executive, Guinness Trust Group

Mike Cohen is Chief Executive of one of Britain's largest and oldest charitable housing associations, the Guinness Trust, founded in 1890. In 1994, it owned 14 200 homes, the vast majority houses and flats for rent. Operating in all Housing Corporation regions, it has developed over 5000 homes under the 1988 Housing Act regime. It works extensively with local authorities, accepting nominations and building on land owned by councils or gained via planning obligation. As it is a major voluntary housing player, the views of its forthright Chief Executive are worth noting, since the policies of such bodies directly affect the ability of councils to enable social housing.

Noting the dramatic increase in the role of associations in accepting nominations of homeless households from councils, he highlighted the need to become much more than housing managers, and to deliver back-up services in relation to welfare support. Of the 1988 local authority nominations in the year to 31 March 1994, almost one-third were statutorily homeless. He urged against packing estates, however nicely designed, with 'single parent families, and couples with young children', the dominant intake from the homeless nominations route, arguing that this would lead to unrealistically high child densities and imbalanced communities; but if housing associations are to take their share of responsibility for addressing the urgent housing needs of homeless people, it seems inescapable.

Another theme was that of the mutual importance of partnership. The permanent reduction in Housing Association Grant levels entails a need to work closely together. He stated that this should always have been the case, and that housing associations have never done anything successful except as partners. Building on the observation that associations have around 80 per cent fewer properties than councils, it would be naive to expect associations ever to be the main providers of social housing: he regards an independent voluntary sector as complementary rather than as a replacement.

Partnerships must be freely entered into, not enforced. On compulsory competitive tendering of housing management, he suggested that no sensible association would tender unless local authorities wished it, which few do. It would be difficult for associations to outbid in-house or private tenders; the winners might excel at securing contracts rather than housing management. It is unlikely that Guinness will be at the forefront of CCT competition in 1996: its Chief Executive was wary about taking over perceived council staffing problems, and questioned whether associations had sufficient knowledge of their own costs to work up realistic bids. This cannot be based upon lack of experience of the nature of council housing and issues facing authorities: the Trust works with 97 of them. The positive aspect of CCT was that it will force those delivering services to publicise the actual costs of provision, engendering healthy public scrutiny.

On private finance, Cohen suggested that larger associations have relatively few problems in raising money from the markets, but that reducing grant rates make lenders increasingly nervous about loan security. Another major issue affecting lender attitudes is housing benefit: threatened or actual restrictions might affect confidence in cash flows and so ability to repay. However, he was emphatic that Guinness rents would never reach 'poverty trap' levels: the association has a rents matrix according to its view of affordability, and would stop developing rather than charge unaffordable rents. New rents are kept down through pooling and use of reserves. Guinness has shied away from using low-start finance, as tenant incomes do not appear to be rising; it would therefore be unjust to increase rents on a regular basis for that reason alone. He was highly critical of the new grant regime which was appropriate when developed, at a time of low land costs, relatively low interest rates, ample council land, and a recession in the building industry. These factors have now changed, and this is incompatible with continued rate cuts.

Low-cost home ownership was seen as very much a secondary activity; the Corporation had been forced by government to increase its share of the Approved Development Programme; and it was definitely the wrong time for such initiatives. He dismissed Do It Yourself Ownership as something which was not appropriate association business.

In conclusion, Cohen sees housing management and not development as the key association activity, and has no problem with stopping new-build if grant rates reduce further, to avoid shoddy housing with falling space standards, as tenants may have to remain in the property allocated for considerably longer than tenants in other types of tenure. It is heartening to find a key player who is not obsessed with the numbers game and who puts quality first; hopefully it is a line which will be promoted generally, and may force a rethink of development finance so that good-quality affordable homes can once more be produced in the quantities needed to relieve the current housing shortage.

PSLG, March 1995

Questions

1. Why does Cohen consider that associations have a welfare as well as a housing management role?
2. Why might compulsory competitive tendering threaten the good partnership relationships which many councils have with associations?
3. How does the Guinness Housing Trust avoid charging high rents on new developments? Is this sustainable?

The future of the Housing Corporation

The Housing Corporation is a major player in social housing, financially assisting housing associations to provide affordable homes, and working with local authorities in formulating its Approved Development Programme (ADP). Recently, however, there have been a number of critical reports suggesting far-reaching changes in its structure and operations, stimulated by the latest Financial and Management Policy Review (FMPR), which is undertaken every 5 years.

The National Federation of Housing Associations (NFHA) issued its submission in February 1995, and suggested that the Corporation be abolished in its present form by 2000. Whilst acknowledging that the Corporation has played an important role since its inception in 1964, it argues that its regulatory and funding functions should be taken over by new bodies. The logic is that, with a growth in the size and complexity of the association movement, it is no longer appropriate for one body to be both regulator and funder: there are possible conflicts of interest.

Building on this suggestion, the NFHA proposes that there should be a strategic body for the direction of investment in both council and housing association programmes, complementing the Chartered Institute of Housing's suggestion that D.o.E. and Corporation merge into a single national housing agency.

In the interim, the NFHA suggests a number of key short-term reforms. The Corporation should be given greater responsibility for designing its development programme. At the moment, it is clear that central government predilection for increasing owner-occupation via shared ownership and Do It Yourself Shared Ownership in particular has distorted the ADP away from affordable rented accommodation, a trend made worse by the output cuts entailed by the cutting of £300 million from the planned 1995/96 ADP in December 1994's Unified Budget. This policy line conflicts with the views of several Housing Corporation board members, and runs counter to the wishes of local authority associations.

Another recommendation is that the Corporation be given duties to give and to publish policy advice to Ministers. It is absurd that so much secrecy should surround the Corporation's dealings with the Department of the Environment, as it is a publicly funded body. The recommendation that there should be greater openness in the way that the board is appointed is hard to disagree with. The Housing Corporation is a very influential quango, dispensing much public money, with tremendous influence over the production of social housing at a time when councils, which are more democratically accountable than housing associations, are unable to sustain feasible development programmes. Yet there is no democracy in board appointments: its members are political appointees, and it is transparently obvious that the few members from the social housing world are there as token figures. It is a closed clique, and, as with any other quango, a prime opportunity for the dispensation of political patronage. Social housing is far too important to be left in the hands of such an elitist organisation.

It is ironic that although the Corporation has long supervised the setting of performance targets and the culture of monitoring for associations, it had no duty to prove itself efficient: therefore the recommendation that it should set clear performance standards and adopt a charter just as the major utilities have, with a clear complaints mechanism, must be welcomed. Additionally, the Corporation has no business providing an ombudsman service for housing association tenants. It is far too close to the movement to be effective there, and the task would be better handled by an independent agency.

The generally negative appraisal of the Corporation is mirrored by the responses of local authority associations. In its response, the Association of Metropolitan Authorities suggested the immediate abolition of the Corporation. Funding would be controlled by regional government offices, and local authority housing committees would make decisions relating to the distribution of funding as well as other support measures for housing associations. This is supported to an extent by the Association of London Authorities, which wants local authority control over the ADP, and an elected regional body which would coordinate housing policy in the capital, something long overdue.

It is not surprising that the Corporation has come in for such criticism: it is unaccountable, cumbersome and highly bureaucratic. It would be feasible to transfer the disposition and administration of Housing Association Grant (HAG) to councils, which already dispense local authority HAG, and which are keenly aware of local housing needs in a way which even the regional offices of the Corporation are not. As for registration and regulation, there is a sense in which there are already too many associations for the finance market to support, and regulation would most appropriately be undertaken by those funding them, within a nationally agreed framework. It would be good news for local democracy if the Corporation were to be supplanted by the only truly representative bodies at local level: local authorities.

PSLG, April 1995

Questions

1. Why did the National Federation of Housing Associations consider that the Housing Corporation should be abolished in its present form?
2. What is a quango? To what extent is it true that board appointments lack democratic accountability?

3. What alternative regulatory body is suggested in the article, and is this feasible?

Grant rates: modelling and manipulation

One benefit of the Citizen's Charter initiative is that the model used by the Housing Corporation to determine Housing Association Grant rates is now public. Details were released in mid-September 1994. Those working with associations should study it so that they can participate in arguments with the Department of the Environment about its consequences, as well as for a consistency in approach between the Corporation and government which appears to be lacking.

Standard development costs, including land, building and professional fees, are estimated for each of the Housing Corporation's Total Cost Indicator regions, and modified for different types of scheme by applying multipliers compensating for higher scheme costs associated with, say, special needs schemes. A view on affordable rent levels is then taken, calibrated from income survey data. These notional rents are then capitalised and deducted from estimated development costs. When arriving at 'affordable rents', assumptions have to be made about the revenue costs, that is, management, maintenance, voids, repairs, sinking fund and loan interest rates, expenditure which must be contained within rents set on actual schemes. Low assumptions will clearly result in unrealistically low grant rates.

The sum resulting from deducting the capitalised amount from assumed development costs is expressed as a percentage of the Corporation's development estimates (Total Cost Indicators). This represents the typical or 'norm' grant an association would expect to receive in respect of a specific type of scheme. Rates for the coming financial year are usually published the previous October. True rents must be set to cover loans raised to cover the difference between grant and actual development costs. The National Federation of Housing Associations (NFHA) markets packages to help associations estimate grant rates and revenue costs for association developments known as PAMKIT and REVKIT respectively.

The Corporation model depends heavily upon affordability assumptions. Forecasts of cost inflation and tenant income changes are used to formulate a view on how much tenants should pay, and the effects on rents of different grant rates shown. For 1995/96, the Corporation assumed that tenant incomes would rise by 11.1 per cent and 7.9 per cent for elderly and non-elderly tenants, respectively, and based its tenant income estimates on 1993 CORE data (continuous recording data on incomes supplied by the NFHA on the basis of association returns), assuming the increase factors applied annually over 3 years. The Corporation model assumed that tenants could afford an average of 34.81 per cent of their income on rent (assumption used from 1989 to 1994), based on the result of deducting typical living costs excluding rent from assumed incomes of tenants not in receipt of housing benefit.

Presumably, if tenants generally ended up paying significantly more than this figure on rents, by the Corporation's own standards rents would be unaffordable to those not dependent upon benefit. Research by the NFHA published in October 1994 shows that the 1995/96 target average grant rate announced by the Government in August means that tenants would have to pay 1.3 per cent more from their incomes than reckoned by the Corporation to be 'affordable'. A year previously, it was widely forecast that average grant rates would be set at 55 per cent. If so, the average modelled rent would be around £66.26, with tenants paying around 4 per cent over the affordability odds (38.26 per cent of income). It seems that, to ensure that rents remain affordable even against the Corporation's criteria, grant rates would have to average 60 per cent.

Rather than asking government to reconsider the grant rate announcement in the light of what appears to be a conflict between the results of a rational model and a parliamentary decision based on the overarching desire to further limit public expenditure, the Corporation has waved aside protests that new rents will become unaffordable. It has done so in familiar language: development costs should be well within Total Cost Indicator ceilings, it should be possible to borrow on more favourable terms than those anticipated by the model, economies can be made in management and maintenance, and so forth, so that actual rents should be well within the Corporation's affordability guidelines.

But this does not ring true. In the latter half of 1994 there have been well-documented upward pressures on interest rates; building materials are starting to rise in cost once more, and economic growth usually entails rises in property and land prices. Several lenders, as reported in last month's *PSLG*, have expressed concern over lending to associations against a background of reduced security. It is likely, therefore, that actual rents will exceed the affordability levels, thus increasing benefit dependency, with yet greater cost to the social security budget and trapping many in poverty. It is to be hoped that much will be made by lobbying groups of the consequences of government failing to heed its own quango's advice before April 1995.

PSLG, December 1994

Questions
1. Are grants payable to housing associations sufficient to ensure affordable rents, and if not, why not?
2. What other resources are available to associations to increase the amount of capital subsidy to try to ensure rents within the reach of lower-paid people?
3. Suggest ways in which the grant system might be reformed to guarantee rents which people can afford without undue hardship.

A tenant management co-operative in London

The ideal of customer involvement in the form of tenant management co-operatives is one which has received cross-party support over the last few years. This entails council or housing association tenants managing their homes under contract from the owner of the stock, appointing staff, and managing a delegated budget. Good practice is exemplified by the South Hampstead Tenant Management Co-Operative in Camden, North London, which took over the running of the Ainsworth and Alexandra Estates on 29 April 1991.

Designed by architect Neave Brown, and constructed between 1969 and 1979, the Alexandra was hailed as a design miracle. Running alongside a railway, the four- to five-storey blocks form a series of steps climbing from a sinuous central street, flanked by walkways. It is an imaginative and not unattractive realisation of a clearly envisaged idea. Shops were supplied to the estate, together with a school, pub and a community centre. Densities are high, at 210 persons per acre. There are around 700 flats and maisonettes, ranging from bedsits to four-bedroom dwellings. The award-winning scheme was oversubscribed when built, but design faults due both to materials used and to layout led to unpopularity.

A walk around the estate reveals inadequate and broken lighting to walkways and communal areas, damaged concrete and disfiguring graffiti. Walkways, shielded from view by walls and bushes, offer ample opportunity for attack. Frequent changes in level and broken lifts make the estate user-unfriendly for disabled, elderly or childcarers. Some of these problems should have been foreseen at the design stage, but it is expected that the problems will be lessened through action by the newly formed tenant management co-operative.

In 1987, alarmed by the worsening state of the properties and environment, the active tenants' association investigated the possibility of management, and approached SOLON Co-operative Housing Services to assist. The association's meetings were well attended, and a subcommittee was set up to establish demand for a management co-op. A poll carried out in the summer of 1988 showed 67 per cent of tenants favouring a feasibility study, to be prepared by SOLON. Its report was put to Camden's Housing Committee in September of that year, which agreed to meet half the survey cost, under s. 16 of the 1985 Housing Act.

Several 'open days' were organised to assess problems as seen by residents. High on the list of priorities was the state of disrepair to exteriors of flats: none of the 478 properties in Rowley Way had received external decoration in 10 years. The council claimed it could not afford to undertake the comprehensive refurbishment programme required, owing to capital restraint.

A secret ballot held in May 1989 showed 80 per cent of respondents (there was a 94 per cent response rate) supporting the formation of a management co-op. Camden agreed to fund 25 per cent of the cost of co-op development plus an initial £5000 grant to set up an estate office. A 30-strong steering committee to implement the co-operative was formed and on 29 April 1991 the Tenant Management Co-op was born. Committee membership now numbers 24 (23 tenants, 1 leaseholder), and it employs 12 staff, all of whom were selected by advertisement. The establishment consists of 1 estate co-ordinator, 2 estate managers, 1 administrator, 1 finance worker, 1 resident estate supervisor, 2 non-resident caretakers and 4 resident caretakers.

The co-op controls a management and maintenance budget, funded by Camden, negotiated annually (£606 per unit per annum in 1991/92) and paid quarterly. Although it performs day-to-day functions – collecting rent (passed to Camden quarterly, although the co-op retains interest), undertakes day-to-day repairs and maintenance, handles lettings procedures, and issues NOSP's – major roles still lie with the council: setting rents, allocations, major repairs, and dealing with transfers. Camden has employed a liaison officer to advise on council policy.

SOLON's training and development agency, CATCH (Client And Tenant's Controlled Housing), runs training courses for committee members to enhance their ability to make informed decisions.

The enthusiastic Estate Co-ordinator, Christine McConnachie, speaking from a central and well-equipped estate office, told *PSLG* that the big issue currently is the £6 million Estate Action bid, formulated by the co-op and applied for by Camden, which, if successful, will run over 3 years (1992–95) and enable the repair and replacement where necessary of estate lighting, re-roofing, re-landscaping, re-lining balcony areas, and the installation of a door-entry system to control access to walkways and thereby improve security. Arrears have fallen along with voids, as perceptions about the estate have improved. It is too soon to judge success, but the commitment from staff and residents to turn the area around is evident, and is worthy of study by other groups contemplating such initiatives.

PSLG, 1992 (unpublished)

Questions

1. What was the motivation for the establishment of the tenant management co-operative described in the article?
2. What consultation processes were involved prior to the setting up of the co-operative?
3. How is the co-op financed, and what input is given by the London Borough of Camden?

5 Councils and their tenants

5.1 What is local government?

As the Widdicombe Report of 1986 states, Parliament is sovereign. Local authorities, or councils as they are popularly known, are not local, independent states, but derive their powers and duties, and indeed their very existence, from Parliament. This can be shown by considering the wholesale reorganisation of local government, both in number and function, in 1974 as the result of the 1972 Local Government Act, and in the changes following the local government review of the 1990s.

In 1994, there were 47 county councils and 333 district councils in England and Wales, which owe their functions to the 1974 Act. Additionally, between 1974 and 1986 there were 6 metropolitan counties containing 36 metropolitan district councils, but the former were abolished in 1986 under the 1985 Local Government Act. The Greater London Council was seen as a real political threat to central government; many think that this was the reason it was abolished, rather than primarily to save money.

Local authorities must act within the law; acting beyond prescribed powers is sometimes known as acting *ultra vires*, and can lead to councillors being surcharged or even imprisoned.

There are three types of local authority which have real powers: county councils, district councils and unitary authorities. They are functionally distinct, except that the latter combine all the powers and duties of the first two.

County councils carry out functions such as education, personal social services, aspects of leisure and recreation, provision of libraries, structure planning, many highways functions, police and fire prevention. They also have reserve housing powers and duties, but are not strictly housing authorities, although they own houses, principally for staff housing. County functions are those which it is most economic to carry out over large areas: it would not make much sense, for example, for each rural district to run its own library service, especially where the population is very scattered; a mobile library service, based in the county town, makes much more sense. And strategic town and country planning requires an overview which cannot easily be provided by individual districts, or indeed by associations of such authorities. Not all highways are county responsibilities: the Department of Transport is responsible for motorways and major trunk roads, but it makes sense to entrust major roads to counties because they cross so many district boundaries.

District councils are contained spatially within county boundaries. For example, the City and District of St Albans lies within the boundaries of Hertfordshire County Council, of which Hertford is the county town, the administrative centre. But this is not to say that the county council is in any way superior, except in size, to district councils: they simply perform a different range of functions appropriate to their scale. District councils carry out such functions as passenger transport, where the service has not been privatised, development planning, meaning the devising of local plans, considering planning applications and enforcement, the maintenance of urban and unclassified roads, refuse disposal, the maintenance of parks and open spaces, cemeteries and crematoria, environmental health and of course housing. A number of these functions have been exposed to compulsory competitive tendering (CCT) and are now carried out by private enterprise, although councils still control them and make policy.

Outside London, the 36 metropolitan districts (1994) carry out all of the functions listed above for counties and districts, as do the 32 London boroughs. These are the so-called unitary authorities. Until 1990, London had its own education authority, distinct from the GLC, known as ILEA (the Inner London Education Authority), but it was abolished on 31 March of that year.

Some responsibilities are carried out by both district and county councils, for example refuse collection and the running of museums and art galleries, playing fields and swimming baths; and county councils may contract out certain services to districts, for example the maintenance of major roads.

These are the authorities which have greatest significance. In addition, there are over 11 000 parish, community and town councils in England and Wales. They have small budgets, and can make decisions on minor matters such as the routeing and repair of footpaths, and are consulted by the district council on planning matters. They offer a valuable means for local people to make their views heard, but they have no significant powers or duties. In Victorian times, they were the most significant unit of local government.

Scotland has its own local government system: its nine regions correspond to England's counties, and often have unlovely or baldly locational names such as Central and Highland, although the county names have often been retained for postal and sentimental reasons. Additionally there are 53 districts, and three island councils. As in England and Wales, the districts are the housing authorities. Unlike in England, the island councils are not contained within counties but are unitary authorities, which makes sense for somewhere like Shetland, 13 hours by sea from Aberdeen. In England, the only island to be a unitary authority is the Isle of Wight, since the Local Government Review.

Each form of local government is made up of a council which at its simplest consists of a chairperson and councillors, elected by local people. Legally, it is the councillors who comprise the council. Such bodies are held to be legal persons, 'artificial' persons in their own right, and can contract with other parties, sue them, or be sued. All councils are composed of committees, which are generally co-ordinated by a Policy and Resources Committee, composed of the chairs of the committees making policy on specific areas. But all committees are responsible to full council.

There are some committees which have to exist by law, for example, Education, Social Services and Police committees. However, most are created as standing committees by resolution of full council: for example, Housing Committees are standing committees, appointed annually. The powers and duties of committees are laid down by law. Full council can also define the terms and conditions of a committee by laying down standing orders. Some powers and duties – for example, the duty to set a council tax, the power to raise loans, and the power to make financial demands on other authorities – are vested in the council as a whole.

All councils have committees. There are a number of advantages, including specialisation, less formality than at full council, smaller numbers making for greater efficiency, and perhaps a greater chance of more fruitful and easier contact with officials. Disadvantages include the excessive bureaucracy which accompanies this system, problems in getting people together, and perhaps over-specialisation.

Councils are political in that they form policies which affect the lives of those who live in their areas, and involve debate. Political parties are represented, although the views of councillors may depart from the national party line, as has been shown time and time again: witness the resignation of many Conservative councillors on the introduction of the ill-fated community charge (poll tax) in 1990, and the differences between the Liverpool City Council of Derek Hatton in the mid-1980s and Neil Kinnock's Labour Party. In some predominantly rural areas, independent councillors dominate. Under the 1989 Local Government and Housing Act, the strength of political parties on the councils as a whole must be reflected in the make-up of committees.

Local authorities are democratically accountable to those they represent: therefore in the majority of cases, their deliberations are open to public scrutiny. There are a few exceptions to this: committee meetings, or those parts dealing with issues such as personnel matters, awarding of specific contracts, details of childcare cases, may be held in camera, under the Local Government (Access to Information) Act 1985.

Such is the nature of local government business that some decisions can be delegated to small 'urgency' committees: for example, those making decisions to evict squatters to ensure the integrity of the housing stock, officers and chairpersons, subject to strict legal safeguards. This is because issues arise on a daily basis, needing urgent decisions, which would not be made if it was necessary to assemble the entire housing committee: for example, dealing with minor repairs contracts, decisions to evict tenants in arrears, or to lease properties from private landlords; also, because if these matters had to be decided at full committee, there would be insufficient time.

As is the case with central government and housing associations, the day-to-day work of the council is performed by paid officials, who do not make policy, but carry it out. The views of senior personnel will be sought out by councillors sitting in committee and recommendations will be made by senior officers to committees for decision; so although officers do not make policy, they strongly influence it. It is necessary for committees to take notice of what officers say, as their advice is necessary to solve problems and to avoid breaking the law. Officers are specialists in their fields; committee members are dedicated amateurs, although some may be professionals in a technical field in another authority. (However, there are restrictions on the membership of councils on the part of local authority employees of another council above a certain grade.)

There is increasing divergence from common grading systems, although the assistant officer, senior officer, principal officer, assistant chief officer, chief officer hierarchy is still in use in many authorities. Pay rates are often locally determined, but may still be expressed as scale points as negotiated nationally between the local government unions, principally UNISON, and associations of employers. Staff in particular areas, where there is great competition from the private sector – for example, legal and valuation staff – may receive a premium in addition to the usual scale to attract and retain them.

The duties of local government officers may be divided into statutory and local policy elements. For example, a homeless person's officer's work will be dictated largely by national legislative requirements, although the local authority may well have a policy regarding number of points to be given to advance a homeless person's case for rehousing, which the officer performs. A housing management officer will ensure that the terms of the Tenant's Charter section of the 1985 Housing Act are adhered to, but will also enforce local by-laws regulating tenancies. Over the years, the statutory element of officials' tasks has become greater than locally determined policy, as the number of duties has increased in relation to powers, leading to the oft-heard assertion that local government is little more than an agency of central government.

5.2   Relationship between local and central government

There is little doubt of the direction of influence in the relationship between central and local government: it is generally acknowledged that the power of the centre has increased over the past decade, as instanced by the capping of community charges, and later the council tax, and increasing controls over capital and revenue expenditure. The 1989 Local Government and Housing Act, following on the Widdicombe Report, *The Conduct of Local Authority Business*, places limits on who should and should not serve as a councillor beyond those already existing (relating to age, mental health, residence, etc.) which are quite unprecedented, and a significant departure from past central government practice.

More formally, there are several ways in which central government can, and does, control the operation of local government, principally legislative, administrative and judicial control.

5.2.1   Legislative controls

Legislative controls include the various Acts of Parliament passed in respect to local authority powers and duties, as will be illustrated for housing. General legislation imposing duties and allowing powers are known as Public General Acts. Statutory instruments empower Ministers to make regulations: for example, regulations regarding housing subsidies, published annually, which have the force of law in relation to a specific Act of Parliament.

5.2.2   Administrative controls

Some statutes impose a duty on Ministers: for example, the Police Act 1964 imposes a duty on the Home Secretary to provide an adequate police force. Surveys of local authority efficiency are conducted from time to time under administrative powers. If a local authority refuses to carry out a duty, the relevant department of state can appoint commissioners to carry out the business, in addition to applying any legal sanctions it sees fit.

Ministers will frequently issue circulars explaining how legislation should be applied; and local authorities can, and do, ask advice from ministers on these matters.

Financial control is exercised through the use of auditors. The District Auditor is an officer of the Audit Commission, a body appointed by Parliament, which is charged with inspecting local authority accounts to ensure that money has been raised and spent lawfully and prudently. Sometimes, as in the case of the Westminster inquiry into the sale of council housing under the so-called designated sales scheme, which resulted in charges of gerrymandering, District auditors seem to stray away from purely financial matters; but this particular case none the less involves local authority income and expenditure. District Auditors can refer any question of legality to a court for a ruling.

Occasionally, Ministers appoint inspectors from their department to conduct an inquiry into local authority practices, where it is thought there might have been some irregularity. Inspectors are appointed to monitor certain council services: for example, the education service.

In certain cases, ministerial approval is needed before a local authority carries out a power. An example is a case in which a local authority wishes to buy residential property, which is known as municipalisation; or where it wishes to assign the management of its housing to another body, although this is subject to review. (*See* Chapter 7, which deals with CCT.) Ministers have default powers, and can act in place of a council which is held not to be implementing legislation properly, as in the case of Norwich in the early 1980s, where commissioners were appointed briefly to operate the Right to Buy. Finally, under rare circumstances, the Minister may appoint and dismiss chief officers, though these are 'reserve powers'.

5.2.3 Judicial controls

Local authorities are corporate bodies, capable of being sued, and are subject to laws relating to contract and tort, etc. In some cases, a council may be found to be exceeding its powers, known as acting *ultra vires*. Sometimes, conversely, councils fail to perform their duties. An example of the former is where a local authority budgets to produce a deficit on its Housing Revenue Account, or spends more than its cash limit. An example of the latter is where a council fails to secure accommodation for someone to whom it has a duty under the homelessness legislation (Part 3 of the Housing Act 1985). Any citizen, or group of persons, may take legal action against a local authority in a court of law by taking out a writ. The forms of court order are as follows:

5.2.3.1 Injunction

A court may restrain a local authority from proceeding along a certain course; the usual reason is that the council would otherwise be acting *ultra vires*.

5.2.3.2 Mandamus

A court can command a council to do something which it has a duty to do: for example, in the case of unlawful refusal to sell a council property under the Right to Buy.

5.2.3.3   Prohibition

Prohibition applies in the case that a local authority threatens to do something which it has no legal power to do, or threatens to carry out a lawful act in an unlawful matter (for example, evict someone without going through all the proper court procedures).

At the time of writing, the structure of local government is being reformed. The existing two-tier system of local government already described is being replaced in many areas by a unitary system, whereby one authority will undertake all the duties and powers presently performed by districts and counties. Some areas will retain two tiers. The last great reform was in 1974 under the 1972 Local Government Act, following from the Redcliffe-Maude Commission's report. This reform replaced a number of different forms of council – parishes, town councils, urban district councils, rural district councils and other forms of administration – with a two-tier system of counties and districts, as described. This was done on the grounds of greater efficiency, as functions were often duplicated between authorities, and to achieve greater cost-effectiveness. The reforms placed housing firmly in the court of districts, although counties retain some reserve housing powers, on the basis that they were smaller and therefore likely to reflect local interests; and it is easier to manage properties over a smaller rather than a larger area.

The reforms were not universally popular. Some counties with no historical precedent, such as Avon, were created. Scottish counties were abolished for all but postal purposes, and replaced by regions with anodyne names such as Central and Highland. Local authority election turnouts were often low, showing that local people felt little allegiance to such authorities.

Partly in response to the unpopularity of some of the 1974 reforms, and in an attempt to obtain greater efficiency and cost-effectiveness, a Local Government Commission under Sir John Banham, former President of the Confederation of British Industry, was charged with reforming the existing system. The Commission came up with a number of unitary authorities which more nearly reflected the aspirations of those living there. These authorities would undertake all functions presently covered by counties and districts. The matter is yet to be fully resolved at the time of writing. One advantage of merger may well be that housing and social services departments will be under one political roof, which might enable them to work together more fruitfully. An article at the end of the chapter, 'Local Government Re-organisation and Housing' (p. 180), examines progress in reorganisation, and discusses the positive and negative effects on the housing service.

5.3 Councils as housing providers and enablers

Councils have been providing housing since the latter part of the nineteenth century, but the existence of separate departments dealing with housing has a shorter history. The statutory powers to provide housing and therefore a management service are contained within Part 2 of the 1985 Housing Act, about which more later. There are few standards of housing management explicitly laid down by law, although much guidance exists as to who should be housed.

A number of advisory reports have been published regarding council housing. The 1938 Advisory Report, *The management of municipal housing*, published by the then Ministry of Housing and Local Government, followed the 1935 Housing Act, and recognised the value of the 'good and enlightened management of properties', suggesting that it was part of the function of councils to transfer good standards to tenants, to educate people unused to decent housing as to how to look after it, suggesting the paternalism of the Octavia Hill approach.

The 1959 Advisory Report stated that council housing should be seen as a national resource rather than a series of local resources. Housing management was seen a serious enterprise, broader than purely providing social welfare, and the report stated that housing should be the responsibility of a distinct housing committee, responsible for maintenance, allocations, strategic planning and new housing to meet need, rather than just ensuring that tenants behave themselves and look after their homes. It suggested that housing functions be unified into a single department, and divided functions into two groups.

Table 5.1 Housing functions – 1959 Advisory Report

Personal	Structural
Rent collection	Repairs
Management	Maintenance
Transfers/exchanges	Building work
Repairs requests	
General tenancy problems	

The role of housing managers as designers of estates was pushed for the first time: but there was no mention of tenants' input. The 1960s saw an increase in slum clearance and the development of high-rise flats on a large and rapid scale; and housing management became a major council function, requiring changes in its organisation. Along with this, the 1960s saw the rediscovery of poverty, and the development of a broader view of housing.

The 1968 Seebohm Report was concerned largely with the reorganisation of social services departments, but recommended the idea of comprehensive housing services: that is, that councils should concern themselves with facilitating access to all types of tenure, and provide advice on tenancy and related matters to councils and also private tenants and owner-occupiers. The Cullingworth Report in 1969 (full title, *Council housing: Purposes, procedures and priorities*) recognised the existence of special needs groups who were relatively unserved by other sectors, and whose needs should be prioritised for special attention. These included elderly persons, homeless persons, large families, homeless households, ethnic minority households, single people and students. The report recognised that much of the increase in demand from these groups related to the decline of the private rented sector. Its central recommendation was that some sort of priority ordering system should be used in the allocation of council housing, the so-called points systems which by the mid-1980s were almost universally in use.

The 1960s and 1970s brought new pressures for change on housing management. Repairs backlogs and design defects had become apparent; the collapse of the tower block Ronan Point in East London in 1968 highlighted the former point. Societal changes – increasing divorce rates and greater longevity leading to the formation of smaller households, the increasing demand from people belonging to ethnic minorities for housing – imposed the need for change in housing. The 1977 Housing (Homeless Persons) Act saw local authorities become the chief means of rationing scarce housing, although building programmes were still relatively healthy.

The 1980s saw the introduction of the Right to Buy, which began the residualisation of the sector – council housing as welfare housing – with the reduction in the quantity of desirable housing. This was compounded by financial cutbacks, causing council building programmes to diminish. With the continued decline of the private rented sector, council housing became much less a genuine tenure choice, more the last resort of those unable to satisfy their housing need elsewhere. Increasing proportions of lettings were going to homeless households, and the income characteristics of council tenants decreased, with greater benefit dependency. Residualisation brought with it the requirement for more sensitive housing management, and greater knowledge on the part of management staff on issues such as welfare benefits, as well as social services procedures.

The 1980s also saw the development of tenant involvement, with bodies such as the Tenants Participation Advisory Service (TPAS) and the Priority Estates Project stressing the importance of engaging tenants in managing and refurbishing their homes, especially in an estates context. Additionally, the local authority product became more diverse, with the development of low-cost homes initiatives, principally shared ownership and management co-operatives. Decentralisation of services developed in several authorities on the premise that a more locally based presence partially removes the 'us and them' mentality which can alienate tenants. Customer care policies started to become important in the late 1980s, although these were not fully developed until the next decade, under legislative pressure.

As cutbacks began to bite, councils increasingly found themselves having to work with other agencies to provide social housing, becoming 'enablers' rather than direct providers. The housing association movement grew rapidly in the 1980s, and received much assistance in the form of local authority Housing Association Grant (HAG) and other grants, and also through planning powers and the sale of land at discount. Nominations and referrals became more important. Some local authorities began to question the value of continuing as housing providers and managers, owing to the increasing difficulty of doing so. They resorted to large-scale voluntary transfer, selling their remaining assets to housing associations, often formed at the behest of the council, hoping thereby to guarantee the provision of social housing by avoiding the Right to Buy for new transfer tenants, and taking advantage of a looser financial regime for housing associations.

The 1990s has seen the further development of these themes. Customer care policies have become almost universal, with many authorities appointing officers solely concerned with this aspect. The Citizens Charter has implied new complaints procedures; the 1989 Local Government and Housing Act entailed annual reports to tenants detailing all conceivable housing policies and practices. Tenant consultation has become highly developed – rightly so, as rents now pay for the lion's share of services. The quality industry has invaded the discipline, with Total Quality Management techniques and British Standards accreditation, especially ISO 6000, being applied for and used to improve the housing service product, often in conjunction with business planning.

The issue and nature of performance indicators are discussed in an article on p. 175, 'Indicating performance in council housing'. Another article (p. 178) highlights the Council Tenant's Charter, which is part of the Citizen's Charter initiative.

The enabling role has increased: by 1994, 35 authorities had divested themselves of their stock under Large scale voluntary transfer (LSVT), mostly shire district councils where the transfer price easily cleared both housing debt and a substantial share of general debt. With council building programmes virtually at a standstill, and most capital activity related either to renovation or to government-directed initiatives such as Estates Action and City Challenge, working with housing associations has become the only feasible way to develop social housing. The Housing Action Trust programme initiated by the 1988 Housing Act has resulted in some housing estates, both inner city and suburban, being lifted out of the local authority arena and into the hands of semi-independent boards akin to development corporations, with a brief to do them up and sell them on.

A final major theme in the development of council housing services has been the impact of CCT, which, if it succeeds, will take housing management out of council operation but not control in a large number of cases by the turn of the century, just as has been the case for parks maintenance and refuse disposal, amongst other services. This, along with LSVT, housing companies and business methodologies, is part of the general commercialisation of municipal services, something that deserves, and gets, its own chapter (Chapter 7).

The net effect of all these changes is that it is unlikely that council housing, either as a product or a service, will survive as a substantive local authority operation far into the twenty-first century, having lost its production role and with its management role under threat.

5.4   Legal powers and duties of local authorities

Local authorities' legal powers and duties are an ever-changing area, and the following sets the scene at around 1994. The principal legislation governing the operation of local housing authorities is the 1985 Housing Act, although it has been extensively modified since then. The Act is a consolidation of earlier legislation, and brought little new to the law regarding housing. I shall outline those aspects which relate to local authority housing management.

Part 1 defines a housing authority. Categories are a district council, a London borough council, the Common Council of the City of London, and the Council of the Isles of Scilly.

Part 2 deals with the provision of housing accommodation. There is a duty, under s. 8, to review and consider housing conditions and need from time to time. Local authorities regularly carry out research to establish this, and present evidence annually in their Housing Strategy and Investment Programmes. This information is also used by housing associations, and the regional offices of the Housing Corporation, to inform decisions as to what schemes to forward and support. Section 9 gives the housing authority powers to provide housing by building, conversion or acquisition, although the latter power requires the permission of the Secretary of State. The power to alter, enlarge, repair or improve such properties is also granted. Section 10 grants the power to furnish and fit out such properties, and to supply cooking and laundry facilities if thought appropriate. Councils have in fact done many of these things: Glasgow City Council, mindful of the cost of acquiring furnishing and that offers may be turned down, was one of the first authorities to furnish flats intended for young single persons in the mid 1980s. Many authorities provided laundry facilities in tower blocks at a time when the cost of owning a washing machine was prohibitive to many families. Common cooking facilities are often provided in hostels under these powers.

Section 12 confers the power to provide shops, recreation grounds and other 'beneficial' buildings and land, subject to Secretary of State consent. It is good practice to provide estates with appropriate infrastructure: an example of a beneficial building might well be a tenant's association office or meeting room. Section 13 provides that councils may also lay out roads and open spaces.

It is possible for councils to supply housing in the ways mentioned previously outside their geographical area, but only with Secretary of State consent (s. 14) and having notified the county council. This may be the case where there is insufficient land in the council's area for development, or where a development spans a district boundary. Occasionally, it is necessary for one authority to arrange for someone to be rehoused in another area. This is often done by mutual agreement; but s. 15 (1)–(4) applies this to London boroughs, and contemplates payment from one authority to another. Section 17 gives specific permission for local authorities to acquire land for housing purposes, including the power of acquiring land for the provision of houses for disposal – that is, for sale. Many authorities have undertaken shared ownership schemes in partnership with builders or housing associations to increase the supply of low-cost housing in their areas. Local authorities may acquire land on a compulsory purchase basis for this purpose, but only if authorised by the Secretary of State. Such acquisition is comparatively rare these days. As previously stated, councils are no longer mass developers, and so many of these powers remain unused unless in partnership with other bodies. Once the houses have been built, s. 18 charges the council with the duty to make such properties available for letting as soon as possible.

It is a commonly held belief that the various committees of local authorities own pieces of land or property. They do not: they merely control the use of them. The council as a corporate entity owns property. Section 19 makes it clear that a council may appropriate any land held by it for housing purposes.

Under s. 31, where local authorities sell land, they must do so for 'best price' although cheap land deals may be struck with associations. If maximal nomination rights are obtained, this is regarded as equivalent to the best price, but nil or low rights may well cause the council to forfeit the ability to spend money.

Issues relating to housing management are dealt with between s. 21 and s. 27 of Part 2 of the Act. Much amendment of these sections is proposed during the 1990s to facilitate CCT, and the necessary changes are referred to in Chapter 7. Section 21 is a case in point: this states that the general management, regulation and control of housing must be vested in and exercised by that authority. Clearly CCT envisages that such management duties may be exercised by another body, thus this section requires amendment. However, strategic and control issues will remain with the local authority as the client.

Section 22 states that housing authorities must give reasonable preference in allocating its housing to:

- persons occupying insanitary or overcrowded housing;

- large families;

- those in unsatisfactory housing conditions; and

- persons found to be homeless.

No order is implied in this, but some form of prioritisation is, according to need. This section legitimises the points system methodology of allocation which is adopted by most councils in an attempt to ensure that those in greatest housing need are assisted first. There is no further definition of need, and how it must be met, although at the time of writing it has been suggested in the Homelessness Review that there should be a universally adopted points system to ensure uniformity of treatment nationwide.

Section 23 confers powers to make by-laws for the management, use and regulation of houses, although much relating to such powers is dealt with under the Tenant's Charter section of the Act, which defines tenancy conditions.

Section 24 allows councils to make reasonable charges for the occupation of dwellings, and imposes a duty to review them from time to time. The Act does not clarify the term 'reasonable' but it is generally taken to mean within the reach of the low-paid in employment, although a major consideration must be to balance the books, as deficits must be avoided and cannot in any case be carried forward for more than a year. In relation to rent reviews, councils make reviews at least annually, in line with budget estimates and subsidy settlements. The 1989 Local Government and Housing Act modified this to insist that council rents of different properties bear roughly the same proportion to the rents of similar-sized properties in the private sector. That is, if the rent for a two-bedroom flat is generally twice as much as the rents for one-bedroom flats in the private rented sector area, the same differential should be reflected in the rents of one- and two-bedroom flats. This requirement was introduced to ensure that councils give realistic pricing signals to their tenants – that more rent is paid for better or larger accommodation – although it is hard to apply this exactly, given the vast variation in market rents within areas. Nor is it clear that the private sector differentials are any more rational than those found in the public sector.

Section 27 confers the power to enter into a management agreement with a housing association or co-operative, subject to Secretary of State approval. The need to obtain such approval will be waived when CCT becomes active. This applies currently even where the local authority does not own the property, for example where it has leased it for private sector leasing, and has entered into a management agreement with a housing association. Some London boroughs forgot to do so in the early 1990s, although retrospective permission was forthcoming in those cases. However, under s. 21, it is clear that ultimate control still resides with the council.

As stated previously, the Act has been modified from time to time. Perhaps one of the most telling insertions was that made by the 1989 Local Government and Housing Act (s. 161), which inserts into s. 9 of the 1985 Act the phrase that 'nothing in this Act shall be taken to require (or at any time to have required) a local housing authority itself to acquire or hold any houses or other land for the purposes of this Act'. This confirms the enabling role of councils: indeed, by 1994, 36 councils had disposed of their entire stock, and so held no stock under Part 2 of the Act, conducting their business through third parties.

The Act also contains regulations relating to the Right to Buy, secure tenancies and other Tenant's Charter matters, consolidated from the 1980 Housing Act.

Other relevant legislation which affects local housing authorities includes the 1986 Housing and Planning Act, the 1988 Housing Act, the 1989 Local Government and Housing Act, and the 1993 Leasehold Reform, Housing and Urban Development Act.

The 1986 legislation gave local housing authorities the power to transfer (sell) their properties to another landlord, subject to ballot of tenants. This is so-called large-scale voluntary transfer, and is discussed elsewhere. Initially it was thought that building societies, given rights to act as developers and landlords in the same year, would wish to buy council estates. They did not. Councils have used this legislation, as modified by the 1988 Act, to get round the financial restrictions imposed by the 1989 Act and to conserve social housing, as tenants taking up tenancies after transfer do not have the preserved Right to Buy.

The 1988 Act gave local housing authority tenants the right to choose another landlord, once again subject to ballot, and to the approval of the landlord by the Housing Corporation. This scheme has not been desperately successful: at the time of writing, there has only been one such Tenants' Choice sale. It was the sale of an estate of street properties in West Central London by Westminster City Council to the Walterton and Elgin Community Homes co-operative, formed by dissatisfied tenants. The properties were given a negative valuation, because of the appalling conditions, and The new body was paid a dowry of £17.5 million by the local authority. The same Act also established the Housing Action Trust initiative, discussed in Chapter 6.

The 1989 legislation changed the finance rules applying to housing authorities, and has already been discussed. Essentially, it redefined Housing Revenue Account Subsidy on a notional account basis, imposed restrictive credit approval rules on borrowing, and further curtailed the ability to use Right to Buy receipts, prioritising their use for the repayment of debt. It also limited the involvement of councils in the affairs of housing associations at a time when councils were setting them up to be LSVT recipients. If more than one-fifth of the membership of a housing association board is comprised of local authority persons, and it has a business relationship with the local authority, it is regarded as a controlled or influenced company and is treated financially as a local authority. This would obviate the advantages of transfer.

The 1993 legislation was principally intended to modify the law relating to leased property, allowing lessees to force the lessor to sell them the freehold collectively if two-thirds or more of the lessees wish it, but there were several important modifications to local authority housing powers and duties. Councils can now deny the Right to Buy in relation to dwellings

Fig. 5.1 Community centre, Charecroft Estate, London Borough of Hammersmith and Fulham

adapted for the elderly without reference to the Secretary of State. The rights respectively to a local authority mortgage, to defer completion and to shared ownership terms were abolished, largely because of the introduction of rent to mortgage, whereby a qualifying tenant's rent is converted into a loan sum, which represents a share of the value of the property. The rent sum is then used to cover a loan to buy a given share of the property's value, and the unsold portion is treated as an interest-free loan until death or resale. This is only available within certain value limits, and to those who are not claiming or who would not be eligible to claim housing benefit, so it has only limited appeal.

A new Right to Repair was included. New arrangements for consultation with tenants on proposed disposal of stock by Housing Action Trusts were added. Local authorities were allowed to charge welfare services to the Housing Revenue Account (HRA), resolving a controversy brought about by the Ealing judgment in 1990, where a tenant claimed that the rent rise imposed was unjustified partly because rents were being used to pay for things which should properly have been funded through the General Fund, that is, caring services akin to social services, specifically those performed by wardens of sheltered schemes. However, this power can be revoked at any time by the Secretary of State.

Issues relating to the delegation of management were referred to, but at the time of writing still require clarification by regulation. It is essential that this be done in time for CCT in 1996.

Finally, restrictions on the size, and number of LSVTs were imposed, as well as a 20 per cent levy on transfer receipts by the Treasury to part-fund

Fig. 5.2 Tower block, William Church Estate, London Borough of Hammersmith and Fulham

the increase in housing benefit subsidy which switching from public to private sector housing benefit entails, owing to the differing subsidy systems.

5.5   Tenants and customers

5.5.1   Secure tenants

The 1980 Housing Act represented something of a milestone for council tenants. It granted greater security of tenure, and also the Right to Buy. The tenancy provisions of the Act have been consolidated into Part 4, ss. 79–117 of the 1985 Housing Act. These rights are often known as the Tenant's Charter. Prior to the 1980 Act, council tenants had few rights other than those conferred by the contractual agreements with their landlord.

The rights of secure tenants include the right:

• to quiet enjoyment;

Fig. 5.3 A Part Three home run by social services

- to exchange;

- to repair the property themselves and to charge the landlord where the council defaults on its duty, to one succession (succession means the inheriting of a tenancy; the tenancy can be passed on only once on the death of the tenant);

- to take in lodgers and sublet with landlord's consent;

- to make improvements subject to landlord's consent;

- to buy subject to various qualifications (Part 5, ss. 118–188);

- to convert rental payments to a mortgage under the Rent to Mortgage scheme introduced under the Leasehold Reform, Housing and Urban Development Act;

- to choose another landlord under the Tenants' Choice rules introduced by the 1988 Housing Act; and

- to receive a considerable amount of information, including full tenancy conditions, allocation rules, and a mass of performance data about the council's housing services.

Additionally, there are extensive rights to consultation on management changes.

Local authorities can obtain possession on a wide range of grounds, although only three are mandatory, and in each case the court must be satisfied that suitable alternative accommodation is to be made available before possession is granted. There are 17 grounds set out in Schedule 2 of the 1985 Act. Grounds where the court can order possession if it considers it reasonable include (ground number in parentheses) arrears (1), nuisance

Fig. 5.4 Children's play area and tower block, Edward Woods Estate, North Kensington

(2) (which includes racial harassment, although some councils have instituted a separate ground here), making false statements to obtain a tenancy (5), and having obtained a tenancy from another tenant on payment of a premium (cash for a tenancy) (6).

Grounds where possession must be ordered if the ground is proved, though only if suitable alternative accommodation is available, include where the property is overcrowded (9), where the landlord intends to demolish or reconstruct the premises (10), where the landlord wishes to dispose of the entire estate on which the tenant lives and needs vacant possession to do so (10A), and (for charities only, and therefore not a case applying to councils) where the landlord is a charity and the tenant's continued occupation conflicts with the objects of that charity (11).

Grounds where the court may order possession, but only if suitable accommodation is available, include: where the letting is a service tenancy, the tenant has ceased to be an employee, and the property is required for someone else (12); the premises are ones normally let to someone with special needs, where the existing tenant does not fulfil this description, and where the premises are needed for someone with special needs (15); and, finally, where the tenant is a qualified successor to a deceased tenant, and the premises are larger than are reasonably required by the new tenant (16), although this latter ground must be invoked between 6 and 12 months after succession, and other circumstances such as the age, length of occupation there, and degree of support given to the deceased tenant must be taken into account.

The rights enjoyed by a secure tenant, and the degree of security, are far greater than those applying to any other form of tenancy. Initially, they were set up to compete with the regulated form, but it can be seen that they are far superior to those rights, except that council tenants cannot register fair rents. The Right to Buy is unique to this form of tenancy, resembled only by the leasehold enfranchisement aspects of the 1993 Leasehold Reform, Housing and Urban Development Act.

5.5.2   Other aspects of the Tenant's Charter

Prospective tenants, or indeed anyone, are entitled to a summary of the council's allocation, exchange and tenancy rules on request from its offices, and a full version for a reasonable fee (s. 106 of the 1985 Housing Act). This was initially suggested by the Cullingworth Report, already referred to. Applicants are also entitled to a résumé of the information given by them when applying for housing; this entitlement is augmented by the Data Protection Act 1984, which entitles them to a transcript of any computerised information held on them. Any information supplied must be in plain English, although many councils supply such information in translation where appropriate.

The terms of secure tenancies have already been referred to: tenants are entitled to tenancy conditions information when granted the tenancy (s. 104); and most authorities have complied by compiling user-friendly handbooks. Some have even done so on tape; and in 1990, Welwyn Hatfield District Council won a Plain English Award for its effort. Overseen by a Customer Care Manager, this laudable enterprise of ensuring that council communications are understandable without a dictionary or a degree in law or bureaucracy was extended to newsletters and other publicity.

Consultation of tenants is another important aspect of the Charter. Section 105 of the 1985 Act provides that public sector landlords (except for county councils) must consult their tenants on matters of housing management which substantially affect all or a category of tenants; and tenants' views must be taken into account when management policy is changed. The following aspects are specified: those relating to management, maintenance, improvement or demolition, or change of practice or policy. Matters relating to rent policy are excluded from the definition, though tenants' views on rent must be taken into account before changes are made. Newsletters are the commonest form of information dissemination, although some councils have Customer Panels made up of tenant representatives which are used as a vehicle for consultation. There is no doubt that the Tenant's Charter provisions have markedly improved the legal position of council tenants.

5.5.3 Performance

Read 'Indicating performance in council housing', an article on p. 175, for a discussion of the introduction of this system, and the envisaged pitfalls and advantages.

In April 1991, councils first had to publish annual reports to tenants about their housing management practices. This duty was instigated under s. 167(1) of the Local Government and Housing Act 1989, with a bizarre title, *Reports to Tenants etc. Determination 1990*. The specified objectives, stated in the government's consultation paper of 10 October 1989, were to provide useful information to tenants about the performance of their housing authority; to promote their interest and involvement; and, through the stimulus of customer demand and interest, and through target setting and measurement, to enhance standards of housing management. The idea was that local authorities set targets themselves, measure their performance in key areas, and then inform tenants of results. These reports have been used to help the D.o.E. assess housing management performance and have influenced both revenue subsidy and credit approval determinations.

Areas of measurement include information on the stock, including numbers of dwellings, typical rents and housing revenue subsidy received; details of rent arrears and collection success; details of repairs and maintenance targets, policies and tenant satisfaction; information on how houses were allocated, including those let to homeless persons; details of voids and nominations; the average time taken to determine housing benefit claims; numbers accepted as homeless, and by category, and numbers in temporary accommodation by type; numbers and cost of staff; descriptions of complaints procedures; and details of tenant consultation procedures.

There are clear advantages to this requirement. Among them are that it gives customers an indication of the breadth of services provided by the council, the constraints under which it labours, and an indication of how effectively rent money is being spent, important as rent money bears the lion's share of costs in most housing authorities. However, there has to be an opportunity cost: that of devoting staff time and money to the task of providing and collating information when other work could be done. Then there is the question of how such information will be used: there is a suspicion that its prime purpose is to measure inefficiency and to calibrate subsidy allocations rather than to provide meaningful information to tenants. The other question is: what are tenants supposed to do with the information? Housing associations also have to produce performance reports, in a very similar format. Perhaps the intention is to encourage Tenants' Choice, but the financial and legal regimes are very different. Such reports will of course be hugely useful to those contemplating competing with councils under the CCT regime, as they contain vital information regarding stock, rents and staffing.

In March 1992, the Council Tenant's Charter, part of the Citizen's Charter initiative, was launched. (*See* 'A charter for council housing', p. 178). It was not itself legislation, but highlighted tenancy rights in popular form, and offered policy and practice advice to councils. Much of it is rather obvious, and good councils would already be following these practices. It is largely a consolidation, in fairly straightforward terms, of existing rights and best practices, but in addition it points out that tenants can choose another landlord, including Housing Action Trusts, if they are dissatisfied with their council's performance. Nowhere does it mention the reductions in subsidy and capital programmes which have made their landlord's life much harsher over the past decades.

5.5.4   Customers or just consumers?

All in all, the 1990s have seen the emergence of customer culture in local authorities, of a greater accountability if only through larger amounts of information disseminated in a more user-friendly fashion from town halls. This is surely right: where rents support housing services, there must be a reciprocal right to information as to how that money is spent. But are council tenants, or applicants, really customers, and, even if they are, have they really any more rights or opportunities than they did prior to the emergence of such a culture?

On the face of it, the answer is 'yes'. After all, tenants have the right to buy, the right to change their landlords, the right to repair, and even in certain cases the right to convert their rents into mortgages. That is quite a good package of choice. And choice, surely, is one of the defining characteristics of what it is to be a customer. But the situation is not quite so straightforward.

Applicants for council housing cannot really be regarded as customers in the normal sense. Customers are generally those who exercise effective demand by choosing the product they consider to be most suited to their requirements within their price range: there is generally a choice of outlets, and there is usually a package of rights of redress in the form of guarantees and legislation if things go wrong. Those serving customers usually compete for their custom, as there is usually more than one potential supplier. These aspects arguably mark the customer out from the mere consumer.

However, council housing has become housing of last resort. It is welfare housing, as illustrated by the high percentage of lettings (in the mid-1990s, over 80 per cent in many inner city authorities) to homeless households, and high welfare benefit dependency amongst newer tenants. No sane person would choose to live in some of the decrepit sink estates of what amount to latter-day slums in many inner cities, or down-at-heel, structurally challenged suburban enclosures with their high crime rates, alienation and sense of hopelessness, which characterise many edge-of-city housing projects, if they truly had a choice. It is generally the case that people are forced through socio-economic contingencies to seek council housing rather than through any exercise of the will.

Of course, it would be ridiculous to stigmatise all council housing in these terms, though much of it leaves a lot to be desired. But even if one wished to become a tenant, in many areas it would be impossible in the short or medium terms, owing to the need to ration such accommodation through severe shortage. Thus council housing as a tenure choice is an illusion. A homeless household given one offer of a 20th-floor council flat in the middle of urban desolation have found themselves in that accommodation, having no more exercised choice than a newborn infant over its birth.

Tenants are more like customers in the sense we can understand, with a formidable package of rights, even that of buying themselves out of the tenure. But CCT runs counter to this trend. Tenants cannot veto the choice of contractor, although they must be involved in specification discussions prior to tendering. It seems ironic that they can vote to change their landlord, but cannot select their managers. On the other hand, there is plenty of scope for tenants to take over their own management, by forming tenants' co-operatives, and by involvement in estate management boards, and in tenants' associations. By so doing they can have more control over key aspects of their lives.

None of the above excuses councils for not treating their applicants and tenants as if they were customers in the fullest sense of the word, and customer culture is to be welcomed.

The article 'The key relationship' (p. 176) highlights one local authority's customer care initiatives, and exemplifies a council which has a dedicated section to deal with customer issues.

5.6   The Right to Buy

Historians looking at social housing in the last quarter of the twentieth century may well conclude that the most bizarre aspect of its chequered history was the Right to Buy. Council housing was built for rent to meet social needs. The ability to buy implies that one does not need recourse to the social sector. And yet by 1990, almost 2 million such dwellings had been sold to sitting tenants at discount – and this at a time when homelessness and poor housing, combined with lengthening queues for social housing, indicate that there are shortages in this area.

This is to see the situation from the global viewpoint; but to council tenants this is a valuable right, a choice of tenure, and purchase could be a sound investment, given the right conditions in the property market. The right was conferred in 1981, under the 1980 Housing Act, now consolidated into Part 5 of the 1985 Housing Act. Prior to this, councils were empowered to sell council houses to sitting tenants if they so wished. It has been amended from time to time since then: the right to shared ownership has come and gone; local authorities are no longer obliged to grant mortgages; and there is no longer the possibility of deferred completion on payment of £150. The Rent to Mortgage scheme, introduced under the 1993 legislation, has widened its scope. The promise of the Right to Buy is sometimes credited with the success of Thatcher's Conservative Party in the 1979 elections.

Tenants qualify for the right if they have been a public sector tenant for at least 2 years. This can have been achieved without having been a council tenant: service tenancies of any public sector institution, for example the armed forces, count for both eligibility and discount purposes. Most council properties are included, except certain service tenancies, properties designed for people with disabilities, and certain types of dwellings designed for the elderly, principally those in a scheme part-serviced by social services. The landlord is generally a local housing authority, although secure tenants of many non-charitable housing associations also have the Right to Buy. If a local authority secure tenant becomes a tenant of a housing association owing to the transfer of stock, the Right to Buy is preserved.

The Right to Buy involves sale of property at discount. The discount starts at 32 per cent of the valuation for houses and 44 per cent for flats, if the tenant satisfies the 2 years' minimum qualifying period. The discount for house purchase increases by 1 per cent for every year of public sector tenancy, and 2 per cent in respect of flats, to a maximum of 60 per cent for the former and 70 per cent for the latter. The maximum discount in 1990 was £50 000, and the discount is not allowed to reduce the price below the cost of building or improving the property within an 8-year rolling period: for example, if the application was made in September 1994, the cost floor limitation would apply if the house had been built during or after September 1986.

If the property is resold within 1 year of purchase, 100 per cent of the discount must be repaid. This reduces to 60 per cent if the sale is within 2 years, and 30 per cent if within 3 years: but after that time, liability to repay discount ceases. As with the discount rules, this has become more generous since the inception of the Right to Buy.

There are advantages and disadvantages to tenants of the Right. If the purchase is in a popular area, with the ready possibility of resale, and prices are rising, subsequent sale, after the discount redemption period, can lead to the realisation of a substantial cash sum in addition to a deposit for another property. The asset can be inherited by the purchaser's heirs, and can be used for security for relatively cheap loans; there is freedom from rising rent regimes, and some of the bureaucracy of housing departments. There is greater freedom to rent the property out, to make improvements and undertake business from the property.

On the other hand, not all of these desirable conditions may be realised. Those buying flats have often underestimated their liability for service charges. In the event of the major repair of a group of flats, council tenants of that block do not pay their exact share, because the costs are usually pooled across the council's entire stock. But leaseholders have to pay their proportion of costs as if they were divided amongst the householders of just that block. Although service charge estimates for the first 5 years, must be given prior to the purchase, and charges cannot exceed those estimates over that period, after that time there is no such guarantee. Also, flats have often proved unsellable on the open market, as many building societies have refused to grant mortgages on properties built in a certain way, in certain locations, and above a given floor level.

The popularity of the Right has waned since the late 1980s, partly as a result of a general slump in property prices and partly because the best stock has already been sold. The main controversy as far as housing policy analysts are concerned is over the use of receipts: it is easier to use one's own money than to borrow, and funds realised from Right to Buy could be put to use in building much-needed social housing rather than merely debt redemption. The reasons for restricting such expenditure have much to do with a neo-monetarist concern with controlling the amount of money in circulation by restricting public spending, and thereby, at least theoretically, keeping inflation down.

5.7   Where is council housing going?

On the face of it, there is very little future for council housing. Over the 1980s and 1990s, very few developments of any significance have been undertaken, except for some renovation projects. Housing associations have taken over as providers: councils are enablers, providers of cheap land, grants and land via planning deals. By 1994, 35 councils had transferred all their assets to associations, and many more wish to follow suit. The best stock has been sold under the Right to Buy. The sector has become residualised welfare housing. And yet there is no reason why this had to come about, and every reason why the decline of council housing should be halted.

Had councils been able to develop good-quality accommodation during the 1980s and 1990s, homelessness would have become a thing of the past. Had council house sales been left as an option rather than enforced, and had councils been able to spend all their sales receipts on improvements, repairs and new-build rather than prioritise debt repayment, the sector might well have become one of high-quality housing in which people would have been proud to live. After all, what is inherently wrong with well-designed, hygienic accommodation, located close to shops, employment and services at low rent, which can be swapped when family circumstances change? Far better, perhaps, for a household to have the opportunity to live in decent low-rent accommodation and be able to live comfortably than to have to struggle with a large mortgage and be stuck in unsuitable housing when the property market falls, or when prices of housing of the right size soar beyond their means – or to have to resort to short-term, expensive lettings in the private sector, with the uncertainty of what happens when the term expires. The behaviour of the property market in the 1990s has once and for all given the lie to the assertion oft heard in the 1980s that owner occupation was one of the most sure-fire investments possible.

It is otiose to suggest that council housing should not be a choice because it is state-subsidised housing. Most households live in state-subsidised housing: everyone who pays a mortgage interest tax relief does, benefiting from an interest rate subsidy in the form of mortgage, worth a great deal more in the mid-1990s than the cost of Housing Revenue Account subsidy. Even if it were abolished tomorrow, the vast majority of owner-occupiers would have benefited from this subsidy. And in several authority areas, no HRA subsidy is receivable. Additionally, is there anything wrong with benefiting from state-subsidised goods or services? Tax money is applied to roads, parks and all manner of services which everyone enjoys, quite uncontroversially. There is (at the time of writing) a state-subsidised National Health Service; and it is still possible to get a good education paid for through taxation. There is no question of being barred from these services on grounds of having too much money. As long as a realistic rent is payable, what is so wrong with councils providing housing on a level playing field with other providers? The availability of relatively low-cost rented accommodation would do wonders for job mobility; and its construction would stimulate the building industry, a well-recognised source of economic multiplication in that it stimulates other areas of the economy.

Unfortunately, there appears to be no understanding of these points at present. Council housing is a dinosaur: its only role is to provide accommodation of last resort. Its functions would best be performed by other agencies. It is a second-class form of tenure. Its advantages have been completely overlooked by governments which regard privatisation as the only way to stimulate efficiencies, and which look on owner-occupation as a natural form of tenure in spite of the evident problems associated with it. Against such ideological bias, there seems little hope for council housing – until the problems of poverty, homelessness and bad housing become impossible to ignore. Then, perhaps, local authorities will be allowed to build again in the quantities needed.

Articles

1. 'Indicating performance in council housing'

2. 'The key relationship: good practice in public relations'

3. 'A charter for council housing'

4. 'Local government reorganisation and housing'

Indicating performance in council housing

It is likely that council rents will increase considerably from April 1991, following full implementation of the new housing finance rules. In view of spartan D.o.E. assumptions in the 1990 Housing Revenue Account Subsidy Determination, improved management, repair and maintenance services will not automatically flow from rent rises, which might have been expected by those unaware of the perversities of council finance. Not that private sector rent increases automatically bring improved landlord performance!

That said, it is surely reasonable that information on how spending is conducted, and assurances on quality, should accompany public sector rent rises. This thinking supports a new duty imposed on councils from April 1991, that of having to produce a report to all tenants giving 'performance indicators' for the previous year. Section 167 of the 1989 Local Government and Housing Act, interpreted by D.o.E. Circular 19/90, requires councils to produce these within 6 months of the end of the relevant year. Indicators include a stock description; total rent collected; arrears; repair and maintenance costs; number of tenancies granted through new letting or transfer, including nominations to housing associations; numbers of vacant dwellings and average void periods; average time to process rebates; volume of homeless acceptances and temporary accommodation used; number of staff involved and cost of management; and, finally, details of tenants' complaint and consultation procedures.

More work will be piled on stretched policy and research units. Although such information is probably already recorded, it is unlikely to have been collated in this form, though it might be found in a comprehensive Housing Strategy Statement produced annually to justify spending permission. Where such units do not exist, staff will have to be redeployed, or cash found to engage personnel to compile the reports either directly or through one of the burgeoning housing consultancies. Presumably the cost will appear in Determinations! (this being the D.o.E.'s decision on the amount of subsidy a council should receive).

In a sense, this continues the tenant-as-customer philosophy emergent during the 1980s reflected in the Tenant's Charter items of the 1980 (now 1985) Housing Act, D.o.E. exhortations via circular, and in the work of the Priority Estates Project in facilitating decentralised, tenant-oriented management of run-down estates and the Tenants Participatory Advisory Service, which advises housing organisations on tenant involvement in policy formation and delivery. The customer approach has been widely adopted: and housing associations have made progress in this area.

But there is a less obvious dimension. The voluntary transfer provisions of the 1986 Housing and Planning Act and the Tenants' Choice element of the 1988 Housing Act were designed respectively to encourage council tenants to consider the supposed advantages of being transferred to or opting for another landlord. But although there have been some estate transfers under the 1986 legislation, many proposals have fallen by ballot, and Tenants' Choice competes for success with housing action trusts. It seems that tenants consider legal security and low rents before the elusive advantages of alternative tenures, except when it comes to the Right to Buy.

It may be that the new requirement is based on the idea that if tenants knew how inefficient and ineffective their council landlords *really* were, they would consider the options offered by other landlords more readily, thus rescuing earlier privatisation initiatives. This, combined with inevitable rent rises narrowing the gap between new-regime housing association and council rents, would provide an incentive towards making the move into ownership or the private or voluntary sectors. The consequence of this would be reduced real public expenditure, a major plank of government policy in controlling inflation and macroeconomic management generally, as the need for Exchequer support falls with stock levels.

If this is an intention, there is a real possibility of disappointment. A well-known D.o.E.-commissioned report, *The Nature and Effectiveness of Housing Management in England* (1989), shows that council tenants are generally satisfied with their accommodation and services: there is greater satisfaction with repairs performance than for other forms of tenure. The requirement to produce indicators may be a blessing in disguise, helping councils to sell themselves as customer-friendly and responsive, hopefully nailing myths of inefficiency and waste – as well as spurring policy reviews, and necessary action to ensure that spending supports efficient and effective services.

This will be helped if details of financial constraints and their sources are clearly spelt out with the document to defuse unreasonable criticism, and councils should use the opportunity to highlight the advantages of their product, whilst taking care not to fall foul of prohibitions on producing 'political' literature. Determinations should be clearly written to avoid misinterpretation and confusion, or the risk that the job will be done badly through sensationalism in parts of the media. It is expected that this challenge will be taken up in a proactive and creative manner: *PSLG* welcomes copies of determinations to gauge success!

PSLG, February 1991

Questions

1. What is the justification for providing annual performance reports to tenants?
2. In what senses are council tenants customers rather than just consumers?
3. Is it likely that adverse performance indications might encourage tenants to choose another landlord?

The key relationship: good practice in public relations

The 1985 Housing Act compels councils to tell housing customers clearly about their tenancy conditions, and consult them on matters affecting the management and maintenance of their homes. This requirement to inform is underlined by the need to produce yearly performance indicators, as featured last year [1992] in *PSLG*. Most local authorities have attempted to provide a more user-friendly range of documents to inform rather than intimidate, perhaps looking over their shoulder at potential competitors.

The London Borough of Lewisham has developed an information strategy which provides a rare example of housing leading from the front in spearheading good practice in the sharing of publicity ideas. *PSLG* spoke to Lewisham Housing's Public Relations Manager, Seth Brook, who, to define the market for the enterprise, stressed that those who are homeless and looking to the borough for advice and assistance, private sector tenants, and those seeking renovation grants join council tenants as customers.

Lewisham faces common challenges – amongst them the need to maximise rent collection, and to eliminate unlawful occupancy to ensure that housing is allocated equitably. A two-stage strategy has been devised to warn those in arrears of the consequences of wilful non-payment. One leaflet gently reminds, and explains the consequences to all tenants of losses through default: the next, sent following the issue of a notice of seeking possession, is uncompromising, and bluntly presents remedies available to the council, whilst offering the tenant the chance to make realistic proposals for clearing the debt. These warnings are backed up by a section dispelling myths about rent arrears, pointing out that, far from no evictions ever being secured on this ground, in 1990/91 190 households suffered this fate, and many were treated as intentionally homeless. The legend at the back, 'Help yourself, act now', printed in large blood-red characters, jars with the assurance that it is printed on environmentally friendly paper, but leaves those in arrears in no doubt as to the consequences of delay.

Squatters are given similar, if controversial, treatment. In many prominent locations in Lewisham – one was below the friendly giant feline welcoming shoppers to Catford's shopping centre – a lurid pink and black poster declared that 'squatters don't pay, homeless families do', in double reference to loss of rental income on properties and to unlawful occupation of a council home by people not selected via the canons of officialdom. Some squatters may claim they are indeed homeless persons who are not assisted by Lewisham because they fail to meet the definition of 'priority need'; but Brook claimed that the campaign has been received sympathetically by council tenants, if not by those in his sights.

In common with other London boroughs, Lewisham has been attempting to crack down on 'key sales': and Brook's section established a hotline in 1991 to encourage tenants to inform on the perpetrators of what is seen as an instance of particularly heinous anti-community fraud. The council's report to tenants for 1991 was produced on time, and made available in English, Bengali, Turkish and Cantonese, reflecting the ethnic mix of the borough: the cartoon representing its multicultural society, whilst rather stereotypical, may lead some to turn the page rather than dismiss it as yet another council handout. As well as being the annual report of a sizeable social housing concern, it also tells how to complain and obtain representation through the local tenants' body. Photographs augment the straightforward text and diagrams outlining departmental statistics on the development programme, rehousings and rent levels. It is a guide to housing services based, says Brook, on the premise that tenants have an active interest in services provided on their behalf and paid for largely by their rents.

Lewisham housing communicates with the world via several media and liaises with the central Press Office, and has a major input into the council newspaper, Outlook, distributed to every home in the borough. It uses posters, radio, television, leaflets and advertising on bus-shelter adshells, at hoardings and at prominent junctions.

Each neighbourhood within decentralised Lewisham produces at least two newsletters to tenants annually, and it is hoped to increase customer input within the year. The council funds the Federation of Lewisham Tenants and Residents Association and resources its newsletter.

Brook is compiling a Good Practice Guide for housing workers, aiming to assist in implementing quality control across neighbourhoods, and has been active in setting up an interdepartmental publicity standards group, enabling departments throughout the council to swap communications ideas and learn from each other's experiences, fully operational from March 1992. The overall impression is of a housing organisation presenting as a caring although essentially hard-headed landlord, coping well with the challenges of the 1990s despite the funding and ideological constraints under which it labours, and offering a model which would perhaps bear investigation by other less pro-active boroughs.

PSLG, 1992 (unpublished)

Questions

1. How does the London Borough of Lewisham approach the arrears question? Is this approach likely to be universally effective?
2. How does the borough ensure that its literature reaches a wide audience?

A charter for council housing

The Citizen's Charter reflects a belief that consumers of public services should have enhanced rights of redress as well as a louder voice in specifying what services remain in the public domain. Although the details require further articulation, the principal housing elements include replacing the 1980 Act Tenant's Charter with a Tenant's Guarantee modelled on that introduced for assured housing association tenants, expanding the Right to Repair, not only for council but also for association tenants, the extension of Tenants' Choice, and compulsory tendering of local authority housing management. The housing aspects must be set in the context of the strengthened powers of the Audit Commission to publish council performance league tables, together with a requirement for councils to respond in public to criticism, and spell out programmes for rectification. The administration clearly hope that the above will appeal to the electorate, viewed by Central Office as deeply distrustful of town hall bureaucracies and their effectiveness.

In a sense, little is new: a series of measures were enacted during the 1980s with the intention not only of increasing access to information, but of strengthening consumer choice. The Right to Buy is perhaps the most dramatic expression of the latter, allowing most secure tenants to opt out of one tenure entirely, without the collateral guarantee of re-entry if desired or necessary.

Councils must publish clearly their allocations and management policies. Tenants can already contract out of council management through Tenants' Choice. Performance indicators, both for housing associations and local authority housing, spelling out targets and measuring progress, have to be published annually rather in the manner of reports to shareholders.

What should particularly disturb public servants is the underlying philosophy. It is clear that central government considers that they, and the organisations they administer, are in a fundamental sense second-rate, very much the creatures of outdated municipalism characterised by the nineteenth-century Birmingham of Chamberlain and his Liberal burghers, finding its most unacceptable expression in the GLC of Livingstone and the Militant minefield of Liverpool. More, that 'ordinary people' share this view, and, in recognising the sense of this reform, will usher Mr Major's heroic regime back in for another glorious decade combining individualism with the virtues of the Active Citizen.

This view of public service is, of course, a parody, as anyone who works within it or with it, or holds a councillor's office, will know. Hopefully, people of sense will see it in these terms, whilst quite rightly demanding good-quality services from public providers. Local authorities have been poor self-publicists, though admittedly they are limited here by the 1988 Local Government Act's restrictions on political publication, and some media presentations, typified by the *Summer on the Estate* portrayal of a dreadful Hackney enclosure and Bleasdale's *GBH*, have done little to assist. It is hoped that authority associations as well as individual administrations will do all they can to resist misleading folk-images which have burgeoned of late.

To return to the specifics of the Citizen's Charter, it is as interesting for what it leaves out as for what it includes. There is a striking absence of any guarantees to homeless people concerning the standard of temporary accommodation that can be expected. What real redress is there for a young family living in a crowded room which may well fall below any reasonable decency threshold? And how is the proven deleterious effect on children's schooling and health, which may have far-reaching consequences in behavioural and attainment terms, to be compensated for? What assurances can be offered to those who do not fit neatly into priority categories that they will ever receive decent affordable rented accommodation? The ability of tenants to change landlords, to contract out, to change tenure is all very well, but those awaiting decent accommodation from hard-pressed social providers are citizens too, too often forgotten, perhaps because they are perceived as having little political clout. The Citizen's Charter is stacked in favour of those already reasonably housed, and fails to address the needs of those who lack decent housing or manifestly require something better, and therefore cannot properly be said to be a charter for all.

To supplement the charter, public and social housing agencies should be required to publish maximum wait-times for social housing, subject to the availability of identified resources from specified sources – and not without those conditions. Unfortunately, because housing finance is seen as subservient to economic nostrums which happen to govern general public expenditure policy, it is unlikely that this corollary will ever be added. Arguably, then, the Citizen's Charter has failed to address rather fundamental issues of provision: one cannot help thinking that the fact that trains from Waterloo will at last run on time and be stocked with acceptable sandwiches provides scant consolation to those sleeping on the platform.

PSLG, September 1991

Questions

1. Why did the government promote its Citizen's Charter initiative in all major public services from the early 1990s onwards?
2. Is there a hidden agenda underlying the Council Tenant's Charter, and, if so, what is it?
3. Are would-be customers of council housing services treated as positively as existing consumers, and, if not, could the Charter be amended to reduce this imbalance?

Local government reorganisation and housing

Less than 20 years ago, the implementation of the Redcliffe Maude Report dramatically altered the local authority landscape, creating a two-tier system of district and county councils, followed by unitarisation elsewhere. A direct result of this was that the new districts became housing authorities, with counties retaining a residual role. There was demarcation of functional responsibility between the tiers, without implying a command relationship. The Local Government Commission, under the chairmanship of Sir John Banham, is currently examining options for another wholesale re-organisation in the light of perceived failures of the present system. An outline of preferred strategies is emerging, allowing argument over the position of housing function in the revised structure.

The Commission has decided to test the concept of the unitary district authority as a model for evaluation before planning wholesale changes. The first stage of reorganisation envisages 24 new unitary authorities, 10 unitary districts within existing district boundaries, and one county – the Isle of Wight – becoming a unitary authority with no boundary changes. Detailed working out of the proposals is currently awaited, which leaves the field open for suggestions from all interested parties.

Unitary authorities have several advantages in housing terms demonstrable at both strategic and operational levels.

District authorities are responsible for assessing housing need in their areas, and devising provision plans, as enablers: but they cannot do so effectively without the co-operation of county councils, as structure planners, providers of social services and educational authorities. Different authorities inevitably have differing perspectives on need and provision; far better to ensure co-operation by merging the functions. At the moment, it is far too often the case that good strategic relations emerge by chance rather than by design. Relying upon happy coincidence of aims is surely a recipe for eventual disaster.

Council housing, in so far as it is still provided by councils, is fast becoming welfare housing, with implications of social services' involvement at an operational level to a far greater degree than hitherto. The ageing of the population, with the growth in the number of very elderly, means that pressures in local authorities to provide or enable care in a housing context, to fulfil Care in the Community responsibilities, will inevitably increase – again entailing far better and closer links between social services and housing. The 1989 Children Act and devolution of aspects of residential health care to councils both imply a multidisciplinary team approach between differing authorities to ensure that clients receive maximal assistance.

A positive trend to emerge from central government policy toward local government during the late 1980s and early 1990s is the emphasis on customers as ends of provision rather than simply as clients to any number of services, and this philosophy demands that modern local government adopts a unified approach to welfare needs. For all these reasons, the emergence of unitary authorities is to be welcomed.

There are several conditions to be fulfilled prior to final decision. It is crucial that the quality of existing services is not disrupted by reorganisation, and therefore a phased approach is essential. Considerations of scale are essential – great play has been made by the Commission of the right size for new unitary authorities, to reflect residents' sense of natural community and relationship to service delivery. This is very difficult to assess, but crucial in acceptance of any new regime. It is doubtful whether the demise of Avon will be much mourned, because the area patently bears no relation to either historical or geographical-economic precedent. Strategic planning at unitary district level, with service delivery on a decentralised basis, might be a good model: it has worked well in district housing authorities, as well as in existing unitary councils. Local community areas could define the boundaries of service delivery, but the definition of such areas should be subject to public consultation on what precisely constitutes community. It is likely that public consultation will reveal a hierarchy of communities depending upon how people use local areas.

For example, work over the past 20 years by councils and consultants such as the Tenants Participation Advisory Service and the Priority Estates Project has shown the high value placed on housing offices within walking distance, in estates or shopping areas, especially where social and other welfare services are also available. Whatever the outcome of the survey, it is essential that more than lip-service is paid to preference, otherwise the customer may be even more alienated than at present. And democratic accountability needs to be built in at local level, perhaps by strengthening the voice of parish and community councils, so that residents have ownership of the new structure.

Whatever the outcome, customers have a right to a unified service provision: that should be the aim, and bureaucratic reorganisation must be subservient to it to avoid another wholesale review in 20 years' time.

PSLG, September 1993

Questions

1. What considerations should affect the decision to change local authority boundaries and functions?
2. What advantages for customers of council housing departments would the wholesale implementation of unitary authorities bring?
3. Are there any disadvantages in combining all local authority functions within a single body?

6 Planning and housing development

6.1 Introduction

Local authorities are both providers and enablers in the sense that they still, in some areas, build homes, and help other organisations to provide affordable housing. Mention has already been made of council grants to assist housing association capital schemes; but they are also crucial in other enabling contexts. Planning is the preserve of district and unitary authorities, and provides the basis for rational land use. Additionally, the system can be used to secure private land for social housing through so-called planning obligation deals with developers, a valuable form of subsidy which can help reduce rents. Thus, an understanding of the planning system and its possibilities is essential to a full appreciation of social housing development.

Development is a challenging and complex field, involving a knowledge not only of planning, but also of design, contracts and finance. The financial constraints upon social housing developers are enormous, and it is a wonder that as many new homes have been produced under the financial regime for associations following the 1988 Housing Act changes as there have. This chapter seeks to explore the possibilities of the planning system, and describe and explain in outline some of the issues which surround social housing development.

6.2 Planning

6.2.1 Development planning

Planning may be divided into two main areas: that of the development plan-making system, and development control.

Development planning, through structure plans and local plans, provides a strategic framework for all varieties of land use development. The various types of council have been outlined: county councils are responsible for the formulation of Structure Plans, which are strategic, broad-brush plans for their areas, whilst district councils are responsible for the development of Local Plans, which deal in greater detail with land use control issues, as well as setting out the criteria for grant of planning permission, and enforcement of those decisions.

The necessity of some form of strategic planning can be illustrated by considering the development, or rather misdevelopment, of nineteenth-century industrial cities in Great Britain. There was a distinct lack of planning: incompatible land uses often resided next to each other, with polluting factories cheek by jowl with mean housing for workers. There was lack of attention to roads, sewerage, recreation space – in fact, everything that we take for granted in today's society. The result was an environmental disaster, with clear health and safety implications. The history of urban planning in the twentieth century has revolved around clearing up the mess of the past, and attempting to ensure that it is not re-created in today's cities: witness the Garden Cities movement of the first quarter of the century, and the New Towns policy following the Second World War.

There were notable exceptions to the unplanned urban sprawls of the nineteenth century. Some more enlightened industrialists built rationally planned settlements for their workers away from the polluting factories, exemplified by Cadbury's Bournville, near Birmingham, and Lever's Port Sunlight on Merseyside. But these were the exceptions rather than the rule. The concept of town and country planning is not new: Plato mentions the existence of town planning in ancient Athens. Strict land use regulation is exemplified in Roman cities; and Machiavelli's *The Prince*, written in the fifteenth century, makes clear recommendations on the siting of market centres and military fortifications.

The development planning system is presently defined through the 1990 Town and Country Planning Act (here referred to as the 1990 Act), which was modified by the 1991 Planning and Compensation Act. It defines development as 'the carrying out of building, engineering, mining or other operations in, on, over or under land' (s. 55). The plan-making system is designed to regulate such development, of which residential production is a small subset.

It is in some respects surprising that there are no regional plans or planning authorities. There were: but the Regional Planning Councils which used to produce them were abolished in 1979, with Regional Planning Boards consisting of local authority representatives retained as talking shops, although the advisory documents they produce are still referred to by plan-making authorities. The Greater London Council used to produce a London-wide strategic plan, but was abolished in 1986. Since then, regional planning advice has come from the Department of the Environment in the form of guidance notes and circulars, to which local planning authorities must have regard.

There are arguments for and against regional planning authorities. Those for include the fact that the UK is a small country, and land use issues often overlap county or district boundaries: for example, the issue of the siting of a fourth London airport, or the line of the Channel Tunnel rail link. A regional planning authority would be an ideal body to adjudicate on the different views of various councils, and to reconcile these with the overall need for the development. Supporters point to the strengthening of central government control over local affairs by divide and rule, through circulars and legislation and by the abolition of regional authorities. This may have been the reason for the abolition of the GLC: or is this just conspiracy theory?

Arguments against include the cost of setting up such bodies, and the additional bureaucracy they would generate, which might slow down the planning process unacceptably. It is also held that the Department of the Environment provides an ideal forum from which the national planning needs of the country can be assessed. In 1994, there were no plans to reintroduce any form of regional planning.

County councils have a duty, under Part 2 of the 1990 Act, to produce Structure Plans, which are valid for between 10 and 15 years. They contain policies of a large-scale, strategic nature. First, a survey of the county is undertaken, which includes such matters as its physical and economic characteristics, the size, composition and distribution of the population, its transport system, and conservation issues. Any projected changes are also identified at this stage. Following this, a Written Statement is prepared, formulating the council's policy and general proposals in respect of the development and other use of the land in its area, considering the impact on any neighbouring counties of such proposals. Extensive public consultation is required before such a statement can be adopted as planning policy, although the essential vagueness of such plans makes it difficult for specific objections to be made. The scope of such plans is vast. The policy must relate to:

- distribution of population and employment
- housing
- industry and commerce
- transportation
- shopping
- education
- social and community services
- recreation and leisure
- conservation
- townscape and landscape

- utility services.

The plan must cover:

- the existing socio-economic structure of the area
- projected changes and opportunities
- population trends
- regional and social policies
- resources available to the local planning authority
- broad criteria for development control
- relationship between formulated policies
- inter-county considerations.

County councils must consider the views of district planning authorities, whose local plans will have to take account of the Structure Plans, as well as any public representations. It used to be the case that, when completed, Structure Plans had to be submitted to the Secretary of State for the Environment for approval, but the 1991 Act abolished this requirement. However, the plan must be made available for public inspection for at least 6 months after being drafted, to allow for objections, before being adopted. These plans are revised from time to time: as they can take up to 5 years to prepare, the data upon which they are based quickly become out of date, which is one of the problems with such plans. However, Local Plans (*see below*), which are far more important in deciding actual planning policy and its implementation, are revised more frequently, so perhaps this is not fatal to the concept.

From time to time, there are proposals to scrap the structure planning process. It was last referred to in a D.o.E. Guidance Note, PPG15, issued in May 1990; but nothing had been done about it at the time of writing (1995). It was suggested that the bulky Structure Plans be replaced by more straightforward and smaller Statements of Planning Policy, at county level, giving indications of broad planning philosophy. Districts and boroughs would produce local plans with a great deal more emphasis on public participation at the point of formulation. In many ways, this would be a retrograde step: at least the structure planning process allows for a more general consideration of land use issues, and places local plans in a meaningful context, in the absence of regional plans. It is undeniable that watered-down county statements would speed up the plan-making process, but would they be sufficient to ensure a co-ordinated approach to, say, housing development where one part of the county is growing economically, with pressures for in-migration, but another part is declining? London's horrific, uncoordinated road system is as good an argument as any for retaining some form of regional planning, even if only at county council level.

Local Plans are prepared by district councils, and appear more frequently than Structure Plans. They are more detailed, and include a map indicating specific development sites and land use areas rather than a plan. The policies they contain deal with the same issues as structure plans, which they must have regard to. The Local Plan consists of a Written Statement, comprising a detailed formulation of proposals for the development and other use of land in their area, and proposes measures to improve the physical environment and traffic management in particular. Although the Local Plan covers the whole district, it may contain specific plans and policies relating to distinctive areas within it, or on themes such as conservation.

Public consultation is more rigorous than for Structure Plans. Prior to devising a local plan, the planning authority must consult the general public, and any body which has an interest in the plan: for example, local civic societies which are concerned to preserve the historic character of towns. As previously stated, the bodies to be consulted include the county council, in respect of the Structure Plan. Once the plan has been prepared, it is certified as conforming with the Structure Plan. Copies are made available for public inspection and comment, and the plan is sent to the Secretary of State for the Environment for scrutiny. There is a minimum period of 6 weeks to allow the public to object to the plan. The Secretary of State must appoint an inspector to conduct an inquiry if substantive objections are made to it, and, unlike the case with Structure Plans, objectors have a right to appear at the inquiry. Any recommendations made by the inspector as a result of this process, as well as public objections, must be taken into account by the planning authority; and a number of government departments, including the Ministry of Agriculture, Fisheries and Food, can order changes. Only after going through these stages can the council formally adopt the plan.

Unitary Development Plans are essentially a combination of Structure and Local Plans. They arose following the abolition of the Metropolitan County Councils, including the Greater London Council, in 1986 and the subsequent creation of unitary authorities; for example, the London boroughs. They are subject to strategic guidelines issued by the Secretary of State, such as the Strategic Planning Guidance for London (SPGL) set out in Regional Planning Guidance Note 3 (PPG3). Additionally, they take account of joint local authority bodies such as the London and South East Regional Planning Conference, which produces SERPLAN, and the London Planning Advisory Committee (LPAC). As with other plans, they also take account of relevant general circulars and must conform with the 1990 Act.

The SPGL issued in 1989 (the latest issue at the time at writing) sets out seven planning objectives which reflect the scope of the planning problem that besets London boroughs. They are to:

- Foster economic growth considering the importance for the national economy of London's continued prosperity.

- Contribute to revitalising the older urban areas.

- Facilitate the development of safe, efficient and environmentally friendly transport systems.

- Maintain the vitality and character of established town centres.

- Sustain and improve the amenity of residential districts.

- Allow for a wide range of housing provision.

- Give high priority to the environment, maintain the Green Belt and Metropolitan Open Land, and preserve fine views, conservation areas, surrounding countryside and the natural heritage.

Such are the pressures for development in London that it is frequently hard to meet all these objectives, and compromise must be struck. London is essentially a coalescence of older towns, which each retain something of their former character, and it would be a shame if poor planning policies resulted in the uniformity of development which is found in many cities. The main objectives of the current *Unitary Development Plan* of the Royal Borough of Kensington and Chelsea exemplify these concerns (*see* pp. 16–17 of the *Plan*), and are not atypical of those of London boroughs generally:

6.2.1.1   Strategy 1

To give priority to the protection and enhancement of the residential character and amenity of the Royal Borough.

6.2.1.2   Strategy 2

To seek an increase in residential provision within the Royal Borough by restricting the loss of land and buildings with existing residential use and changes to uses other than residential of land or buildings with potential for residential use.

6.2.1.3   Strategy 3

To seek the continued economic growth of the metropolitan area by supporting change and development in those parts of London and the Royal Borough that are recognised as having capacity for additional commercial or industrial activity.

6.2.1.4   Strategy 4

To seek a safe, efficient and environmentally acceptable transport system for the metropolitan area, whilst protecting the residential character, amenity and quality of the Royal Borough.

These strategies nicely illustrate the development pressures to which the inner part of large cities are subject. Over the century, there has been considerable conversion from residential to commercial uses, as commercial users have bought up large houses and converted them into offices, or demolished what was there and raised blocks, often changing the character of areas. Additionally, retail uses have competed for land with other developments, to provide the patchwork of uses we see today in cities. Increased personal mobility has brought traffic management challenges, some of which may be dealt with through the planning process, in relation to the siting of roads, and the avoidance of areas near to busy routes for residential development. One of the most significant issues is striking a balance between conservation and the need to retain an economically viable city.

Reference has already been made to Planning Guidance Notes. These do not have the force of legislation, but local planning authorities must have regard to them. One of the most significant to influence housing is PPG3, *Land for Housing*, which is revised from time to time, and was last issued in April 1992. Essentially it allows local authorities to take account of a community's need for affordable housing when formulating its development plans, and where there is a demonstrable lack of affordable housing to meet local need, the authority can indicate an overall target for its provision, both at district and at site level, although a good case needs to be made out for such a decision. It even suggests that willingness to provide affordable housing should be a material consideration when a planning decision is made, although this is also facilitated under what is known as planning obligation, dealt with later. However, local plans must not favour a given form of tenure, or indeed define affordable housing in those terms. Planning is supposed to be tenure neutral, although local authorities are supposed, under PPG3, to say what they mean by affordable housing. Thus, affordable housing should not be equated with, although it includes, social housing. For example, Wimpey Worldwide may propose a development of relatively cheap housing destined for the owner-occupier market on land acquired on favourable terms from a farmer who has decided to take some land out of production under the Set Aside rules; this may be more 'affordable' than housing built on more expensive land, but would hardly be termed 'social' in the terms we have discussed. PPG3 entails that local planning authorities take a more pro-active stance towards the provision of affordable housing, although there are limits to what the planning system can do in itself to facilitate this objective. However, if the planning system increases the supply of land for affordable housing through such policies, it is conceivable that its scarcity will diminish and the price of land in certain areas will fall, thus reducing capital costs and thereby rents, especially important in an environment of falling Housing Association Grant (HAG) rates. For all that, it should not be seen as a substitute for public subsidy to produce housing within the reach of lower-income people.

6.2.2   Planning permission

District and unitary authorities are responsible for considering planning applications, granting consents and enforcing the terms of planning consents. Although this is generally true, various development corporations have been established to cover areas which government wants to see revitalised, and these may cut across borough boundaries, as in the case of the London Docklands Development Commission. Established in 1981, it was formed to co-ordinate the revitalisation of London's Docklands, which had lost its economic base through the closure of the docks as a result of containerisation and therefore the declining suitability of river sites as entry points for sea-borne traffic. It is the planning authority for the area, and has relaxed planning criteria in order to minimise barriers to the redevelopment of the area.

Generally, whenever it is desired to change the use of a piece of land or a building, or to construct a property, it is necessary to seek and obtain planning permission from the local planning authority. Land uses are classified according to the major use, and are subject to the Use Classes Order which defines them, and permitted changes without planning consent. Classes A1 to A3 specify retail uses; classes B1 to B8 are business and industrial uses; classes C1 to C3 are residential and hotel uses; and classes D1 and D2 cover a variety of non-residential uses and assembly and leisure. Material (that is, substantial), changes of use require planning permission; however, it is possible to change from certain classes to others without it. Such exceptions are specified under the General Development Order, issued under the 1990 Act. This is usually where there will be no detriment if the change takes place. For example, it is possible to change from A3 [use for sale of food or drink (consumption on premises) or of hot food (consumption off premises)] to A1 (use as shops) without seeking planning permission, because the result will probably be environmentally cleaner: the reverse is not possible without permission, because of the public health implications. In some cases, a piece of land may not have any use, or a building may have fallen out of use: in this case, the applicant can apply to the local authority for a determination as to the use class.

Certain other forms of development are excluded from the necessity to seek permission, including the extension of a house, as long as it is within the curtilage (boundary) of the property, and it does not exceed the cubic content of the house or original height by certain limits, or extend the house to within 20 metres of the highway. Most forms of demolition do not require planning consent. Clearly the above is not true if the building is 'listed' as having some architectural or historic interest. However, although the above seems liberal, Article 4 of the General Development Order (GDO) awards the right to local planning authorities to suspend permitted developments, although this power requires the consent of the Secretary of State. This is not required where buildings of special architectural or historic interest are concerned.

There are four other cases where specific planning permission is not required. First, Special Development Orders (SDOs) are made by the Secretary of State to bypass local authority planning procedures, and apply to specific projects. For example, the plant used to reprocess nuclear waste at Sellafield (when it was called Windscale) was made the subject of an SDO, in the teeth of considerable local opposition. They are commonly made in urban development areas. Their use is a significant erosion of local democracy, although it could be seen as reinforcing the power of the state to intervene in securing strategic objectives of national importance.

Second, Enterprise Zones are areas designated by the Secretary of State for special treatment, and allow developments of a certain sort as specified by the scheme without local planning permission. For example, the Isle of Dogs Enterprise Zone in London's Docklands, created in 1982, managed to attract major newspaper producers and financial service industries partly as a result of such intervention. It has now been declassified: but Canary Wharf is a testament to its operation. The problem with such zones is that they are often unresponsive to local feelings: there was some direct action on the part of residents to try to influence decisions there, without avail. One of the problems in Docklands has been that comparatively few jobs for local people have been created, and the social housing component of the scheme has not been significant.

Simplified Planning Zones are in effect local General Development Orders made by local planning authorities, again to encourage the development of certain classes in their area. They have often been used in respect to residential development, especially urban renewal; but planning guidance (PPG5) suggests that they should not be used in a commercial context.

Finally, Deemed Planning Permission is where no application is required, because permission is deemed to have been granted under the 1990 Act. This has relatively limited scope, applying mainly to outdoor advertisements, but significantly to developments which have been authorised by government departments, and are therefore in the national interest, such as those by the Ministry of Defence.

The most common form of planning permission is the grant of Express Permission: that is, where an application is placed before the local planning authority for decision. Local authority developments have special rules applying to them, but the effect of the 1991 Planning and Compensation Act was to make the process rather more like any other application, although this is difficult, as the local authority is both developer and planning body in these cases.

It would be a very foolish developer who acquired land with a specific purpose in mind without having permission for a certain class of development (which generally goes with the land, regardless of ownership changes), except where no application is necessary, under the GDO. Land with planning permission for, say, residential or industrial use usually commands a higher price than land without it. There is no necessity for the applicant to have a legal interest in the land, or even to obtain the owner's consent, although those having a material interest in the land must be given notice of the application. This is part of the consultation exercise; later, the public have a chance to object to and influence the proposal. However, it is not generally necessary to publicise the application to third parties, except under specific circumstances, such as where the building will be more than 20 metres high (a block of flats), where it is proposed to work minerals, where buildings will be constructed and land used in relation to refuse disposal or as a scrapyard, or where a cemetery or crematorium is proposed. This is because such developments will have a significant impact on the local environment. However, many authorities publish a schedule of planning applications in the local press to give notice to residents of all applications in the area. Publicisation usually means publishing a notice in the local paper, and fixing notices on the site boundary indicating the nature of the proposal. Those having a material interest in any development have 21 days to make representations to the planning authority. Objections can only be considered on planning grounds, not for social reasons. For example, it is not legitimate to object to the development of a hostel for homeless people next door because it would 'lower the tone' of the neighbourhood (or bring down property prices); but breaches of certain design or conservation considerations specified in the local plan might be grounds for objection, even though this has nothing to do with the use as specified. If the proposal involved a change of use outside the GDO, then a case could be made against such a development: but it is up to the planning authority to decide whether it is a planning matter.

Applications may be made for either outline or detailed planning permission. An outline application is often made to test the water, especially in the case where local policy is unclear, or where the proposal is on the edge of acceptability, and does not include the detailed drawings or siting information as required in pursuance of detailed permission; detailed permission must be sought afterwards before development can go ahead. There is nothing sure-fire about outline permission, since it can be revoked after having been granted, though only after consent by the Secretary of State. If it is, the planning authority is required to compensate the would-be developer, and so revocation is comparatively rare. Whatever the nature of the application, it must identify the land, and give plans and drawings describing the development. Of course, if the developer has studied the local plan and is sure that the proposal falls within its scope, there is no reason why detailed permission should not be sought in the first instance, although the fees of professionals involved in working up plans – architects, surveyors, planning consultants and the like – may make it financially prudent to go for outline consent first.

Although it is up to the local planning authority to decide planning applications, there is a duty to consult with various bodies if appropriate. For example, if an application affects trunk roads, the authority must consult with the Secretary of State. In certain cases, where there may be an impact on the physical environment, it must carry out an Environmental Impact

Assessment. This requirement was brought in to comply with European Community directives. Examples of applications requiring this are holiday villages and industrial estates. HM Inspectorate of Pollution must be consulted where poultry- or pig-rearing are proposed.

Generally, planning authorities must have regard to the details of the Local Plan when making their decision, and are not allowed to depart radically from it. This presumption in favour of the Local Plan rather than the developer was strengthened as a result of the 1991 Act. Departures have to be publicised, and in some cases the Secretary of State must be notified. It is therefore essential that housing developers have a good detailed awareness of the content of the housing and related chapters of the local plan, especially if they are proposing something on the edge of acceptability.

The decision may be one of three: unconditional permission; Conditional permission; or Refusal (s. 70 of the 1990 Act). It is a deemed condition that the development should commence within 5 years of grant; and applicants must be notified of the decision within 8 weeks of submission. Conditional permission is common in sensitive areas: landscaping may be required, or design modifications, so that the development fits in with whatever is already there. Permission to develop comes about only when the applicant is notified.

Appeals against the decision can be made only by the applicant, and are made to the Secretary of State within 6 calendar months of the authority's decision. There is an opportunity to appeal in front of a planning inspector; the appeal may take the form of a public local inquiry. The inspector's decision is usually regarded as final, although there is a further opportunity to appeal on matters of law to the High Court.

If developments are of a large-scale nature (for example, the proposal to develop a private new town or an airport), the 1990 Act provides that a Planning Inquiry Commission is to be set up, which investigates relevant issues and presents the matter to the Secretary of State for decision, as if he or she were the planning authority.

Once planning permission has been granted, it applies to the land for 5 years, regardless of ownership, and can enhance the value of land, although the subsequent development must follow the detail of the consent. However, in the case of grant of planning permission to a council, consent is personal to the authority.

Prior to planning regulations issued in 1992, it used to be relatively straightforward for a council to obtain planning permission for its own developments, but the effect of the regulations has been to make the whole process more open. It may seem odd that local planning authorities are both developer and adjudicator, but the alternative would be for a completely independent body to make a judgement. As long as the authority is seen to comply with the letter and spirit of its own development plan, there is no reason why one should be suspicious of such procedures, as long as they are open – and the regulations ensure this. In essence, councils are required to submit their proposals to the planning office like any other applicant, and must publicise their proposals. The application must not be decided by the officer, subcommittee or committee responsible for the management of land and buildings covered by the planning application. Planning permission granted by the council to itself cannot pass on to subsequent owners, for example a transfer association; and the Secretary of State must be notified in cases where local authority development proposals depart from the Local Plan. These rules apply not only to the local authority's own development, but also to joint housing association–council ventures, for example where a local authority supplies cheap or free land.

6.2.3   Planning obligation

Land costs are often a major capital element in the development of housing schemes. Typically such costs account for around one-third of total costs; therefore anything which can reduce these is welcome. If a council sells land cheaply to a housing association, the discount is treated as public subsidy, and deducted from HAG to ensure that total public subsidy does not exceed the appropriate grant percentage. This requirement can be waived only in return for substantial nomination rights. Such practices can also affect the local authority's spending power: credit approvals to the value of the discount can be effectively frozen, under s. 61 of the Local Government and Housing Act. This would effectively prevent them from borrowing the equivalent amount; that is, unless substantial nomination rights are granted. On the other hand, such rights may not matter, in these days of common waiting lists.

Another way of securing cheap or free land for social housing is to use planning powers known as planning obligation. Put crudely, this entails a local planning authority negotiating with a private developer for some gain, as described, in return for the grant of planning permission which might not normally be given, owing to the fact that a scheme might depart slightly from the spirit of the plan. For example, it might entail a change of use which the authority can legitimately refuse, or be at slightly higher density than normally allowed. This gain for the community can only be passed to a third party, for example a housing association. Prior to the 1991 Act it was known as 'planning gain', and was introduced as s. 52 of the 1971 Town and Country Planning Act. It is now to be found in s. 106 of the 1990 Town and Country Planning Act as amended by s. 12 of the Planning and Compensation Act.

Under section 106, anyone with an interest in a piece of land (practically speaking, developers) may enter into a planning obligation (agreement to do something in relation to a grant of planning permission on the land) either via an agreement with the local planning authority, or as a 'unilateral undertaking'. That is, a developer can present the planning authority with a proposal to offer some benefit to a third party in connection with the application, without first entering into negotiations. Prior to the amendment, it was up to the council to commence negotiations to secure 'planning gain'.

In a sense, planning obligation deals can be seen as profit-sharing deals which benefit the community. It may well pay developers to enter into such agreements: the cost of appeal against refusal of permission, and delays in commencing work and selling or leasing properties on the site, may well eat into profit margins. It would be wrong to see planning obligation as a kind of bribe for the grant of permission: a scheme which in no way conformed with the spirit of the local plan would not be passed anyway, even if planning obligation was in issue. It should be seen as an opportunity for local authorities to obtain community benefits in return for granting permission in marginal cases.

Although the main form of planning obligation is in the form of free or cheap land or housing passed to a third party, the agreement can also be to restrict the development or use of land in a specified way, or to require certain operations to be carried out in, on, over or under the land (example: a bus waiting area as part of a shopping scheme), and may even take the form of a sum or sums of money to be paid to the local authority on a specified date or dates, although such payments are subject to strict regulation. However, it is the possibility of land or buildings being passed to housing associations which concerns us.

A planning obligation is enforceable not only against the developer who entered into it, but also against others to whom the land might subsequently be sold, although it may be made personal to the developer who entered into it by agreement. The agreement has the status of a local land charge. The obligation may be modified or set aside by agreement. Five years after it has been entered into, if nothing has happened, the developer (or successor) has the right to appeal to the planning authority for it to be modified or discharged. If the planning authority refuses to modify it, the developer can then appeal to the Secretary of State, whose decision is final. In practice, planning obligations are cumbersome and can be long-winded, but have generated social housing gains.

An example of planning obligation is given in an article at the end of this chapter, 'Housing gain for the community' (p. 224), where the developers of a creekside site agreed to provide social housing on part of the land in return for enhanced planning permission. It illustrates the necessity for planning and housing departments to work closely together to maximise the production of social housing at arm's length.

6.2.4 Enforcement

Enforcement is required to deal with cases where development is carried out without planning permission, or in breach of conditions and limitations: and the enforcement powers of local planning authorities were strengthened considerably by the 1991 Act. There are various methods of enforcing planning law, ranging from acceptance, if the development conforms to the local plan, to ordering it to stop, or even demolition.

The mildest form of action is the issue of a Planning Contravention

Notice, which enables the authority to obtain information about the suspected breach, and invite the recipient to discuss the matter with either officers or council members. New planning permission can be applied for, an offer to modify the scheme can be made, or other appropriate action taken. If the terms of such a Notice are not complied with, a fine may be levied.

Breach of Conditions notices are issued when the conditions applying to planning consent have not been observed, and again fines may be levied.

The Enforcement Notice is the basic tool, and is applicable either where a development has been carried out without planning permission, or where a condition or limitation applying to it has not been observed. Before issuing such notices, the authority must consider whether it would have granted consent if permission had been applied for, and that entails referral to the development plan. There are time limits after which enforcement action cannot be taken. In the case of building, engineering or mining, the limit takes effect where 4 years have elapsed since the development; similarly where there has been a change of use of a building to a dwelling house. Any other breach has a 10-year time limit. In appropriate circumstances, the authority will issue such a notice not only on the owner, but on the occupier and anyone else with a material interest in the land. Fairly obviously, the end result may be that somebody loses their home, and it is reasonable for notice to be given of this. The notice must say what the breach is, what steps must be taken to restore the situation, the date of effect of the notice, a period for compliance, the reason for issuing the notice, and the boundaries of the land to which the notice relates. Prior to modification by the 1991 Act, the notice was void if the authority omitted some of the details specified, but now it is enough that the recipient knows what the situation is: formal accuracy is no longer of the essence.

If the planning authority considers that the development would have been granted permission if applied for, it can issue a Certificate of Lawful Development, which will fend off any enforcement action. There is a right of appeal against enforcement action to the Secretary of State, who may uphold, quash or vary it.

Finally, a planning authority may issue a Stop Notice, but only after having issued an Enforcement Notice. The effect of this is to prohibit the carrying out of an unauthorised activity (for example, use as a caravan site), but only where the use has been carried out for less than 4 years. In the case of caravan sites, it used to be the case that such notices could not be used where the caravan was a person's main or only home, but this has now been set aside. The notice comes into effect immediately, and non-compliance is punishable by a daily fine. The consequences of this are considerable, especially as local authorities now no longer have a duty to provide caravan sites for Gypsies or travellers, and there are bound to be increases in such unauthorised activity. The effect of this, and enhanced powers to remove unauthorised occupants of land and premises under the Criminal Justice Act, has been to increase homelessness amongst certain groups. However, there has to be some way of enforcing planning controls, otherwise unsatisfactory developments would threaten the built and natural environment without redress.

Given the importance and scope of planning regulations, it is essential that social housing developers have preliminary meetings with planning officials, as well as a thorough knowledge of development plans, before working up schemes. It is also important that such organisations take part in the public consultation stages of development plan formulation, especially in the writing of the housing chapter, and as potential recipients of planning obligation land and housing. Use of the planning system is a principal way in which local authorities can enable social housing, and such powers should be used to the full, in partnership with developers.

It is clear that some reforms may be desirable. There is scope for a regional overview of planning issues, perhaps through the revitalisation of Regional Planning Authorities, as many developments, for example that of hypermarkets, have a significance which transcends county boundaries. Such bodies could also act as quality controllers of Local Plans to ensure some consistency, strengthening the existing requirement to conform with Structure Plans, especially where the authority is a unitary council. In housing terms, the existence of a regional dimension would allow the analysis of the effects of inter- and intraregional migration and economic development on housing policies in a more formal manner than at present. If such bodies were made up of local authority representatives, it would strengthen rather than diminish local democracy, through sharing of information and views. The last thing that is needed is another quango, which would simply reinforce the government line. Local people have to live with developments on their doorstep, and so it should be their representatives who determine the nature of development, albeit in a good-quality, consistent way.

In terms of planning permission, it would assist developers greatly, especially developers of social housing, if planning authorities were required to publish examples of acceptable types of scheme, rather than rely on the interpretation of myriad regulations. This not only would help associations, but would help the public consultation process during the process of revising the Local Plan. And Local Plans should be written in plain language to assist comprehension, for the same reasons. Much more exciting and interesting publicity needs to be given to applications, so that local interest is generated. Once a development has been completed, it is far too late. The whole planning obligation process should be simplified, both in detail and timescale. It is at present inordinately cumbersome, and insufficiently used. There is also no reason, apart from ideology, why local authorities should not be direct recipients of gains through the process; after all, they act as arbitrators on their own developments, and as long as the process is subject to public scrutiny, there is no good reason why the stock of council homes should not be increased on the back of a retail development.

6.3   Development

6.3.1   Overview: partnerships

Housing development includes the creation of new homes by construction or conversion and the renovation of old stock. It is a crucial activity of social housing organisations, but sadly has been underfunded for some years now. There are vastly more households in need of decent accommodation than there are suitable homes available, as evidenced by homelessness.

The main players are housing associations, although they could not effectively operate unless in partnership with local authorities. It is salutary, therefore, to start this brief consideration by considering the ways in which associations and councils can work together in providing social housing.

6.3.1.1   Money

Local Authority Housing Association Grant (LA HAG) is a significant source of capital for housing association development, both for rent and for sale. It is available to registered housing associations, and is derived initially from capital receipts or basic credit approvals. On payment to the housing association, the Housing Corporation reimburses the council; thus the only costs are staff time in working up assistance, and financial arrangement fees. Naturally, the authority cannot borrow against approvals used in this way to undertake its own work, and any monies received from the Corporation have to be used to repay debt. On the other hand, assistance of this sort makes sense. Not only is it evidence of local authorities working in their enabling role, but, as the grant is normally less than 100 per cent of capital costs, more properties can be developed than could be by the council itself. The average grant rate in recent years has fallen to around 50 per cent of qualifying costs; this means that, roughly speaking, the council can facilitate two homes for the cost of one.

Schemes supported by LA HAG usually attract nomination rights for the funder. Although only registered associations can obtain such capital support, smaller sums can be advanced to non-registered associations through s. 74 of the 1988 Local Government Act. Councils can also give valuable revenue support, although not necessarily through housing budgets. For example, social services can part-fund the running costs of special needs schemes with a care element, on the basis that they would have had to supply the facility themselves under other circumstances. This is especially relevant under the Care in the Community regime.

Housing benefit is an important source of revenue to associations, as an increasing percentage of new tenants are dependent upon it. Many associations attempt to secure housing benefit direct rather than relying on tenants to pay the rent to guarantee cash-flows, increasingly important as lenders look to income streams rather than assets when making loans. Effective use of housing benefit relies upon good liaison mechanisms.

6.3.1.2   Site

The cost of land can amount to up to one-third of scheme development costs; thus the availability of cheap or free land is a definite asset. Local authorities are such a source, although care must be taken in utilising this resource, as there are financial implications for both council and association. As a general rule, councils are supposed to obtain best consideration for their assets, although sales under the Right to Buy are a clear legislative exception. Sales of land at under value run counter to this. First, it is generally necessary to obtain the Secretary of State's consent to such disposals, except in the case of land for low-cost home ownership, where a general consent operates. Then, the discount is treated as if it were a capital grant: its value is deducted from any HAG payable under the scheme, in all cases but ownership schemes. Additionally, an amount equivalent to the discount is excluded from spending permission under the rules governing basic credit approvals. This latter feature, instituted under s. 61 of the 1989 Local Government and Housing Act can be avoided only if the council secures generous nomination rights to the scheme. If 100 per cent, then there is no restriction on expenditure, and so on, on a *pro rata* basis. However, the Housing Corporation frowns upon very high nomination rights, as associations are supposed to be independent of local authorities – this is a condition of registration – and so 100 per cent rights are comparatively rare, except on first lettings.

In addition to providing cheap or free land from its own resources, it can facilitate it from private developers through the medium of planning obligation (s. 106 of the Town and Country Planning Act), as already described. This method has the advantage that it does not entail grant rate reductions or expenditure restrictions on local authorities, although such negotiations can be cumbersome and long-winded, and work well only where there is a market for development. They are most effective where a developer applies for change of use, as local planning authorities have greater power in this area.

6.3.1.3   Planning

In addition to the above, it must be remembered that local authorities are also planning authorities. The issue was discussed more fully in the preceding section: but associations and councils must work closely together here to make the most of the system. A major opportunity is provided in the current PPG3, *Land for Housing*, which makes the provision of affordable housing a material planning consideration. There is every reason why associations should be consulted at the Local Plan formulation stages to ensure that this opportunity is maximised, and that they are involved in evaluating their potential contribution on a site-by-site basis as applications are tendered.

6.3.1.4 Process

The construction process involves the local authority through building control: officers from this department will inspect works at various stages including prior to covering of foundations, when the substructure has been erected, and on practical completion, to ensure that works have been completed to a sound and satisfactory standard. Additionally, periodic inspections of the site will be made to ensure that health and safety rules are being observed. On completion, planning officials will check to ensure that the conditions of permission have been observed, and undertake any necessary enforcement action.

6.3.1.5 After construction

The issue of nominations has already been raised. Additionally, referrals might be made to schemes. These do not in themselves guarantee assistance: and such referrals may be made from a diverse group of agencies, for example, citizens' advice bureaux, housing aid centres and the like. Common waiting lists make it most likely that those in greatest need will be assisted, whatever the route of application. Additionally, joint management arrangements are fruitful examples of local authority–association partnerships. The 1989 Children Act duties of council social services departments have already been discussed in the Chapter 3. It is hard to see how social services departments can discharge their duties unless by working closely with housing associations that make special provision for this group, and it seems natural that there should be some social services staff and management input here.

This brief consideration shows how profitable co-operation can be, and the interdependence of associations and councils. One of the reasons that many associations have expressed reluctance in competing with councils in compulsory competitive tendering (CCT) is that they are natural partners, and competition may spoil this relationship.

6.3.2 Development of housing programmes

The term 'programme' is taken to mean a collection of schemes, to be undertaken over a specific period. Major considerations in preparing a housebuilding and improvement programme include the following:

- length and size of the programme;
- availability of resources;
- prioritisation between new-build and improvement.

6.3.2.1 Length and size of programme

The programme should correlate with projected financial resources. The use of information technology, especially spreadsheets, is of significance here. One problem is that budgets are usually certain only over 1 year, and schemes may take longer than this to develop. There are usually a number of imponderables, such as the availability of capital receipts from sales, and that of earmarked funding (for example, from the Single Regeneration Budget). The programme should be flexible enough to respond to policy changes at central and local government levels. This is often easier said than done, as changes in council composition can bring major reorientations on matters of finance and development policy. Moratoria on spending have frequently been forced by cash crises caused in part by building costs inflation and calls on capital for other purposes, as well as by determinations by Secretaries of State – for example, when leases of over 3 years were deemed to incur capital expenditure up to the market value of the property, in the late 1980s. It is difficult to see how any medium term programme can survive such uncertainty.

For a local authority, the programme should be designed to meet predetermined housing needs, as signalled in the Housing Strategy and Investment Programme document. For a housing association, it should be designed in relation to the Housing Corporation region's strategy statement, as mediated by the aims and objectives of the organisation. It is essential that the programme can be sustained by an adequate supply of land. This may well entail deals with other organisations, such as councils or farmers, and definitely involves close working with planning.

The development programme should also be sustainable in revenue terms: all development incurs management and maintenance costs, and these must be borne in mind, as they will affect rent-setting policy and so affordability. Notoriously, some schemes entail higher costs than others because of the nature of the client group: for example, clustered units for elderly people, requiring more intensive management than general needs stock, perhaps the presence of a warden or care workers. Hostels require more intensive management owing to high client turnover; and some structures seem to attract more than their fair share of revenue costs, for example blocks of high-rise flats, where lift maintenance and communal area decoration are perennial issues, along with security installations including concierges in some cases. To summarise, finance, land and labour costs should be key considerations in the planning of capital programmes.

6.3.2.2 Availability of resources: development programmes as part of capital programmes

It should be remembered that the development programme does not constitute the entire capital programme, although it may be a major element, both for housing associations and local authorities. As well as ensuring that

Fig. 6.1 Refurbished system-built house, Swansea

there is a balance between new-build and renovation schemes, it is essential to balance the total programme against other requirements such as portable discount schemes, using capital to undertake major repairs, loans and grants to other housing bodies, moneys held in reserve, and so forth. Allowance must be made to continue to finance schemes which have slipped into the current financial year from the previous one, as well as plans made for slippage into the next year. Bodies should attempt to ensure that 'committed' schemes are given priority.

In the context of development, commitment can mean a number of things. There is contractual commitment: where the body has signed a contract with a developer to undertake a project, and where pulling out might lead to severe legal costs. This is sometimes unavoidable, and perhaps contingency funds should be established to insure against such an eventuality, given the relatively short-term nature of capital planning both in the housing association and the local authority context. There is the commitment given by the governing body to go ahead with a scheme, exemplified by a committee decision to undertake development to meet a specified need. The cost of abandoning such schemes may well be considerable loss of goodwill amongst those standing in need of housing in the local area, as well as a loss of credibility generally. Many local authorities earmark funds from projected budgets on a points system, with those scoring highest getting priority for funding should that money become available.

Land is a crucial resource. Much has already been said about the use of planning obligation, use of cheap or free council land and PPG3. In general, the number of sites should be sufficient to meet predetermined needs over a rolling timescale, say 5 years (as recommended in a previous PPG3). Land audits should be regularly carried out by councils: a local authority

Fig. 6.2 Access to service vehicles must be provided

should certainly know which parcels it owns, which committee controls it, what the designated land use is, how large the site is, its current value, and any conditions which might complicate development (for example, its geological structure, what lies beneath the land, the nature and extent of any contamination, topographical features, conservation considerations, and availability of services to or near the site).

6.3.2.3 Prioritisation between new-build and improvement

A number of factors affect the issue of prioritisation between new-build and improvement, including the current condition and estimated life of existing stock, and demand for new housing. Some estates, especially those built before the 1970s, may now be in need of major renovation, which may well impinge upon the size of any new-build programme. For housing asso-

Fig. 6.3 Traditional house types with easy access to cars are preferred

Fig. 6.4 Flats need not be monoliths

Fig. 6.5 The depressed state of the housing sales market in the 1990s provided acquisition opportunities for housing associations

ciations, the relative Total Cost Indicators (TCIs) and grant rates will also play a major part. Sometimes, this decision is affected by unexpected events: for example, the extent to which some sorts of steel-framed concrete houses had deteriorated was realised only in the early to mid 1980s: awareness of this was sudden, and capital programmes had to be adjusted to cope with renovation or demolition demands.

The demand for new housing units may be fulfilled both by new-build and conversion of existing large dwellings, and by the rehabilitation of void dwellings. Following the abolition of the Greater London Council in 1986, the successor body, the London Residuary Body, transferred significant amounts of stock across to London boroughs. In Southwark's case, over 30 000 properties were so transferred, many of which were void and in poor repair, but potentially usable. Much capital was diverted to their renovation both directly and indirectly, through use of housing associations. This scheme is discussed in detail in an article at the end of this chapter, 'Short-

Fig. 6.6 Homes should be adequately screened from major roads

life: the logic of necessity' (p. 222). The availability of land for new development will clearly help condition the balance between new-build and renovation or conversion.

It should be remembered that D.o.E.-granted credit approvals can influence the balance of programmes for local authorities. Much credit approval is allocated in the form of Single Regeneration Budget-related schemes such as Estates Action, which is primarily directed towards renovation. This is not surprising, as housing associations are regarded as the prime agent for the creation of new social housing.

6.3.3 Key stages of development

Development should be a systematic process, proceeding logically from idea to completion. The fine details depend upon which organisation is developing, but the basic format remains the same. Brief descriptions of key stages, and important questions, are given below.

6.3.3.1 The idea

What needs are to be addressed? What is the guidance from funding or other influential or regulatory institutions. For private developers, what is the state of the housing market both nationally and locally?

6.3.3.2 Site identification

How large a site is needed? What is available? What do available sites offer in terms of use, class, location, value, etc? What is the competition likely to be for the site? Can it be afforded, and, if so, what influence will it have upon the out-turn cost of the development, and therefore rents or sale prices? Can the developer obtain a site through planning obligation: is the council prepared to sell land cheap or at no cost?

6.3.3.3 Feasibility

How many units, and of what type, can be fitted on the site? What would be the approximate capital and revenue costs of alternative strategies? What basic designs will be used, given the nature of the site and client group? Will outline planning permission be granted?

6.3.3.4 Funding

Where will the money come from? What are the sources for capital and revenue aspects? Is there a special pot of money or specific borrowing permission available for this type of scheme? Will rents or sale prices be affordable, and if not is there the possibility of cross-subsidy, or alternative sources of help? Does the scheme satisfy the funder's requirements? What are the strings attached? When will the funding become available? What is the mix of grant and loan, if applicable?

6.3.3.5 Land acquisition

Now that it is known that the local planning authority will agree to the proposed scheme in outline, it may be prudent to buy the land, or at least commence negotiations for it. Lawyers should be instructed, a formal valuation performed, and the title deeds to the land examined for restrictive covenants or any other conditions pertaining to the land. This stage should include a detailed survey of the land, although the land should have been scrutinised in some detail at site identification stage.

6.3.3.6 Detailed design and full planning permission

Design and build (that is, a package deal offered by a developer) or in-house/commissioned design? Should an in-house or external design team be used? What are the appropriate design standards? Can Parker Morris (p. 204) be used without exceeding cost limits, and, if not, what are the minimum design requirements which can be accepted? What is Housing Corporation or D.o.E. guidance saying about this type of dwelling? What does the local plan say about design and density standards? If the dwellings are designed for special needs groups, should they be designed to meet full wheelchair or mobility standards? What about any landscaping issues, parking provision, roads, paths, communal facilities, playgrounds, security considerations, shielding from noise or danger, etc.?

Will the completed design obtain full planning consent? Having been to the planning committee, can the developer live with the conditions (if any) attached to the consent? What modifications are necessary to satisfy the planning committee?

6.3.3.7   Development schedule

There are various considerations. Which contract to use? Formation of the development team. Selection of contractors, subcontractors, clerk of works, and other key personnel. Architect briefed to steer the development as the agent of the employer. Target times for completion of key tasks devised, for example exchange of contracts, start on site, practical completion, projected handover date, and tied in with dates for certificated payments to the contractor. This is crucial, as overruns may be expensive in terms of development loan servicing: delays may be remedied by legal action in extreme cases, although the formation and monitoring of a viable development team should obviate this.

6.3.3.8   Monitoring of contract

Monitoring of the contract is essential for reasons already stated. At various stages, building control will want to examine the progress of works, to ensure that health and safety considerations are observed, and that the structural aspects are properly performed. Payments must accord with the dates stated in the contract, unless there are good reasons for delay. There is need for the employer to liaise with the contractor via its agent (Architect) and the Clerk of Works.

6.3.3.9   Handover and allocations

The final payments and final reconciliations are made. Effective use is made of the defects liability period after practical completion to identify any faults in the dwellings for which the contractor is liable. How are the units to be allocated? This will depend upon the priority system in use: most social housing organisations will use some form of points system to determine eligibility. Is pre-viewing by prospective tenants possible? Is it possible to make any customised alterations to suit the needs of the specific tenant (for example, stair-lifts, flexible sink units, long-handled taps)? A tenant satisfaction survey should be initiated after a reasonable time of residence, say 6 months, to learn from any mistakes in design, and to note good points which can be replicated in further schemes. The issue of possible tenant involvement in the management of dwellings might be addressed at this point.

6.3.4   Development issues specific to housing associations

Housing association development planning is structured in the way described above. There are, however, specific financial issues which impinge upon the process of feasibility assessment. Some of these points have been made earlier, but the following gives an overview.

At the heart of the feasibility study is the assessment of capital and revenue funding. Most associations use a National Federation of Housing Associations computer package called PAMKIT to assess the development costs, and to work out rough rental figures, for their schemes. This is a database-based package. They also use REVKIT to work out different loan schedules and detailed rents. These programmes can be updated with regulation changes and annually according to new TCI and HAG rates. A further package called SALEKIT is also available to work out the details of low-cost home ownership schemes.

Housing association development has, as emphasised previously, become more onerous during the 1990s because of reducing grant rates, and an article at the end of this chapter, 'The end of housing association development?' (p. 226), explores the causes of this situation, and suggests that some associations have cut standards too drastically in order to maximise the number of properties they produce, to stay in the development arena. It is suggested that associations must do more to lobby government to increase grant rates to secure affordable homes without excessive reliance upon housing benefit. At the time of writing, the White Paper proposal to limit new housing association property rent rises to Retail Price Index plus (or minus) X per cent – the so-called X factor – amounts to suggestions of rent control, or limitation. If so, it must follow that grant rates will have to be adjusted, perhaps upwards, to ensure that rents fall within prescribed limits. The only alternatives would appear to be drastic cuts in management budgets, or further expeditions towards cheapest building contracts, which could spell disaster for living conditions and service delivery, and deliver the slums of tomorrow. This would be a poor legacy for the future, as well as doing little or nothing to meet housing need in a quality manner.

What follows is an attempt to explain in simple terms the stages of costs assessment for non-programme associations.

1. *Determine site size, cost and density limits*. This is important, since all local planning authorities specify maximum development densities, for example, in terms of habitable rooms per hectare or acre (1 hectare is 2.471 acres; 1 acre is 0.4046 hectares): for example, 75 habitable rooms per hectare. A habitable room is a room which can be used to live in, and is subject to minimum space and other standards. Basically, bedrooms, discrete dining rooms and lounges count; bathrooms, toilets, halls and kitchens do not. So a typical three-bedroom semi-detached house with two reception rooms could be described as having five habitable rooms. As well as determining square meterage, it is important at this stage to estimate how many people will be housed in each dwelling, as this affects the assessment of cost limits (TCIs) later in the process. Density limits will determine the number and type of dwellings which can be placed on a site. Site cost will be determined by comparing that

site with similar ones, or by assessing the asking price in relation to an independent valuation. When the square area to be occupied by each dwelling has been determined, land cost per dwelling can be estimated; or such costs can be allocated equally, or in proportion to number of habitable rooms. Planning authorities may be prepared to be flexible over densities which slightly exceed those stated in the development plan, provided they are convinced that design is good, and that a contribution is being made to meeting housing needs.

2. *Determine construction costs.* This can be done by using a quantity surveyor or by discussion with a building contractor; or on the basis of similar scheme costs as experienced by the organisation on other schemes, or other bodies. Oncosts (fees, etc.) should also be estimated at this stage.

3. *Add land, construction and oncosts together to determine total qualifying costs.* This is the estimated total cost of the scheme, which will qualify for grant.

4. *Estimate cost limits for the scheme.* This is crucial. HAG is generally either the appropriate percentage of total qualifying costs, if such costs are at or under cost limits (known as Total Cost Indicators or TCIs) or the appropriate percentage of TCI, if qualifying costs are higher, subject to tolerances which change periodically. If estimated scheme costs exceed TCI by more than 130 per cent, non-programme schemes may not get Housing Corporation approval in any case. It is obviously important to attempt to stay within cost limits, since the greater the gap between HAG and total development costs, the larger the private loan, and hence the higher the rents, unless some way can be found to cross-subsidise the scheme.

TCI tables are issued annually by the Housing Corporation. The procedure involves selecting the base TCI for the right type of scheme and the right TCI Area. England is divided into seven areas which represent different building cost areas, as TCIs are supposed to represent the average cost of building dwellings in the private sector. Most of London is in TCI Area A, the highest band. The base TCI varies with square meterage, bedroom number and occupancy. This TCI is then modified by applying a key multiplier, which varies depending upon the nature of the scheme. For example, Acquisition and Development schemes, where land is bought and properties built on it, have a key multiplier of 1; 'works only' schemes have a lower multiplier. Effectively, then, TCIs are based on new-build acquisition and development schemes, and multipliers are used to vary this base figure in recognition of the different costs of other forms of development. This modified TCI is then changed again, in the case of special needs-type properties, by applying a supplementary multiplier, which is supposed to increase the cost limit in relation to the cost of specialist features: for example, mobility or wheelchair design aspects, which may increase the cost of a scheme. Eventually, the TCI (cost limit) is determined for each unit.

5. *Compare total qualifying costs with TCI.* This is important for reasons already stated. If estimated costs are far above TCIs, now is the time to attempt to shave costs if at all possible. Care should be taken not to compromise quality – although affordability must be a major consideration. The reconciliation of these two has proved difficult for many associations.

6. *Estimate housing association grant.* Around autumn, the Corporation publishes HAG rates for the coming year for the guidance of associations, at about the same time it publishes TCI tables. The grant rate is expressed as a percentage of total qualifying costs, or TCI, whichever is lower, and varies according to scheme type and TCI area. The appropriate rate is determined by inspection. One scheme might comprise several property types, so it could take a while to assess grant rates for the entire scheme; but the aggregate grant is important in determining the size of the development loan, and therefore rents. The difference between total HAG and either TCI or total estimated qualifying costs is the amount which will have to be raised. In most cases, the grant rate will be substantially below total costs: in 1995/96, the average HAG rate for general needs schemes was around 58 per cent. Only special needs schemes attract rates of 100 per cent, and also revenue subsidy known as Special Needs Management Allowance (SNMA). It is clearly in the interests of the association to minimise the gap between HAG and costs.

   For-sale schemes attract grant on the difference between the initial equity purchased and the development costs; otherwise the procedure is similar for the determination of grants for rental schemes.

7. *Estimate loan finance requirement, and investigate different forms of loan.* As already discussed in Chapter 2, loans can be raised in different ways. The Housing Corporation used to assume that associations would use low-start finance, but there has been a reluctance to use this, because it commits the association to raise rents according to a schedule dictated by the form of loan, and may be difficult to justify to tenants, or on affordability grounds. Most associations schemes must use private loans: these are the so-called mixed funded schemes, as they combine private loans with public grants. REVKIT can be used to simulate loan schedules.

8. *Estimate revenue costs and reconcile these with rent policy and affordability criteria.* Rents have to cover loan charges, management and maintenance costs, voids and repairs sinking fund. These figures must be determined. Each association has its own method of assessing management and maintenance costs, based upon experience and policy, although the Housing Corporation publishes 'management and maintenance allowance' figures annually, which are intended primarily as assumptions used when working out typical HAG rates, but are also used as measures against which real rents can be compared. Ideal figures are also

given for repairs sinking fund estimates: in 1992/93, these were estimated at 0.8 per cent of project costs. Again, much will depend upon the design of dwellings, and experience. The same goes for void estimates, although anything much below 2 per cent would be hard to sustain. It is better to overestimate rather than underestimate costs at this stage, so that realistic rents can be assessed.

The resulting rents can then be compared with the rents which the association would ideally charge, in the light of its rents policy, based on notions of affordability. Some associations refer to affordability tables published annually by the National Federation of Housing Associations to calibrate their policies, although clearly they have to balance their books. It is not in the interests of associations to set very high rents, because that would not only restrict the type of clients who can be housed, but also engender benefit dependency by placing people in a poverty trap, preventing them from getting work. By the same token, associations have to make up their own minds as to the policy they will adopt in the light of affordability but also financial management considerations.

Rents having been determined, decisions can be taken as to the viability of the scheme as it stands. Perhaps rents can be reduced by reducing capital costs: perhaps cross-subsidy, say from surpluses generated from the proceeds of for-sale schemes or rent surpluses from other schemes, can bring rents down. Perhaps revenue costs can be reduced by lessening staff : tenant ratios, reducing maintenance, or some other device. It may be possible to apply the proceeds from semi-commercial ventures, for example takings from charity shops or management charges for services rendered to clients (e.g. management fees from Housing Association as Management Agent or Private Sector Leasing schemes), to the scheme. It may be that the scheme cannot produce affordable rents, and therefore a radical rethink has to take place, or the scheme may be scrapped entirely.

Ultimately, the decision to proceed or not must rest with the committee, and may be dictated by the Housing Corporation. The complexity of financial assessment makes it unrealistic to reach such a decision without the use of information technology.

6.4   Design matters

Design is a specialist area which cannot be left to the specialists, as has been demonstrated time and time again in the residential sector. Leaving design to the 'experts' resulted in tower blocks and faceless estates. Design, like fashion, varies with culture both spatially and temporally, and it is difficult to agree on what good design standards should be. To say that a well-designed home should be fit for its purpose and good to look at sounds right, but it is rather too simplistic to constitute a full policy.

Design issues centre around the interior and exterior of individual dwellings and their adequacy to meet the needs of those for whom they are intended, their relationship to one another, and the environment in which they are set. Over the years, there has been plenty of guidance over what constitutes good design in all these respects, and views have changed quite radically, sometimes driven by changing aesthetic fashions, sometimes by the adverse reactions of users, at other times motivated by financial restriction, and occasionally for no good or discernible reason whatever. It is the purpose of this section to examine some key recommendations which have been applied to social housing.

6.4.1   Parker Morris: 'Homes for today and tomorrow'

The Parker Morris committee was appointed by the Central Housing Advisory Committee to consider designs for family dwellings whether built by the private or the public sector, and to recommend standards. Its report, *Homes for today and tomorrow*, was published in 1961. Although much of its text appears rather dated to modern eyes, its methodology is sound, and the design standards which it recommended are generous by today's standards. It was one of the first reports to look at lifestyles and the way they determine accommodation use. It is perhaps best known for its space standard recommendation, although its significance is greater than this.

Recommendations included:

- improved access to terraced accommodation;

- two lifts in blocks of flats over six storeys;

- the need to preserve privacy for individuals and groups.

It also contained a series of safety recommendations including the sequencing of kitchen equipment, which is followed universally in good design today, segregating incompatible uses by worksurfaces. A typical sequence would therefore be: cooker/worksurface/fridge/worksurface/sink/worksurface. It recommended that bathrooms have non-slip floors. There were other safety points regarding the height of risers and the width of stair treads, lighting and especial attention to safe windows which could be cleaned from the inside in multi-storey buildings.

Floorspace recommendations were far in excess of those of previous reports: it was suggested that a five-person terrace house should be of at least 910 square feet, with 50 square feet of storage; houses for similar occupancy prior to that were typically 60 square feet smaller, including storage. The table of sizes is reproduced in Table 6.1.

Table 6.1 Parker Morris floorspace and general storage space recommendations (sq. feet)

Type of house	No. of people					
	6	5	4	3	2	1
Floorspace						
Three-storey house	1050	1010	–	–	–	–
Two-storey terrace	990	910	800	–	–	–
Two-storey semi or end	990	880	770	–	–	–
Maisonette	990	880	770	–	–	–
Flat	930	850	750	610	480	320
Single-storey house	900	810	720	610	480	320
General storage						
Houses	50	50	50	50	50	50
Flats/maisonettes: inside	15	15	15	12	10	8
outside	20	20	20	20	20	20

Source: *Ministry of Housing and Local Government (1961)*

These standards were more or less reproduced in the Institute of Housing/Royal Institute of British Architects (RIBA) recommendations, *Homes for the future*, in 1983. The report considered storage not just in volume terms, but in location, based upon tenants surveys.

The report's recommendations continue in many respects to be valid. A theme of the relationship between rooms runs through the report, in terms of family use. Two distinct reception rooms are recommended, so that different pursuits can be carried on by distinct groups in the family; and recommendations which have long been accepted as essential, such as that there should be access to the toilet from all bedrooms without passing through any, and that washing facilities should be immediately adjacent to the toilet, were made.

Until the late 1970s, councils followed Parker Morris standards, as subsidy was denied if they were not met, and some excellent building was done, in terms of interior design, if not necessarily in appearance. From the late 1970s, these standards were all but abandoned, as subsidy no longer related to them, and standards started to fall once more.

6.4.2 'Homes for the future'

The report *Homes for the future* was intended to update Parker Morris in the light of current lifestyles, and in response to financial stringencies suffered by local authorities. It noted that demographic trends had changed since the 1960s, and that house design should reflect this, highlighting the growth in the number of smaller households due to the increase in divorce rates and the ageing of the population, but also increases in demand for social housing due to continued decline in the private rented sector which traditionally catered for such households. It also mentioned the need to cater for special needs groups, such as disabled persons, by sensitive design. The gaps in Parker Morris had to an extent been plugged by D.o.E. publications such as *Wheelchair Housing* and *Mobility Housing* in the mid-1970s. The report noted changes in lifestyles: for example, the growth and change in the nature of leisure pursuits, the rise in the number of appliances, especially in the kitchen, and the increased importance of energy conservation. Principal recommendations included the retention of Parker Morris space standards where possible, and that greater space to facilitate the plumbing in of washing machines, and installation of fridge freezers, should be made possible through the exclusion of built-in cupboards if space standards could not be increased. It was recommended that a separate utility room be provided to isolate vapour-producing activities likely to cause condensation, and that such a room should be provided with a window, to facilitate extension if necessary. Standards for disabled people are reiterated, as with the recommendation that minimum corridor-widths should be 900 mm with doorsets of the same width.

A very useful checklist of questions is provided, against which designs can be assessed. The questions include:

1. Does the plan meet changing demands? This is posed both in terms of different times of the day or week, and at various stages of the family life cycle.

2. Are the issues of privacy and quiet addressed?

3. Are the right spaces next to each other?

4. Is it possible to get from one room to another without embarrassment or inconvenience?

5. Is there adequate provision for entering, leaving and dealing with callers?

6. Does each room and space perform well in relation to lighting, aspect, prospect, heating arrangements, ventilation arrangements, sound insulation, and intended use?

The report, then, is a logical development of Parker Morris, and has been widely followed by social housing providers, although sizes have tended to decrease because of further problems with funding and land availability. From time to time, the D.o.E. and Housing Corporation issue design bulletins and circulars to guide development.

It would be a shame if cost constraints led to the diminution of new-build and conversion standards, not only for the comfort and convenience of today's owners and renters, but for that of succeeding generations. Past ages are often judged by the dwellings erected then: what will future generations make of the rabbit hutches that often pass for homes which are too often constructed against today's cost limits?

6.4.3   Estate design

Large new housing estates can be found on the edge of many towns and cities. Some are predominantly owner-occupier territory, others social housing areas. All have had their problems, and have been subject to recommendations over the years.

It is clearly very convenient to develop housing estates: it is possible to rationally plan dwelling mix, facilities such as retail, recreation, health and places of employment and even worship, and road layout for the convenience of residents, without trying to graft these on to an existing layout which may be inadequate, and where conflicts may arise, especially during the development period. Ideally, an estate should develop a sense of community amongst those living on it. This is the ideal, but experience has often shown a rather pessimistic alternative: witness the high crime rates, and levels of vandalism on many a soulless 1960s concrete estate in inner and outer cities. In many instances, this is because the scale of the development is too large, or because there is no or inadequate local management presence, or it could be that the estate suffers from excessive child densities or unemployment.

It is certain that design alone cannot explain rioting and other forms of unrest which have occurred on estates; nor can alienation or other problems associated with the absence of local management presence or concern, and perceived powerlessness and lack of ownership on the part of residents. Rather, both aspects need to be examined in tandem to ensure that such estates are decent places in which to live.

Many of the design principles found in today's estates had their origin in the Garden Cities movement of the late nineteenth and early twentieth centuries, given expression by Ebenezer Howard's experiment in combining the advantages of town and country at Letchworth, and successive settlements planned along similar lines such as Welwyn Garden City and Hampstead Garden Suburb. An emphasis on segregation of incompatible land uses, the rational planning of road layouts and care taken to define neighbourhoods have become accepted planning lore. New towns were designed along similar lines, albeit with less care taken over aesthetics and density, and many a private estate built in the post-war years on the edge of town, with its green verges, cottage-style or standard semi-detached villas, arcade of shops and recreation ground, attempts to reproduce the neighbourhood concept beloved of Howard and his followers.

Of particular importance is the concept of community. It is debatable as to whether this can be achieved by design, and there can be little doubt that good design is a necessary rather than a sufficient support to a viable community. What is known is that an absence of a coherent community – of *gemeinschaft* – can lead to dysfunctional behaviour. For example, an alienated group may display displeasure by causing social disturbances. It is likely that a development which is planned such that all have more or less equal access to essential facilities, such as health centres, shopping and public transport, as well as recreational facilities, will be a more pleasant place to live in than one where insufficient thought has been given to these factors, and will therefore give rise to a feeling of focus, of mutual benefit.

Design is not the end of the story in ensuring community solidarity. An article at the end of this chapter, 'Estate-based employment initiative' (p. 228), discusses a venture in North Kensington, London, between Kensington Housing Trust (a local housing association) the local authority and a further education college in providing work and construction training for unemployed people on the estate. Through such vocational initiatives, residents are given the power to enhance their own environment, and thus feel less alienated. Could this be part of the key towards community harmony and reductions in vandalism and other manifestations of dysfunctional community organisation?

The issue of crime, and attempts to design it out, must be considered. Most crime is opportunistic, and can be aided by poor design. For example, overhead walkways between blocks of flats, designed initially to segregate traffic from pedestrian flows, are havens for muggers, and offer ready escape routes for burglars. Underground car parks, which are often unsupervised and out of the public gaze, provide ample opportunity for car theft and related crimes, and personal attack. Communal entrances and lifts serving tower blocks are often unwatched, and are often the sites of vandalism and attack. Car-parking areas which are behind walls, or formed into a block in an area which is not overlooked, are obviously insecure. The list is potentially endless. Various police forces issue design advice through the services of their Architectural Liaison Officer, along the lines recommended in the publication *Secured by design*. The issue has also been addressed by Alice Coleman and the Priority Estate Project initiative, albeit from differing angles.

In relation to tower block security, many authorities now favour the concierge–CCTV (closed-circuit television) system. This can be expensive to install, but pays dividends in terms of decreased crime rates, as evidenced in the article about Glasgow at the end of the chapter (p. 221). Concierges are essentially officers who are stationed in offices at the entrance of blocks, and who get to know who lives there. Their duties vary with the organisation and situation concerned, but a common feature is that they are able to inform residents of intending callers, and let them through if the resident wishes. They can also take initial action in the event of vandalism or intrusion. Closed-circuit television allows the concierge to view common parts, including those above ground floor, and outside the entrance area, to detect vandalism or crime. Incidents can be recorded, and photographs are admissible as evidence in prosecutions. I visited the CCTV–concierge system installed at the Alma Road estate, owned by the London Borough of Enfield. The scheme was installed in response to high crime and vandalism rates in the four tower blocks which form the nucleus of the estate. Estates Action funding was secured to undertake the capital works, and the revenue costs are spread over all tenants in the borough. Lessee service charges are set to cover the proportion of the system used by each flat. Crime and vandalism rates have fallen significantly since inception: the location of a neighbourhood housing office in the once void area below one block has reduced alienation by increasing accessibility of management to residents, and there is general satisfaction with the scheme. Many metropolitan boroughs have similar schemes: a particularly notorious block called Trellick Tower in the Royal Borough of Kensington and Chelsea was turned around by installation of CCTV and a concierge from a vandal-ridden haven for drug dealing and petty crime, a place with high voids and desperately unpopular, into a highly desirable block. There is no reason why tower blocks should not be excellent places to live as long as they are secure, the lifts work and management is responsive. The views from upper-floor windows are often unsurpassed, and they provide an ideal solution to the problem of insufficient development land in already congested cities. When Le Corbusier initiated the concept in the early twentieth century, he envisaged villages in the sky, with a full complement of services, such as shops, health facilities and other services distributed throughout the block. However, the idea was simplified into the people-containers they are, with all the problems which are often but not necessarily associated with high-density living.

'Tackling high rise crime' on p. 221 discusses actual initiatives designed to reduce crime, highlighting the Glasgow case, and making a strong case for linking concierges to CCTV systems.

The publication *Homes for the future* (1983) suggests in Part 4 the following schema for analysing estate design.

6.4.3.1   Essential features

There should be adequate expenditure on the housing environment, with 2 per cent of scheme costs set aside for soft landscaping (i.e. plants).

Spaces on the estate should be clearly defined, with responsibility for them identified. There should be protection of private spaces.

There should be adequate provision for vehicle manoeuvre and parking. Parking spaces should be well integrated and distributed for convenience (for example, outside the residence); but the domination of vehicles in the street scene should be avoided if at all possible.

On the issue of provision for traffic: estate designers in the 1950s and 1960s often used the Radburnisation concept when providing roads. This is based on an idea developed in the United States of America, in the construction of a new settlement called Radburn, New Jersey. The essential concept is that traffic and pedestrian flows should be segregated for health and safety reasons. A perimeter road would have spurs running off it, serving clusters of houses, which would be connected together by walkways: thus pedestrians would have no need to use roadside paths. Another expression of the same idea is found in the pedestrian underpasses often running beneath busy roads and roundabouts. The idea sounds good, but the isolation of such footpaths and pedestrian ways from traffic flows can render users vulnerable to attack, which is why pedestrian underpasses are often unused, and in some cases they have been blocked off. I lived for a short time in the new village of Bar Hill, just north of Cambridge, the transport system of which was designed along similar lines. At the time, large ruts were worn in the grass alongside the pavement-less ring road, as residents voted literally with their feet, preferring to risk the dangers of walking beside a busy road rather than fear attack or simply the loneliness and in many cases the inconvenience of the footpath system.

Play area provision should be related to age-range, and designed to avoid estate nuisance (noise, visual intrusion, etc.).

6.4.3.2   Desirable aspects

Density considerations should be subservient to good design. The dwelling types should be mixed, and dwellings designed for special needs or elderly people should not be segregated into a corner of the scheme.

Larger estates should be subdivided into clusters. This will help the sense of community discussed earlier. It also fits in well with the concept of defensible space, advanced by Oscar Newman (1976). That is, for their psychological well-being everybody needs to feel that they have control over a given amount of territory, or at least be able to identify an area as to do with them; that is, to have a sense of ownership (even if not in the legal sense). This can be expressed not only in the form of, say, a garden fence, but also in a finite cluster of dwellings which can be identified as distinct from another cluster.

Dwellings should be oriented to maximise views and sunlight.

There should be provision for cars adjacent to the dwelling, and a hard standing or storage within the curtilage (the boundary) of the dwelling.

It is important that there is adequate lighting for security, and the use of vandal resistant materials.

Also, the headings of Part 4 of *Homes for the future* provide a good schema for the analysis of an estate, or indeed any group of dwellings. They are:

- density and form of development
- orientation and outlook
- definition of public and private spaces
- privacy and security
- gardens
- fences, walls and hedges
- car access and accommodation

- children's play

- landscaping

- footpaths

- changes of level

- street furniture

- provision for the disabled

- estate management.

The reader could profitably use this schema when considering the merits or demerits of housing areas.

Finally, the views of potential residents, and pertinent survey information, should be taken into consideration when it is proposed to build a housing area.

6.5 Conclusion

It must be stressed that this is a summative chapter only: nothing has been said about contracts and their management, tenant participation in the design and evaluation of dwellings and estates, and about techniques such as critical path analysis, which can assist in the efficient progression of projects. Little has been said about the requisite standards for disabled and elderly persons. Development is a wide yet detailed area of housing work, and it is to be hoped that social housing organisations will be continued to allowed to provide good-quality homes at affordable rates, whether owned or rented, for the foreseeable future. It is hoped that the following articles will stimulate further thought on the matter.

Articles

1. 'Tackling high-rise crime'

2. 'Short-life: the logic of necessity'

3. 'Housing gain for the community: planning agreement in Greenwich'

4. 'The end of housing association development?'

5. 'Estate-based employment initiative: the Wornington Green Building Centre, North Kensington'

Tackling high-rise crime

The 1950s and 1960s saw considerable new-build activity by UK housing authorities, in an attempt to replace substandard housing and ensure that secure homes
were available to all. One of the manifestations of this policy was the construction of high-rise apartment blocks. Many homes thus created are spacious,
are convenient for local facilities, and offer superb views, even if they do not
mirror Le Corbusier's initial ideas of 'villages in the sky', lacking the complement
of shops, recreational facilities and community centres within blocks which he
envisaged. However, they are not universally popular with residents, as some suffer high crime levels, including burglary, assault and damage to common parts.

The main problems revolve around access to entrance lobbies, often left unsupervised. Once intruders obtain entry, often via door-entry systems rendered
insecure through use of trades buttons, unauthorised duplicate keys or by following behind legitimate entrants, unsupervised access to dwellings via lifts and
back-up stairways is easy, entrance doors can be broken and burglaries effected,
often quickly and without detection. Those intent on vandalising lifts can do so
unobserved, causing distress and inconvenience to those who rely on them.

Crime itself, as well as associated fear, causes letting difficulties, protest
arrears, and high responsive maintenance bills as doors, locks and lifts are
repaired or replaced. For residents, there is the recurrent nightmare that, once
criminals realise the ease of effecting burglaries, the chances of escalation are
increased. In such blocks, insurance may be costly, as premiums relate to the
company's perception of risk, and many on low incomes will be unable to afford
it. They are thus doubly penalised. Residents often feel stigmatised by the unsatisfactory environment in which they subsist. Residents of surrounding areas may
unfairly label the occupants, and they may find difficulty in obtaining credit. The
psychological damage is immense.

It is incumbent upon councils having ownership of such blocks to analyse the
problem and to do as much as is feasible to secure them against such criminal
activity, without creating a prison-like environment which would stigmatise and
alienate the residents. At the recent Chartered Institute of Housing Conference,
Hugh McDonald of Glasgow City Council discussed the way in which that
authority tackled the increasing burglary and vandalisation associated with the
city's 250 blocks, some 25 000 homes. The rise of crime and anti-social behaviour, accompanied by growing unpopularity, was associated primarily with defec-
tive security, inadequate lighting and unmonitored underground car-parks.

The issue was the subject of a study involving police, local residents, elected
members, planners and security firms. By priority, the objectives were to improve
the security of the blocks and reduce crime and the fear of crime; to improve
management standards; to foster consultation with tenants, and to base all this
on a sound forward investment strategy. The successful strategy included the
separation of public and private space by ensuring a one-door entry, electronic
door-access, good lighting to communal areas, and closed-circuit television
(CCTV) monitoring of strategic areas, hinging on a concierge, with caretaking
and supervision duties, on a 24-hour rota basis. The security firm PAC installed
one CCTV station per four blocks, covering about 400 dwellings. Tenant consultation was stressed at every point: post-scheme monitoring suggests high

levels of satisfaction despite initial worries about the 'big brother' effect of some aspects.

Crime rates fell dramatically. In one block, whereas 69 per cent of tenants had suffered burglaries in the year prior to the changes, only 22 per cent had burglaries immediately afterwards. Voids reduced considerably, by 200 per cent in one block. It was estimated that this translates into an additional rent yield of £1.3 million per year. Once security issues were tackled, communal areas were improved, with public telephones which actually survived, and decoration of halls and lifts. The cost averaged £2500 per home, financed through revenue and capital sources, but the return in terms of user satisfaction and safety, whilst not quantifiable, is surely the most important gain. There is no reason why such schemes might not pay for themselves after taking into account reduced repair bills, voids and arrears, and a small rent premium.

If such improvements can be achieved in high-crime inner city areas, so much better the chances in other areas. Concierge and CCTV systems in London councils including Brent, Hammersmith and Fulham, Enfield and Bromley prove this.

Councils failing to take note of resident concerns, at a time when central government is supportive of such schemes to the extent of making Single Regeneration Budget approvals available to help facilitate them, must face the prospect of tenant management organisations forming under the Right to Manage, and wresting control away from them. At a time when councils are having to sell themselves as responsible, customer-oriented landlords, wholehearted remedies such as those mentioned are surely the stuff of survival.

PSLG, 1994 (unpublished)

Questions

1. Are tower blocks necessarily havens for crime and anti-social behaviour? Why have they acquired this reputation?
2. How was the security issue tackled in Glasgow? How was its effectiveness measured?
3. How can residents participate in making CCTV and concierge schemes successful?

Short-life: the logic of necessity

The government's draft Housing Revenue Account Subsidy Determination, based on the 'notional' housing revenue account reflecting D.o.E. assumptions on current housing expenditure and income, indicates likely central support to council housing running costs and rebates for 1991/92; but void levels of just 2 per cent are allowed for. The optimism of this and other elements will entail insufficient Housing Revenue Account (HRA) subsidy for many authorities, meaning higher rents or cuts in services, unless more empties are filled.

Some voids are needed to ensure lettings, mobility within the stock, and maintenance. Declining capital spending permission over the decade [to 1992] has cut ability to bring all stock to lettable standards – so blame for higher than desired vacancy levels must partly be directed at the Treasury, although some councils hardly exemplify efficient and effective management and maintenance practices, and the discipline of subsidy penalties gives an incentive to greater cost-effectiveness. So how can voids be minimised, to increase income and housing opportunity?

Some boroughs have adopted 'short-life' schemes. In view of the impossibility of renovating all long-term vacant stock, often inherited from other bodies or resulting from compulsory purchase of substandard or blighted private housing to permanent standard, restricted sums have been invested to provide acceptable dwellings for shorter periods. This has involved joint funding initiatives with the voluntary sector, to spread the burden of costs – part of the new enabling role.

One borough that has done so since 1984 is Southwark, which needs to increase income to make up for HRA subsidy losses and has a pressing homelessness problem. It operates two parallel programmes, one for homeless families, the other for single people in housing need. Under the Homeless Families Scheme, vacant properties are licensed to one of three large housing Associations. Using their own reserves, where necessary topped up from the short-life budget, the managing associations carry out repairs and decoration, and furnish the units, which are then let to council nominees who would otherwise be in bed and breakfast. The loan raised by the association, management and maintenance costs and furnishing costs are recouped through rents over a 3-year period.

The 'singles' programme makes properties available to a range of user groups, from large associations to small co-ops, and new and developing associations. Housing Corporation mini-Housing Association Grant funding is used to carry out repairs to bring properties into use, mainly for single people, whose access to other tenures has become increasingly limited owing to the overall housing shortage, and high prices in private rented and owner-occupied sectors. Since 1987, the Housing Corporation has given special allocations of mini-HAG to help the development of black and ethnic minority associations and user groups, for which short-life can provide a useful training ground.

When the scheme was devised, it was seen as a 'holding operation', awaiting a time when enough cash would be available for permanent refurbishment – but with continued cash shortages this has not happened. Policy and Development Officer Marie Price, who has steered the development of short-life in Southwark since 1988, told *PSLG* that the emphasis is now on developing void properties for homeless families' use, rather than use by 'singles' groups, owing to the mounting costs and unsuitability of bed and breakfast hotels as a form of temporary accommodation. With punitive subsidy arrangements for 1991/92 due to be brought in for private sector leasing on leases signed after 22 October 1992, the Homeless Families short-life initiative is likely to play an increasingly important part in providing good-quality temporary accommodation in a relatively cost-effective way.

John Drummond, Hyde Housing Association's Temporary Lettings Services Manager, told *PSLG* that Hyde works with properties in Southwark, Lewisham and Greenwich, and plans to expand elsewhere in south London. Two approaches are used: the 'cost rent' model, where the entire loan charges incurred through initial repairs, as well as running costs, are met through tenants' rents; and a strategy where repair costs are defrayed partly by council cash. Turn-round time from receipt of property to handover is around 3 months, with an average contract sum at £12 000 – remarkable value for money. Rents are commonly no more than £40 per week, higher than average council rents, but lower than bed and breakfast charges. Most of Hyde's schemes are targeted towards the homeless – thus leading to savings on community charge funds. Hyde has 730 properties in management, and a recent tenant survey revealed high satisfaction, with 85 per cent quite or very satisfied with their homes, and 88 per cent satisfied with the maintenance service.

It is encouraging to find authorities pursuing such initiatives, which reduce voids, mean effective liaison with housing associations, help their revenue positions, and serve the interests of those in housing need. It is a pattern which should be encouraged, and which would underline the intent of caring authorities to tackle homelessness.

Paul Reeves *PSLG*, December 1992

Questions

1. What is the main motivation of the local authority in developing short-life schemes?
2. Why is this form of scheme preferable to using bed and breakfast, and are there any disadvantages?
3. What is the nature of the housing association – local authority partnership?

Housing gain for the community: planning agreement in Greenwich

Local planning entails attempting to balance environmental concerns and socio-economic needs with market forces, and developers often find their potential returns constrained by planning agendas. However, mutual advantage is possible through s. 106 of the 1990 Town and Country Planning Act – so-called 'planning gain' – used since the original 1971 legislation to gain community benefits, including social housing, on private land. Essentially, communities share in the extra profit made by developers through planning concessions. In addition to other benefits, land and housing can be passed, often at no cost, to third parties (such as housing associations) in return for an agreement by the planning authority to modify land use, density or other constraints whilst remaining within broad local planning objectives. Reduced scheme costs therefore result from planning gain, but such reductions are not counted as public subsidy, even though facilitated by councils. Housing Association Grant entitlement and thus the possibility of producing relatively affordable accommodation is therefore unaffected, as it would be by council grants made under s. 25 of the 1988 Local Government

Act. As housing authorities struggle against financial restriction, diminishing land supplies and growing need to provide or enable lower-cost housing, planning gain forms a growing part of housing strategies, exemplifying partnership between communities and business as sought by central government.

The London Borough of Greenwich is active in this area. Its territory contains large industrial zones subject to planning application, such as the Greenwich peninsula gas works site, and there are considerable planning gain opportunities along the entire Thames waterfront there. Overall policy involves negotiating with applicants to secure up to 25 per cent of the residential land for social housing.

Deptford Creek lies just west of Greenwich's historic centre, but is unlikely to feature on any tourist itinerary. Obsolete Deptford Power Station, a dirty red structure topped by a sentinel off-yellow chimney, dominates the area. Scrapped cars front the derelict station, heavy demolition and road-stone conveying equipment crawls noisily, and soiled creek waters slither into the Thames. This heavy industrial remnant is bordered to the east by the Meridian Estate, a series of redbrick 1930s council blocks. Across the Thames rise the shining glass offices of Docklands and Canary Wharf's pyramid-capped tower, as much a contrast to Deptford Creek as the nearby *Cutty Sark* and Maritime Museum.

In 1989, some of the site owners formed Greenwich Reach Development (GRD) and submitted a plan to transform the area by substituting an ensemble of residential, light industrial, retail and hotel facilities. Six hundred homes would be provided, half of them flats, at an average density of 120 habitable rooms per acre, with six-storey blocks of flats enjoying riverside views. Work-homes and houses would be located to the centre and rear of the site. Almost 400 000 square feet of business space would be included; 'exhibition shopping' and entertainment facilities would line a boardwalk along the Thames, and the plan includes a passenger liner moored for conference and hotel use. The redundant coal-dock would become a water-garden, and the creek a marina. The development would be made more accessible by a proposed extension to the Docklands Light Railway and a new station. In short, Docklands across the water, reminiscent of Tobacco Dock in Wapping.

Catherine Kell, Development Initiatives Manager representing the housing department in planning gain negotiations, told *PSLG* that negotiations are bearing fruit.

On the back of change of use and relaxation of density standards, we want around 25 per cent of the residential land – just over 1 acre – to be transferred at nil cost to London and Quadrant Trust, a member of a consortium of associations geared to take advantage of Greenwich planning gain. It's intended to provide rented housing: shared ownership would be beyond the reach of the lower-paid in the borough, and wouldn't really meet housing need. Greenwich seeks full nomination rights to ease pressure on our existing housing resources. Liaison between housing and planning departments has been positive, and co-operation with the housing association proves beyond doubt our commitment to the enabling role.

She urged caution:

Housing Corporation money was lined up for a similar development elsewhere, but the scheme foundered, and the grant was reallocated. There's no absolute certainty over whether or when such schemes will be delivered, and the housing association risks considerable sums on appraisals and the like. Another planning gain is frozen due to the property slump.

She is, however, convinced that planning gain will in future be the main way of providing social housing through what amounts to land subsidy.

In facing the challenge of meeting housing need, councils should systematically examine the possibility of planning gain whenever major developments are proposed alongside other strategic approaches. If they do, planning and housing department agendas will merge to supply corporate solutions to the problem of social housing provision.

PSLG, May 1991

Questions

1. What is the planning gain to the community in this instance?
2. Outline the form of the development proposed by Greenwich Reach Development. What conflicts might exist between social residential use and the rest of the scheme?

The end of housing association development?

The average Housing Association Grant (HAG) rate for 1994/95 will be 58 per cent, the lowest yet, although higher than the widely expected 55 per cent. Doubts have appeared amongst housing associations and their funders, as well as partner local authorities, about their viability as developers of affordable accommodation. Several speakers at September's National Federation of Housing Associations (NFHA) Conference suggested that associations should eschew their development role, and Steve Howlett, Chief Executive of transfer association Swale HA, predicted that the emphasis would shift from development to management as a direct consequence of not wishing to produce homes with unaffordable rents.

This is very worrying. The government expects the movement to produce around 50 000 social rented and low-cost homes annually. Now that most councils no longer provide new accommodation, housing associations are the only candidate for the task. What are the problems foreseen by the movement?

Prominent is the reluctance of lenders to make advances to associations in the face of low grant levels. At the NFHA Conference, Adrian Coles, Director General of the Council of Mortgage Lenders, suggested that lower HAG levels, plus doubts surrounding future levels of housing benefit, mean that interest rates will be higher and terms more onerous, excluding many associations from the development process altogether.

'Gearing' – the relationship between assets and money borrowed – is crucial to a lender's decision. If an association is too highly geared – that is, it has a higher than acceptable ratio of debts to assets – lenders will be reluctant to make loans because of low security against which to take a charge. And high gearing ratios render the association vulnerable to interest rate rises, which, in increasing expenditure, jeopardise sound cashflow. Thus lenders, who look at both asset-worthiness and income–expenditure projections, will be doubly wary of the movement. This is a direct consequence of HAG reductions, which entail greater indebtedness.

Associations have not always helped themselves. In their eagerness to secure a slice of the Approved Development programme, many have bid below current HAG rates to convince the Housing Corporation that they are serious about production in an increasingly competitive environment. Reserves have been used to internally subsidise building programmes to ensure reasonably affordable rents. It is clear that this form of subsidy cannot continue, but equally that the wrong signals have been sent to the Corporation and its paymasters, who are confirmed in their belief that associations can do more with less, justifying further cuts.

Housing association professionals are beginning to react against under-bidding, rather too late perhaps. It is clear that substandard homes – in design and space terms – may result from attempted economies in the absence of other external subsidies.

It is questionable whether any principled association would wish to produce the slums of tomorrow. Hardly any association now produces to Parker Morris standards, regarded in the early 1960s as minimum standards, designed to take account of new lifestyles. The director of the Joseph Rowntree Trust, Richard Best, should be applauded by all providers and nominators in his defence, at the conference, of Parker Morris standards as the fundamental basis for lifetime homes. The unfortunate reality, however, is that associations are generally producing smaller homes with higher rents, as revealed in recent research by Professor Valerie Karn. It is certain that associations will be judged not only by the current but by future occupants of cramped homes, who will presumably regard them as fondly as the occupants of some tower blocks do their 'villages in the sky', the early 1960s solution to housing need in our conurbations.

It has therefore become necessary for housing practitioners to lobby government, much more effectively than previously, to secure capital subsidies which will produce affordable homes of a size and type appropriate to their customers, and guarantees that housing benefit – a valuable source of income to associations via rents – will not be cut, to provide reassurance to lenders. If this fails, then the only ways to secure an ongoing housing association programme of any worth would be for the government to resume its role as major lender at favourable rates over extended terms, as was the case for local authority capital projects and during the much-lamented era of the pre-1988 Housing Act financial regime, or to give an open-ended commitment to housing benefit free of the threat of capping. Neither is likely. Land subsidies will wane as council land banks run out. Planning deals are cumbersome and relatively scarce. What is needed is a grant regime based on a model which generates rates based on realistic affordability assumptions arising from research into the actual spending requirements of representative tenants. Until then, associations should refuse to develop, even if housing need remains unmet in the short term, in the hope that drastic action will force a reappraisal of current policy.

PSLG, November 1994

Questions

1. What is 'gearing'? Why are private financiers worried about reducing grant levels?
2. In the absence of realistic grant levels, how can associations ensure affordable rents?
3. What are Parker Morris standards, and why have they been largely abandoned by the housing association movement?

Estate-based employment initiative: the Wornington Green Building Centre, North Kensington

Within a few minutes' walk of West London's cosmopolitan Portobello Road market, and beside the Great Western Railway, stand the red-brick blocks of medium-rise flats and maisonettes of Kensington Housing Trust's Wornington Green Estate. A recent social survey reveals an area suffering from high crime rates, unemployment, and other problems associated with many similar inner city enclaves. The 539-home estate was constructed between 1965 and 1985; the maze of walkways and disturbing graffiti may intimidate, but social deprivation engendered by unemployment is a less visible malaise. Fortunately, this issue is being addressed through a training initiative creating renewed purpose and therefore improving the outlook for everyone living there.

An unpretentious two-bedroom maisonette at first floor level houses the Wornington Green Building Centre. *PSLG* spoke to Stuart Mulholland, Lecturer at Hammersmith and West London College's Faculty of Building Studies and Project Manager, who has been centrally involved in setting up an initiative to improve local residents' employment chances by developing building skills. The college has been able to use its experience in this and related fields practically, to benefit this deprived community.

Mulholland stressed the crucial involvement of Kensington Housing Trust, which is acutely aware of the estate's problems, having commissioned a survey, and who have leased the maisonette to the Building Centre. In June 1990, the college was approached by the West London Task Force, a key funder within the government's Action for Cities consortium, to address various issues revealed by the social survey; and in November 1990, proposals were presented, with implementation following the following January. This illustrates the potential for partnership between government, associations, educational establishments and the community in stimulating positive change in estates that would once have been written off as 'dreadful enclosures'.

The project aims include developing building skills amongst disadvantaged groups, typically members of ethnic communities, women, and lone parents, and to create lasting employment opportunities, with the long-term aim of setting up a building co-operative. Because this is essentially a training initiative, it is one-third funded by CENTEC, the local Training and Education Council. The Centre offers 20-week training courses, free to trainees, with an emphasis on carpentry, joinery, painting and decorating skills, although computing, business, numeracy and literacy courses are offered to complete the package. The equal opportunities credentials of the scheme reflect the social mix of the estate. Of a total current enrolment of 22, 8 are female and 15 other than white.

Of the 27 who enrolled initially, all of whom were without work, 7 have joined further education courses, 7 are employed by other firms, 2 are self employed, 5 have returned to the project to enhance their skills, and just 6 remain unemployed. If this pattern is repeated in further intakes, then the project will have demonstrated its socio-economic worth.

'The knock-on effect for the families of the trainees is incredible,' said Mulholland. 'Although it takes £4500 per trainee to resource, it's very reasonable for a 20-week course; but the positive attitude encouraged, and the implications for improving the physical and social fabric of the estate, must outweigh these minimal costs.' He added that trainees had applied the skills learnt to repair and improve their homes.

The small but well-equipped workshop – a ground-floor room of the maisonette – proves that building training does not require distant and rather institutional provision: it is most appropriately delivered where needed. Being located in the estate means that users have psychological ownership of the project, an ethos reinforced by the supportive and informal atmosphere fostered through user-friendly hours (10 to 4), childcare arrangements, freedom to make refreshments at any time and off-site visits, although attention is paid to health, safety and cleanliness. An indication of community ownership is that the second intake was filled solely by word of mouth locally and by the fact that the Residents' Association rents its meeting room to the Centre for weekly use as a computer workshop. The Association is using the Centre as a consultancy with architects Hunt Thompson to facilitate a self-built estate community centre.

The project is due to finish in March 1992, at the end of the current six-monthly funding cycle, but it is hoped that further cash will materialise. Mulholland wishes to replicate the model in Kensal New Town further north, linked in with an Estate Action initiative.

It is essential that attempts such as this to give relatively deprived local communities hope are fostered, to bolster self-worth and ultimately to stimulate social and economic regeneration, and it is hoped that central and local government agencies will continue to support this form of stimulus. If not, then social costs will far outweigh any notional savings, as witnessed in the urban disturbances of 1991.

PSLG, February 1992

Questions

1. What were the main problems which the Wornington Green Project were designed to relieve?
2. What was the role of the housing association, and why was it crucial to the success of the venture?
3. What is the scope for extending such training initiatives to provide an estate-based repairs and maintenance service?

7 Commercialism and social housing

7.1 Introduction

Over the last 10 years, social housing organisations have adopted a far more commercialistic approach. This is true both of local authorities and housing associations. The manifestations of the new commercialism include products, services and techniques which resemble or even in some cases equal those found in the private sector. Examples are the proliferation of housing for sale, housing associations acting as management agents for private landlords, and the use of business planning to attract private finance and promote organisational change.

Local authorities have to compete with others, including private firms, to run their own housing under compulsory competitive tender (CCT). Many have transferred their assets to more business-oriented organisations, custom-made housing associations initially entirely reliant upon market finance in order to avoid restrictive Treasury rules. In some cases, private firms already run some council housing. Annual reports have to be produced for tenants every year which are not dissimilar to those produced by companies for their shareholders. Some housing professionals welcome the setting up of local housing companies which will share many of the features of public limited companies, and which could stand outside the ambit of Treasury rules.

Tenants and leaseholders are almost universally referred to as customers, and many organisations have Customer Care Officers. User surveys are conducted to establish the customers' views on the organisation. There is talk of paying committee members of housing associations. Town hall departments have often been replaced by Business Units with their own strategic plans, harmonised with those of the corporation as a whole. All this adds up to a commercial ethos which to a certain extent reflects changes in societal attitudes as a whole, and developments elsewhere in the public and semi-public arena.

It is difficult to say precisely why these changes have taken place, or when they started, but useful suggestions can be made on an impressionistic basis. First, the Thatcher era marked a significant tidal change in the operation of local government. Up to the 1980s it had enjoyed a relatively stable relationship with central government, albeit punctuated by crises such as the general refusal to implement fair rents for council tenants as a result of the Housing Finance Act 1972, and considerable unease at the reorganisations of 1974 following Redcliffe-Maude and the 1972 Local Government Act. Nobody seriously questioned their role as significant providers. The Thatcher era started in housing terms with the 1980 Housing Act Right to Buy, which would considerably reduce council stock through sales to tenants – individual privatisation and new, severe cash limits applied to local government expenditure under the 1980 Local Government Planning and Land Act. This was followed up by the 1986 Housing and Planning Act, which gave local authorities the power to transfer their assets to others, including housing associations, coinciding with legislation enabling building societies to become landlords and developers once more. The intention was the privatisation of entire estates. The 1980s saw several types of local authority service such as school catering, parks and refuse, being subject to CCT, the promotion of management buyouts in some areas, and a new language of competition. The era ended with the 1989 Housing and Local Government Act, which severely restricted council spending once more, and made it virtually impossible for councils to develop new housing. Thus, throughout the 1980s, local authorities were forced to search for other ways of providing for local people – in other words, to become enablers, which necessarily meant engaging with bodies with which previously they had but a passing acquaintance.

The changes were consolidated in the 1990s by the emergence of a customer care philosophy, spurred on by the Citizen's Charter, and the requirement to publish performance indicators in the form of annual reports to tenants, from 1991 onwards. As the 1989 Act financial restrictions began to bite, and as it became evident that large-scale voluntary transfer (LSVT) would not be feasible in metropolitan areas where debts exceeded assets, the idea of local housing companies was proposed by a number of policy analysts such as Nick Raynsford, and supported by the Chartered Institute of Housing. The mid-1990s saw the challenge of CCT, and councils scrambling to adopt a more cost-effective, businesslike approach in readiness for such competition.

An article at the end of Chapter 5, 'A charter for council housing' (p. 178), discusses the role of the Citizen's Charter in its housing manifestation, and argues that, although it highlights existing secure tenants' rights, it does very little to address the legitimate requirements of potential customers: for example, those on housing registers. It does, however, offer a series of standards which should be regarded as minima, and which, if followed, definitely enhance the position of tenant as customer.

Housing associations have changed too. Back in the early 1970s, their role was minimal: developments were mainly for rent, and the grant regime ensured that properties were let at fair rents, covering the lion's share of actual costs. By the early 1980s, they had been drawn into the government's vision of Britain as a property-owning democracy and began to engage in for-sale schemes, typically through non-charitable subsidiaries, catering for marginal market demand rather than, strictly, for need. Shared ownership was a distinctive new product, and took its place along improvement for sale and sales outright at discount. In 1983, housing associations found themselves buying private houses for shared owners under the pilot Do It Yourself Shared Ownership (DIYSO) scheme, revived in the early 1990s.

An article at the end of this chapter, 'Home ownership: The housing association connection' (p. 265), highlights the Do It Yourself Shared Ownership scheme, which has entailed greater housing market awareness amongst housing associations, and the need to deal with customers who are expressing effective demand rather than simply standing in need of housing.

The 1988 Housing Act changed the face of the movement for ever, and introduced a wave of commercialism. For the first time, apart from a few limited pilots in the two preceding years, the majority of associations would have to raise private loans to finance the portion of development costs not funded by Housing Association Grant (HAG), which would now be fixed at levels far lower than previously. For the first time, the movement needed personnel skilled in engaging with the private finance market, committee members with business experience, and business plans to convince potential lenders of the value of assets and the soundness of cash flows. Even the accounts were now put into a PLC format to make it easier for private lenders to understand association finance methodology.

This business experience whetted the association appetite for engaging in commercial and semi-commercial ventures. From the mid-1980s, they had been competing with other associations to run council-sponsored private sector leasing schemes as management and development agents, engaging directly with private landlords. They engaged with private developers in the context of planning gain, and later planning obligation. In the 1990s, they broadened their agency activities into managing homes on behalf of private landlords, sometimes over shops, and leasing from owners. Finally, they became competitors for local authority housing management under CCT. Their far wider use of assured shorthold tenancies nowadays, especially for homelessness and special needs schemes, means that their resemblance to private organisations has increased. Reductions in HAG have meant that they have had to balance costs against revenue in a far closer and more businesslike way than before.

In summary, then, commercialism in the social housing field has grown, and is probably here to stay. Could it be that social housing practitioners, perhaps tired of the rather dusty town-hall image which pervades the profession, wished to increase their status in the materialistic 1980s, and decided to adopt a more commercial stance to do so? Certainly, many senior managers have welcomed the changes; and housing conferences, with their plethora of financial consultancies and business-led seminars, reflect this change of ethos, and have moved away from the days when better boilers were the item of the moment. It is to be hoped that the value of social consciousness will not be lost in a collective status-seeking.

7.2   Competition: compulsory competitive tendering

7.2.1   General observations

One can imagine a country where the state is the sole supplier of goods, where essentials are distributed on the basis of needs, and where luxury items are produced to quota, sold from state outlets, and are available in a given limited range of styles. In such a state, there would be no competition amongst sellers to provide better services or products more cost-effectively. There would be no price-undercutting. There would be no real incentive for the state to improve its products or services: as it would be a monopoly supplier, there would be no alternative which could be chosen, no alternative price.

For many years, local authorities were monopoly suppliers of very many services, and some commodities. Social housing was dominated by them until the 1980s. Those requiring such accommodation would approach the council, find themselves on a waiting list, and accept what was offered. Choice was in the form of exchanging one tenancy for another. The only way to escape from monopoly provision was by buying out, either through the Right to Buy, or into the private market. Private rental was often not a realistic alternative, owing to the cost. This was true also of purchase, for the vast majority. Other services, such as refuse collection and parks maintenance, were the preserve of the local authority: only it could do them. As long as one paid the rates, or even in default, the service was provided in a certain way by the municipality. The only sanction against poor services – although this was a significant lever – was deselection through voting the regime out in local elections and hoping the next lot would be better. There were no real incentives for service improvement, as there was no external threat.

All this has changed. Part 3 of the 1980 Local Government Planning and Land Act set out the groundwork for competition, and has been consolidated by successive legislation. The introduction of CCT was justified on the basis that it would stimulate efficiency, enable councils to examine their performance, encourage them to seek value for money, break down entrenched monopolies, and generate large gains in efficiency through competition. Initially, CCT was confined to services provided by manual workers, and to direct labour organisations involved in building. Many boroughs engaged private firms to collect rubbish; and firms based on the Continent often won contracts. Whole departments were disbanded, there were redundancies, and many transferred to new firms which offered less favourable terms and conditions, a practice which has now been ruled out.

The Local Government Act 1988 specified refuse collection, school catering and grounds maintenance as so-called 'defined activities' which a local authority could carry out itself only if it had invited tenders and if its workforce had submitted a tender demonstrating that it could work just as effectively and at a cost no higher than that submitted by external tenderers. This means that council operatives do not have to submit lower tenders than those in the private sector to win contracts, but it does mean that costs have to be examined to ensure that bids will not be higher.

The scope of CCT has been extended by regulation, and through new legislation, principally the 1992 Local Government Act. In addition to housing management CCT, a number of other services either have been or are about to become subject to CCT, not necessarily all at once (the list shown in Table 7.1 relates to metropolitan and London boroughs, to illustrate the timetable). Reorganised authorities will be given a period to adjust to new arrangements before having to implement CCT, depending on the size of the authority and the service in question. There are also separate timetables for Scottish and Welsh authorities. In all the above, consultation papers were issued by the Department of the Environment.

Table 7.1 Contract start dates for compulsory competitive tendering in metropolitan and London boroughs

Service	Contract start date
Legal	October 1995
Construction-related	October 1995
Information technology	October 1996
Finance	October 1996
Personnel	October 1996
Corporate Administration	October 1996
Direct services:	
Security	October 1995
Fleet management	October 1995
Parking	October 1995

The principle is that the local authority will be the client in all cases. It will retain strategic services, and hire other bodies (or even its own departments) to undertake operational work, on a contractual basis. These operatives will therefore be 'contractors'. Most authorities have already reorganised themselves into client and contractor divisions in readiness.

Thus, by the end of the twentieth century, local services will be delivered by a diversity of organisations, with councils acting as co-ordinators and paymasters rather than providers. Their staff will be contract managers, using many of the techniques of business. There is no necessary reason to fear CCT.

Councils will retain their democratic identity, and will still be able to formulate their own policies, to the extent that they can at present, even though
it may be that someone else will be carrying out the council's duties. As long
as the control mechanisms are strong, there is no reason why there should
be any diminution in quality, and there may even be further economies, as
very large firms emerge to deal in the new marketplace. It is to be hoped
that customer responsiveness will not suffer, and that decentralisation will
be adopted, perhaps at estate or community level, to prevent the alienation
characteristic of much municipal management previously.

7.2.2   Application to housing management

The Department of the Environment issued two consultation paper prior
to implementation, one in 1992 and another a year later. Numerous regulations and amendments were made before the first contracts were let, and
several authorities were given the task of setting up experimental tendering exercises to examine the practical issues involved. The issues discussed
in consultation revolved around the scope of the defined activity, the implementation timetable and the size of management agreements; that is, how
many properties should be included in contracts in all or part of an authority. To give an idea of the complexity of the issue, aspects piloted included
the nature of contract specifications, the monitoring of management agreements, the client–contractor split, including the scope of the defined activity, effects of CCT on warden services, impact on small housing authorities,
tenant consultation prior to management agreement, the interface with capital programmes, and the management of cultural change in organisations
subject to CCT.

CCT has been extended to housing management under section 2 of the
Local Government Act 1988. Essentially, departments are required to split
into client and contractor sides corresponding on the one hand to their
strategic or policy aspects, and on the other to day-to-day management
functions. There was much equivocation about what should be in one and
what in the other, but the issue has settled down. The defined activity was
set out in the 1994 Local Government (Competition) (Defined Activities)
(Housing Management) Order, and broadly includes letting and transfer
administration, rent and service charge collection, tenancy management,
management of repairs and maintenance service, cleaning and caretaking,
and voids administration. Eventually, 95 per cent of the activities listed will
have to be subjected to the CCT process. Councils can if they wish add
other housing management functions to the list, but enabling, policy-making and strategic roles are exempt. So the monitoring of contracts, design
of new points systems, decisions relating to evictions and development
appraisals would presumably fall outside the scope of CCT, as would decision-making regarding homelessness and housing benefit, although much
of the administration of the above could presumably be tendered out.

There are so called *de minimis* regulations, which exempt local authorities where the cost of the listed operations in all is less than £500 000 annually.

The decision was taken to phase CCT in: first contracts would be let in April 1996: and all councils will have let at least part of their contracts by the following April. The general principle is that smaller authorities, that is, those with under 15 000 properties, let all their functions in a single year: larger authorities can stage this process over 2 to 3 years. There is also a distinction made between authorities which are judged ready and those not, as the government does not wish the initiative to fail through disorganisation.

Some local authorities have 'jumped the gun' and let contracts voluntarily, perhaps to avoid the onerous regulations besetting CCT, or simply to ensure readiness. Provided certain conditions have been met, they do not have to re-let their contracts until 5 years have elapsed.

There have had to be various legislative amendments to enable housing CCT; and there has been not a little controversy, much of it surrounding the issue of tenant consultation and involvement.

The first and perhaps most controversial issue concerns tenant consultation. During the late 1980s and into the early 1990s, a number of legislative and practice initiatives appeared to increase the ability of residents to have a say in the management of their homes. The 1988 Housing Act had, after all, given them the right to vote for a new landlord, and several tenant management co-operatives were formed to take over the day-to-day running of estates and blocks. LSVT was made subject to ballot; and the Citizen's Charter initiative, combined with the earlier requirement that local authorities publish annual reports to tenants, also signalled greater resident involvement – rightly so, as, owing to subsidy restrictions, more than ever before there was a direct correlation between rent income and service output. This was largely paralleled in the housing association movement, with the requirement that associations involve tenants in management and improve information to them laid down by the Housing Corporation in a series of circulars.

Under s. 105 of the Housing Act 1985, tenants have a right to consultation on management changes. Similarly, s. 27 of the same Act requires consultation prior to the delegation of management functions to another body, as well as the approval of the Secretary of State. This does not, of course, imply that there should be a ballot, but does suggest something more than the dissemination of information and the occasional public meeting. However, under CCT, it has been made clear that tenants will not be consulted individually over the final choice of contractor, which will be decided on the basis of price and quality; and s. 105 has been amended to clarify this. The requirement for Secretary of State approval of delegation of housing management is probably not needed anyway for CCT, as the contracts are for services rather than full delegation, but the law has been amended to make this clear too.

Many councils have implemented full consultation with their tenants and leaseholders in respect of drawing up specifications and other important matters of detail, such as the localisation of management: it has been used as an opportunity for full and frank dialogue in many cases. But certainly between 1992 and 1995, many tenants' groups felt that it did not go far enough, and wondered why the final choice of contractor could not be put to ballot, given all necessary information, especially where bids were very close. After all, Tenants' Choice implies a change not only of manager, but also of ownership, and this is subject to vote. Were tenants not to be trusted to make the correct decision? Was this not the emergence of the old paternalism which had supposedly been swept away by customer-friendly legislation?

There are compelling arguments on both sides. Certainly tenants have to deal on a regular basis with those who manage their homes, and poor-quality service, or even a lack of common grounds and difference in ethos, will clearly impact mainly on tenants, and therefore to minimise the risk of alienation it could be important to involve tenants in the selection process. If people are given ownership of change, there may be a greater chance that it will be effective and relatively unproblematic. On the other hand, council housing is a public asset which belongs to the community rather than solely to tenants in common, and therefore the authority owes a duty of good management to all residents. Thus, to devolve the decision on who should manage the stock to a sub-group, albeit an important one, might be seen as too partial, as if a small, unelected board were to be given the right to decide how a public park should be developed and managed. It is probably otiose to push this argument too far, since unelected quangos do make decisions about public assets: the Housing Corporation is a case in point, as are housing association committees, which spend large amounts of public money every year on management and development. However, if one accepts its validity for the moment, this justifies making the decision as to who manages council stock a council-wide, corporate decision, rather than one to be devolved to tenants, or just to tenants, as the council represents all residents of its area, and has been elected democratically for this purpose. Indeed, if the decision were devolved to tenants, this could be seen as yet one more erosion of local authority powers.

One way to resolve this dispute is to accept that tenants cannot have a final say in who takes over management, but to give them considerable input in designing contract specifications, and then to form a quality monitoring committee on which tenants form a majority, to ensure that the contractor lives up to the specifications laid down. The decision as to whether to institute legal proceedings, and even the remedy for breach of contract preferred, could also be laid at the door of such a committee either wholly or in part. After all, if tenants have a significant say in contract design, and monitoring, and possibly in termination, there is very little space left for further meaningful involvement.

An article at the end of this chapter, 'Involving tenants in compulsory competitive tendering' (p. 257) discusses issues raised at a conference in

May 1994 convened to discuss the issue of tenant involvement in CCT. It was reinforced by the Minister that although tenants could, and should, be involved in the specification process, they should not be given a veto over the actual contractor, as this was the role of the local authority. However, it was stressed that tenants' views had to be taken into account, and that councils disregarding them might be subject to legal action.

The second issue is that of the so-called Right to Manage, strengthened by the provisions of the 1993 Leasehold Reform, Housing and Urban Development Act. There has been a growth in the number of tenant management organisations (TMOs) which have taken over the running of estates or areas on a co-operative basis. Sometimes this has been as a result of dissatisfaction with the local authority, sometimes it has been actively promoted by the council as a method of greater customer involvement and common ownership of problems, such as repairs and security issues. There is nothing to stop a TMO putting in a bid for management under CCT, although many of these organisations have the nature of client rather than contractor. They have been exempted from CCT, except where they employ local authority-seconded staff. However, they are expected to put management contracts out to tender in a businesslike way. Because of the restriction on local authority staff, they cannot be used as a way to avoid CCT by councils.

A third issue relates to transfer of staff from the local authority to any new contractor. It is to be expected that such contractors may well wish to take on such staff, as they have a good knowledge of their areas and of the tenants; thus the steepness of the operational learning curve would be reduced and the contract managed more effectively. This does not naturally follow: much depends on the local authority in question. Legislation deriving its legitimacy from European Union law requires that the terms and conditions of transfer should be no less favourable than those enjoyed previously. That is, where transfers of engagement actually take place. There are many housing associations which have a nationwide sphere of operations and may not need to hire extra staff to manage CCT contracts; others might prefer to engage new faces. Thus there is no guarantee of continued work for existing local authority housing officers.

A further issue concerns the geographical spread of bids. An EC Services Directive of 1993 provides that contracts of an annual or aggregate value of or greater than 200 000 ecu (around £142 000 at 1993 prices) must be advertised throughout the EC, as well as being subject to other EC rules. Thus, it could well be the case that tenants find themselves being managed by a French or Dutch housing organisation which may have little knowledge of local requirements. This has happened in other CCTs, often without particular problems: as long as staff are hired who have local knowledge, and are committed to quality provision, there should be no problem here, except that head office might be rather more remote than the town hall.

A final point concerns the size of contracts. How many properties is it reasonable to expect any one organisation to manage? Many councils went down the decentralisation route, not just in housing, as pioneered by Walsall in the 1970s, in order to provide a more locally responsive service which residents could identify with and reach easily. Estate-based initiatives such as those facilitated by the Priority Estates Project and through Estate Action commonly involve a local management presence. The figure of a maximum 5000 units per contract has been decided. This will apparently avoid the replacement of one management monopoly with another; and contracts should be let on an area basis.

At the time of writing (March 1995), it remains to be seen whether there will be many external takers for CCT. Doubtless some housing associations may see this as an opportunity for expansion, perhaps foreseeing the possibility of cross-subsidising other aspects of their operations through surpluses made through management contracts. There may well be private firms which will be interested in aspects of the management of council stock: for example, Quality Street, which emerged in the late 1980s in response to Tenants' Choice, but has in fact become a significant private lettings and management agency, or one of a number of other building society vehicles created in the wake of the 1986 Building Societies Act to take advantage of their renewed development role. A consultancy has already won a voluntary competitive tendering bid in respect of Rutland District Council's stock, in competition with a housing association. Although around 80 per cent of bids were won by in-house teams on first contracts for other forms of CCT, there is no guarantee that the same will be true of council housing management tendering.

On the other hand, housing associations have a long and successful record in co-operating with local authorities in providing social housing, as has been discussed, through planning, grant finance and discounted land, as well as in co-operative management initiatives in the permanent and temporary housing fields. There is little to suggest that this role will diminish. The desire not to disturb this relationship may yet lead to a most half-hearted response from the voluntary movement when first contracts are let in 1996. There are comparatively few associations with over 5 000 properties in management, and so the issue of experience must be held in question. There are as yet comparatively few large-scale housing association estates, whereas this is the typical council product: will associations be comfortable with the role of estate managers? And will tenants be at all happy with the notion of having a new manager imposed upon them without their direct consent? These are all reasons to be sceptical about the scope for housing CCT.

An article at the end of this chapter, 'Compulsory competitive tender for housing management: the next housing revolution?' (p. 256) could profitably be read at this stage, as it gives a broad overview of the initiative, and the early stages of its planning, as well as questioning whether tenants actually want new managers. This should help the reader to integrate the detailed information which has gone before.

7.3 Selling out: large-scale voluntary transfer and companies

7.3.1 Large-scale voluntary transfers

Local authorities are considerably constrained in what they can and cannot do: and much of this relates to financial restriction. Central government restricts the amount they can spend and borrow for capital purposes because control over public expenditure is one of the chief ways of controlling the amount of money in circulation, and therefore, theoretically at least, the rate of inflation. The same reasoning is applied to revenue expenditure, and the subsidy system, which has been pared down in an attempt to finance tax cuts and promote efficiencies. Many local authority treasurers or chief housing officers must have looked enviously at their counterparts in the housing association or business world, and wished they could operate in a less constrained way to produce greater volumes of social housing in a cost effective manner. The story of large-scale voluntary transfer (LSVT), and the emergence of the housing company idea, is that of the triumph of commercial thinking over the confines of the traditional bureaucratic mind, and represents a sea change in attitudes amongst senior housing professionals.

By 1995, more than 35 local authorities had sold their stock, in whole or in part, to housing associations, most of which had not existed prior to transfer. New names graced the pages of *Inside Housing* and similar publications, and tenants had to get used to seeing the same officials in a new guise. Consultants had a field day in writing business plans, new mission statements and designing company logos, as well as arranging finance for the new organisations and giving any amount of legal advice, and help with the ballots.

LSVT was initiated under the 1986 Housing and Planning Act, which allowed councils to dispose of properties *en masse* to the non-local authority sector. It was changed as a result of the 1988 Housing Act, and has been modified slightly by further legislation and regulation. It is not my intention to consider the legal and financial minutiae of the issue, but to enumerate its main features, and indicate that it is to be seen as a significant reflection of a new commercialism in social housing.

Basically, LSVT involves the sale of stock to a housing association. This can be as a whole, or in blocks, or can involve 'trickle transfer'; that is, the sale of properties when they become vacant. A variant of this is the sale of shared ownership freeholds to an association, which, unlike mainstream LSVT of rented stock, does not require Secretary of State consent. The price of the transfer is generally reckoned as tenanted market value, which is assessed on discounted valuation grounds. This is considerably lower than an estate agent's valuation of vacant stock, but can prove vital in ensuring that the association's indebtedness is not too great, which would have significant implications for new rents, or existing rents after the expiry of any rent guarantee period, where available.

Tenants of the new association become assured tenants subject to the Tenant's Guarantee, but have the preserved Right to Buy. This right was included as a sweetener to ensure that at least some LSVTs went through, as the process is subject to majority ballot of tenants and leaseholders.

The valuation issue is crucial to the deal. LSVT associations cannot obtain HAG to finance the transfer, therefore they have to borrow the sum privately, even if they become a registered housing association prior to the transfer. If they are registered with the Housing Corporation, they may be able to obtain HAG for future developments, like any other association, if their aims coincide with those expressed in the appropriate Corporation regional policy statement, although the simple fact of registration is no guarantee of HAG. Valuations are at tenanted market values, which means that the fact that there is an occupant must be taken into account. A property purchased with a sitting tenant with a long-term periodic agreement is known as an investment property, because what is being acquired is a cash flow: rental payments, to be set aside the cost of managing and maintaining the property, together with other liabilities such as loan repayments. Hopefully, there will be a positive difference between the flow of expenditure and income, otherwise it would be a bad investment. The valuation of cash flow therefore determines the selling price. The methodology is known as Net Present Value (NPV), or Discounted Valuation, and is comparatively simple to understand.

In essence, the meaning of Net Present Value can be understood from a description of the methodology. First, a projection of current expenditure is made over the life of a loan term which the body wishes to obtain, say 25 years. This may include an inflation factor – always a guess – over the term. Items will include management and maintenance costs, estimated losses, the financing of liabilities, and any revenue sums set aside for capital purposes. Then, a projection of current income over the same period is performed. Principal items will include rent and service charges, and interest on any investments. Projected expenditure is totalled and deducted from projected expenditure. The sum is then adjusted for inflation, so that the valuation is at today's prices. This is the net present valuation: net, because it involves deducting expenditure from income once the cash flow has been established; present, because the sum is discounted for inflation (hence 'Discounted Valuation'.) And valuation is obvious. This is the sum which will represent the purchase price. It is common for both prospective buyer and vendor to perform such valuations, and to meet at a negotiated figure.

The very notion of valuing social housing in this way, as a series of cash flows, is evidence of creeping commercialism. Certainly council homes are producers of rent and also objects of expenditure, but they are also somebody's home. They were built not as some asset to be used as security for private finance, but as a foundation for personal happiness and security. The very act of valuation may lead the housing professional to slip away from the idea that the property is a social good to the notion that it is a financial contingency, and this mode of thinking if pushed too far may dehumanise the debate. It should be remembered that the entire motivation behind transfer is, or should be, the betterment of existing and potential customers, through the continued provision of good-quality services and a viable development programme.

Once the price has been determined, then assuming a positive ballot, private finance will have to be sought on the basis of association's business plan. The heart of this will be a series of cash flow projections and statements of present and future assets, to convince the lender that there is sufficient security, taken on assets or cash flow or both, to justify lending at a given rate, but also a statement of purpose, and an analysis of the business environment. The plan may well involve a programme of sales, which may finance some of the capital liability. Some of these sales will be a result of the exercise of preserved Right to Buy; but some may be assumed as a result of voluntary sales policies, embarking on shared ownership, and even land sales. These are all commercial considerations. The association will have to take a businesslike view on rent payment levels, and increases, to meet loan repayments and ensure it has sufficient to run its organisation along cost-effective and efficient lines.

LSVT organisations must ensure that rents and other income are sufficient to maintain loan repayments, along with other outgoings. They operate in a subsidy-poor environment, and are in many respects very similar to public limited companies (PLCs), at least before they can get HAG. They are able to maintain relatively low rents, or at least charges consistent with what tenants paid to their former landlord, because the valuation methodology throws up a lower figure than would be the case under open market valuation. Much of their viability depends upon income generated by the housing benefit system, as it is often the case that a large proportion of tenants will be reliant on social security. Owing to the difference between the ways that private and public sector housing benefit, respectively, are subsidised, the net effect of transfer is an increased cost to the treasury, even though some of the sales proceeds will be used to redeem public debt. A 20 per cent levy on transfer receipts was imposed to help pay for this increased liability. But transfer associations are highly dependent for their cash flow on regular payments of housing benefit-backed rents, and therefore as vulnerable as other housing associations and private landlords to further restrictions on the system, in terms of levels of payment to individuals. Capping may well increase arrears levels, and therefore lead to great uncertainty in the mind of potential private investors, which may yet slow up the transfer rate.

The motivation for LSVT is, as has been stated, a desire to ensure that social housing can continue to be produced under the more favourable regime pertaining to housing associations, and where the proceeds from asset sales can be recycled 100 per cent into the creation of new homes and renovations. It is also sometimes justified on the basis of keeping the social stock together, as assured tenants gaining their tenancy after transfer do not have the right to buy, although they may benefit from any voluntary sales policy operated by the association. There is, however, a worrying accountability problem which feeds the tendency for LSVT boards to act rather like those of large companies. Legislative constraint restricts the membership of such boards by local authority persons to less than 20 per cent, so that councils cannot control or influence them. If the board contains more than this percentage, and there is deemed to be a business relationship between the association and a local authority, the finances of the association are subject to the same restrictions as those of a council. This obviates the point of transfer. Thus, to be a bona fide transfer body, the association needs to be formally independent of the sponsoring council. LSVT organisations therefore bear as little democratic relationship to their customers as do traditional housing associations.

Some may think this sacrifice too high a price to pay for the advantages of such a strategy, and this lack of connection may tempt boards to make high-handed decisions in the knowledge that there is no democratic redress. At least councillors know that bad decisions can result in not being voted in at the next local election. As with any other strategy, the pros must be weighted against the cons, even if it sometimes involves trying to assess quantifiables against unquantifiables.

7.3.2   Local housing companies

One of the oddities of the current UK housing finance system is that local authority borrowing is counted within the Public Sector Borrowing Requirement (PSBR), even though the majority of housing loans are raised privately and repaid through the wallets of tenants. It is strange too that Right to Buy sales, and the use of receipts, are counted in the PSBR, even though purchasers no longer have a right to a council mortgage, and receipts are often used to redeem private debt. The unstated rationale for this is that public expenditure is classified according to who does it rather than the source or destination of funds, and that counting such activities within the PSBR is another way of controlling the amount of money in circulation, and thus, supposedly, inflation.

LSVT is one way of removing part of the housing stock from the confines of the PSBR, as non-HAG housing association activity is not accounted within it. But it is allowed only where the receipt clears housing debts, and it has the unfortunate side-effect of reducing accountability to customers through removal from the democratic process, as previously defined. What if a new organisation could be formed, which could contain a higher level of council representation and yet be free of undue financial restriction, even where the sale receipt realised would not clear all housing debts? This, in essence, is the notion of the local housing company, as floated by Nick Raynsford, Steve Wilcox and others, and which formed the subject of a Joseph Rowntree Trust report, *Local housing companies: New opportunities for council housing*, published in 1993. It is an idea since championed by the Chartered Institute of Housing, and supported by the National Federation of Housing Associations, although at the time of writing it was poorly understood and the subject of research by the Department of the Environment. In 1993, several shadow housing companies were set up to test the notion.

Such companies would acquire the stock at Net Present Valuation or possibly outstanding loan debt. Where the value exceeded or equalled housing debt, the transfer would proceed as with LSVT; otherwise, the property would pass to a local housing company, with D.o.E. subsidy continuing to be made available for loan charges. The argument is that even if some form of subsidy continued, there would be a net gain to the Treasury, as the total amount of subsidy payable would fall, and some public loans would be redeemed.

It is thought that this form of arrangement would be appropriate to many metropolitan boroughs where loan debts exceed valuation. Such organisations would clearly be outside the PSBR, and, as bona fide companies, would be able to raise private finance against assets and cash flows without undue restriction. They would also be able to undertake a greater range of provision: perhaps up-market developments for rent or for sale, to cross-subsidise social housing.

One cloud on the horizon concerns monetary policy. The amount of money flowing in the economy would not decrease, but might actually increase, through the enhanced activities of such companies. If central policy is to control inflation partly by restricting the amount of money in circulation, would not such companies threaten this objective? Money is money, whether spent by public or private institutions.

However, the economic multiplier effects, in terms of creating housing construction and ancillary employment, and the tax yield and savings in social security implied, have to be weighed against any inflationary tendencies associated with such companies. An alternative approach, which appears to be beyond the imagination of the mandarins, would be to count any private loans and expenditure from cash receipts from sales as being outside the PSBR by definition, and let councils get on with the job of providing social housing. However, the notion of working for a housing company might be rather more romantic, if housing work can ever be termed thus, than working for the municipality. Hence, perhaps, the reason why the idea has been pursued so vigorously by professional groupings who perhaps eye their contemporaries in business with not a little envy.

Two articles at the end of this chapter concerning housing companies (p. 259 and 261, respectively), discuss the initiative in some detail. The first examines the Chartered Institute of Housing proposal on the matter, put forward in 1992, and the second, the range of options put forward under the aegis of the Joseph Rowntree Foundation the following year. Of particular significance is the treatment of cases in which the authority's housing debt exceeds the purchase price. Will councils be allowed to carry such

Fig. 7.1 Will high-rise housing be an attractive proposition under compulsory competitive tender?

Fig. 7.2 Homes and people are the assets of local housing companies

Fig. 7.3 Housing associations can manage private rented homes

debts over to their General Fund? In which case, why should non-council tenants be expected to subsidise loan debt on properties no longer in the domain of the local authority? It is unlikely that central government, or lending institutions, will simply write such debts off. Will central government offer to subsidise loan debt repayments when the assets they created have been disposed of in this manner? Much depends upon whether the financial benefits to the state – reduction in overall subsidy liability – outweigh the costs. Another issue discussed is that of local democracy: housing companies are, like housing associations, less accountable to local communities than are councils, even if a proportion of their board can be made up of councillors. This should worry those who believe that local people should have a decision-making stake in the management of homes which were constructed to serve local needs.

7.4 Business planning: the logic of commercialism

Business plans have become as much a part of the local authority and housing association kitbag as repairs and maintenance policies. There are several reasons for this: the greater reliance on private finance, where lenders insist on seeing a credible plan of action as well as an asset valuation; a move towards more commercial methodologies in getting essential tasks done; and perhaps a fashion for things businesslike. There is also a sense in which the marketeers of this form of corporate planning-cum-selling device have created demand for this form of validation exercise.

Definitions vary, but centre on the notion that they are statements of actions and resources which organisations require to sustain and develop their activities over time. A business plan's essential difference from management by objectives is that it is supposed to involve consultation with and input from staff and customers at all levels. At its simplest, it is based around a projected cash flow and statement of assets; but it is far more than this. It involves the analysis of the organisation's purpose.

There is no one format for the business planning process, but all have the following stages:

- *Status review* – that is, an examination of the present nature and position of the organisation, including its environment, challenges and particular strengths and weaknesses.

- *Strategy* – an evaluation of alternative methods of achieving aims and objectives.

- *Detailed plan* – a plan to implement strategy in an ordered manner, with the involvement and consent of all staff and with significant customer input.

- *Implementation* – a timetable with dates against objectives, fully costed, together with a means of monitoring progress.

A typical series of steps, based on a number of consultancies' briefs, might be:

1. *Definition of the mission statement.* This is a simple statement of the values of the organisation, and should define its overall aims. For example, the mission statement of a housing association might be to provide affordable homes for rent and for sale to those covered by the charitable objects of the association. A mission statement is a flag which gives the organisation its distinctive identity.

2. *Definition of objectives.* If the aim is what lies at the top of the ladder, the objectives are the rungs – what needs to be achieved in order to arrive at the aim. For example, if the mission statement is to provide affordable homes, an objective might be to provide 60 new homes for rent by 1998, which, when added to the objective to provide 50 shared ownership homes by the same date, would indicate that the aim had been met, to that point in time at least. Objectives must be quantified in terms of time or money to mean anything, if these measures are at all appropriate.

3. *Business audit or SWOT analysis.* The purpose of this stage is to define the business environment of the organisation. SWOT stands for Strengths, Weaknesses, Opportunities and Threats, which may be internal or external. It is impossible to plan for the future unless the constraints of the present are known. The external strengths of an organisation might include a solid relationship with the local authority

in terms of funding and access to discounted land through council sales and planning agreement. Internal strengths may include a relatively flat decision-making hierarchy, so that decisions of moment can be taken by most staff members, which may be important in terms of personnel motivation, and adaptability to change through being able to call upon the diverse talents of the workforce.

External weaknesses may include difficulties in obtaining private finance on competitive terms owing to a lean asset base, or some feature of the lending market common to organisations of that size, or of the movement as a whole – for example, common worries over the level of gearing (ratio of assets to loans) – and thus security. Internal weaknesses may relate to high staff turnover due to perception of a turbulent environment, or a lack of trust or consultation between senior management and the rank and file.

Internal opportunities may include the possibility of using star teams (that is, groups which are formed regardless of formal hierarchical position to solve or undertake specific problems or projects),which might reduce the alienation identified as internal weakness. External opportunities may include the development of Housing Corporation policy to favour new forms of low-cost home ownership which the association feels happy with pursuing, or local authority policy which favours partnership deals. Currently, CCT may well be regarded as an external opportunity by many an association revising its business plan.

Internal threats may include that of industrial action as a result of an unpopular personnel policy or a wages freeze; or that of customer dissatisfaction with the existing level of consultation or involvement. This latter may well become an external threat if picked up by the Housing Corporation in its monitoring visits, as tenant participation is a key policy area. External threats may include the level of competition for contracts and resources from other associations, and the diminishing HAG level available to support development costs.

The SWOT analysis provides an ideal opportunity for staff at all levels to give their views as to their own sectional environments, and that of the concern as a whole. It provides an excellent forum in which the stuff of informal discussions may be aired and teased through. Management committee and senior management may use the SWOT process to redefine their roles and attitudes, and clarify differences in perspective.

4. *Identification of plan assumptions.* The business environment having been defined, it is now necessary to make assumptions about any changes which may occur in it, and thus impinge on plans. For example, a prudent association would probably have to make the assumption that HAG rates will diminish even further, and possibly that there will be a yet greater emphasis on home ownership in the future. Interest rates may change, as may the availability of loans. Many things will be less

predictable than others: but some crystal ball gazing must be done. At this stage, balance sheets and income and expenditure accounts may be inserted, along with cash flow projections to reflect different possible futures, given changes in the business environment foreseen.

5. *Gap analysis.* This entails attempting to measure the gap between where the organisation finds itself, and where it wishes to go. A model must be built of the organisation's future, perhaps in terms of numbers of units, or a financial state of affairs. The gap can be expressed in terms of time or assets. It is a prologue to devising a strategy to arrive at the desired state of affairs.

6. *Evaluation of alternative strategies.* There may be more than one way of achieving the desired goals. Much will depend upon the realisation of resources, and policy constraints beyond the organisation's control, such as the availability of private finance. For example, the objective of housing a given number of people could be achieved solely through providing housing for rent, for sale, or a mixture of both. The strategy adopted will depend upon external constraints and opportunities further into the plan. It is at this point that much useful work can be done by teams at various levels of the hierarchy in examining alternative scenarios, as well as assessing the realism of any strategies suggested. Computer modelling can help, especially where the projection of accounts is required. Modelling can answer the question as to whether any given strategy can be sustained by projected resources, and which strategies will deliver acceptable results around a margin.

7. *Identification of resources required.* Resources encompass not only finance, but also personnel. Are sufficient skills available to realise the plans, and, if not, which particular ones are needed? Could they be achieved by training existing staff, or is it necessary to recruit further personnel in a targeted manner? A skills audit could be carried out to address this issue. There should be a discussion as to the location of any resources required, and the relative ease or difficulty in obtaining them. The organisation's track record in obtaining such support may be of relevance here: hopefully, a good business plan will increase the likelihood of such resources being made available.

8. *The definition of key tasks (action planning).* It is necessary to set out a plan, with the consent of staff involved in its implementation, which consists of a series of key, measurable steps that can be taken to realise the objectives set out earlier. For example, a new association may have as one of its key tasks the building of relationships with funders and local authorities which will work in partnership with it, as well as a comprehensive understanding of Housing Corporation procedure. Another might be the regular review of committee membership and roles in attempting to maximise the effectiveness of decision-making. A flowchart may be used to define a timetable for the action plan, or a criti-

cal path analysis performed. This is essentially a method of defining the route which will lead to realisation of the desired result, measured in terms of resource input and time, and lends itself to computer simulation. Care should be taken to ensure that these tasks are realistic, which should involve extensive discussion with the staff who will have to carry out the tasks, as well as an audit of equipment needed in the process.

9. *Measurement and control.* The action plan having been defined, there must be some way of evaluating progress. One common method is by recording actual against projected income or outputs and expenditure or inputs: but monitoring is more than this. It also involves analysing the efficiency of the programme, which involves looking at time and staff resources devoted to achievement: some strategies may be more wasteful than others, and there may be a chance to modify the method in the light of such findings.

Performance monitoring is already very much part of the kitbag of associations and authorities, and has even been imposed on them, as previously stated. The results of strategies should be made publicly available, in order to act as a discipline on the organisation and encourage progress as much as for the sake of giving information. This is also a requirement imposed by the D.o.E. for authorities, and the Housing Corporation for the voluntary sector. Monitoring implies that the process can be measured, and a decision must therefore be taken as to the units of such assessment.

Business planning is no longer a luxury which can be passed over: the Corporation recommends that every association has a plan, and in Scotland it was a condition of registration. Private lenders generally insist upon them, as do development partners, if only to examine the congruence between respective organisations' aims and objectives.

This is an area where many organisations choose to use consultancies to assist in formulating and even, on occasions, in implementing business plans. There are advantages to using a disinterested party for this purpose. First, a consultant may be able to reveal and then to take account of any hidden agendas which may be lurking and foul up the preparation of a plan: sectional interests might lead to the issue of restructuring being ignored or obstructed in cases when restructuring might prove necessary to meet new challenges. Second, a good consultant, with experience of plan preparation in an number of like and different bodies, can bring a wealth of comparative knowledge to the enterprise. Third, it might prove necessary to engage an honest broker to mediate between, say, a management or committee, and an alienated workforce who are unwilling or unprepared to accept changes in routine. Consultants are not cheap; and they cannot be expected to formulate the plan without extensive knowledge of the technique, but also of the business environment and the organisation itself. Thus intense co-operation at all levels is required. The consultant will facilitate rather than direct change, and will listen rather than dictate.

In summary, then, a business plan is an excellent tool for getting people who may be poles apart in attitude, influence and operational area together to jointly appraise future directions; and if planning of this sort achieves only this, it will surely have been worthwhile.

One of the articles at the end of this chapter, 'Business planning and housing associations' (p. 263), discusses the application of this technique to the voluntary sector, and concludes that it is a sound method not only in establishing for the Housing Corporation the financial credibility of associations, but also as an exercise in self-analysis, especially where new challenges arise or where restructuring is proposed. It should be noted that, at the time of writing, Scottish Homes no longer requires new housing associations to produce a business plan as a condition of registration, but it is still highly recommended, and it is difficult to see how an association could obtain private finance unless it followed this line.

7.5   Engaging with the private sector as management agents

Housing associations are primarily providers of affordable housing for rent and for sale, but they have diversified their activities considerably. They are now competitors with local authority housing contractors, agents for the government in rescuing an ailing home ownership market through mortgage rescue schemes, responsible for the housing market package where they bought up unsold private homes, and promoters of Do It Yourself Shared Ownership, which is largely motivated by the political necessity of reducing the overhang on the housing market. They promote themselves like private companies, and have logos which are reminiscent of multinational corporations.

In the 1970s, it would have seemed inconceivable that they could or would act as managing agents for private owners, collecting a market rent on their behalf, and charging a management fee above current commercial levels, directly competing for business with private lettings and management agencies. And yet this is precisely what they have been doing since 1994 in the shape of the Housing Association as Management Agents (HAMA) scheme. Under this arrangement, associations enter into a management agreement with private owners, and manage properties let on an assured shorthold basis, accepting nominations of homeless households mainly from housing authorities. Market rents are collected and paid to the landlord net of the management fee, which is generally higher than the commercial rate owing to the fact that the associations offer rental guarantees and promise to return the property in good condition at the end of the agreement. Surpluses accruing from the scheme end up in the Income and Expenditure Account, and can be used to subsidise mainstream rents or other activities – hence the popularity of the initiative with housing associations across the country.

There are advantages and disadvantages to this commercialistic scheme. It is clearly better that private sector properties are managed by competent organisations which at least notionally have some respect for those who live in them as opposed to often unscrupulous and profit-motivated landlords. At least associations will not discriminate against those on housing benefit in the mistaken belief that they are bad payers (what could be more certain than housing benefit direct to the association or landlord, always assuming that the parties can get the paperwork right)? The properties will be allocated on the basis of need rather than effective demand; and repairs will be done. If anyone has to manage dwellings, it might as well be a relatively caring, responsive and well-informed agency.

On the other hand, it is difficult to see how associations can afford not to recharge market rents. No private landlord with any financial acumen, unless they have a severe case of altruism or suspect that it might be a way of reducing tax liability, will accept anything less than a market rent for a property; thus, unless the association can subsidise the rent in some way, it will have to pass on the full rent to the tenant. Anything less would jeopardise associations' ability to finance management and maintenance, and so their ability to be managers of quality, perhaps their best feature. They may argue that since most of those nominated to HAMA schemes will be on Income Support and therefore eligible for full Housing Benefit (Private Sector), the tenant will not feel the full effect of market rents. This argument is reasonable only as long as housing benefit fully reimburses the cost of the rent. Housing benefit capping reduces this liability: excess rent would have to be paid through income support, reducing the income of such tenants below the state poverty line. This cannot be something which organisations with a social conscience would seek to promote.

Further, the effect of charging, or rather collecting, high rents is to force many into the so-called poverty trap. This occurs as a result of the steep withdrawal rate of housing benefit when earnings exceed income support by a small threshold. In 1995, the withdrawal rate was 65 pence for every pound earned above the threshold. If this is added to withdrawal of other benefits, and the cost of travel and other work-related expenses, and possibly the cost of childminding, the result of taking a relatively low-paid job, even if some way above income support levels, may be to make the tenant worse off than if he or she remains on income support. Thus there is a disincentive to take work, with personal and societal implications. And forcing people to take low-paid work would simply impoverish them. One way forward would be to house people in cheaper accommodation immediately they got work: but where? Presumably, if this were an option, they would not be in HAMA-type schemes in the first place. Again, do organisations with a social conscience really want to pursue schemes which may impoverish those they purportedly help? The fact that so many associations do pursue this option shows how far they have moved away from their charitable roots, and have embraced a commercialistic ethos.

The same argument applies to their activities as leasers of private property, or agents for private sector leasing schemes, where to make such projects stack up it may be necessary to recharge something like a market rent. There is an argument which says that this is better than simply refusing to engage in solutions, however short term, to assist those in greatest housing need; but would not collective refusal to engage in this activity force a rethink on a housing policy which entails these rather desperate measures, or a return to the unconditional support of rents at up to market level through the social security system? Associations tend to be pragmatic organisations: survival is a primary aim, and it is not surprising that they latch on to new initiatives, whether or not they are socially sound, just as a private enterprise might diversify its operations as a hedge against a decline in the market for any one thing it produces. This is a reason why something is done rather than a reason for doing it; an explanation rather than any excuse.

7.6 A commercial future

There is nothing wrong with running profitable enterprises which produce objects or services of quality that people want and/or need and that they, or at least some of them, can afford to pay for. Arguably, the profit motive is the single most important engine for economic growth, and the world-wide failure of socialistic modes of production where attempts have been made to eliminate the profit motive at least in the formal sense must support this view. Unfortunately, profit-seeking organisations can flourish only where there is effective demand for their products – in other words, where people can afford to pay for them. Services allocated on the basis of need do not cater for effective demand: they exist precisely because there is a lack of it in that area. Enterprises supplying private goods at profit can flourish only if their consumers' incomes can be artificially boosted so that they can exercise effective demand. This is why the private rented sector cannot be expected to make a significant contribution to meeting housing need in the absence of massive financial support, either to landlord or to tenants, from the state. But one must question the validity of asking private enterprise to do something which could be done by organs of the state, or at least by non-commercial organisations which may receive some form of state subsidy to ensure that effective demand is not the sole arbiter of availability.

For all that, it seems that the private sector is being constantly asked to play a yet larger part in social provision: witness pensions, the health service, education and transportation. Of course, if incomes were to rise in real terms to an extent that most of these needs could be satisfied by most people at the economic price, the issue of social provision would not be a significant one. It could be met through pretty minimal taxation. Unfortunately, this does not appear to be the case. And as long as the private sector is in this position, there will be a case for intervention by social agencies to ensure that it can provide an appropriate level of assistance to those in need.

Therefore, it can be expected that local authorities and housing associations will continue to be enablers of home ownership, which is essentially a private sector concern, through the continuance of Right to Buy, Rent to Mortgage, DIYSO and traditional shared ownership. They will continue to be managers of private accommodation to lease at commercial rates, and to work in partnership with private landowners and developers through the planning system to secure social benefits. Local authorities will continue to divest themselves of their stock to new or existing associations which fund the acquisition privately, or form local housing companies.

The disciplines of commercial management are appropriate to organisations which use public money and therefore must be as accountable as private companies to their shareholders or other investors. There is no excuse for wastage, or of letting arrears spiral, in a lean financial environment. The information technology techniques applied in business, based around spreadsheets, lend themselves to social housing applications. But for all that they might resemble them, social housing organisations are not commercial organisations. Their primary aim is to provide a service or product which is necessary to the integrity of the fabric of society and which cannot be left to the chance that someone will see a buck in providing it – to make it available despite the risk of deficit; that, after all, is the whole justification of public subsidy.

The worry is that as such organisations increasingly follow the commercialistic road, they will lose sight of their major aims and objectives. It is necessary, and healthy, for such organisations to state and restate their core aims and values in every new formulation of their business plans, to remind themselves again and again that, for all their fascination with things commercial, they are there to serve those who have been marginalised by the very success of modern capitalism.

Articles

1. 'Compulsory competitive tender for housing management: the next housing revolution?'

2. 'Involving tenants in compulsory competitive tendering'

3. 'Housing companies: are they the way forward?'

4. 'Housing companies'

5. 'Business planning and housing associations'

6. 'Home ownership: the housing association connection'

Compulsory competitive tender for housing management: the next housing revolution?

In June 1992 the D.o.E. circulated its consultation paper, *Competing for quality in housing management*. The proposal that housing management should be subject to the same sort of compulsory competitive tender (CCT) as waste disposal and maintenance comes as no surprise, as it was a clear Conservative manifesto commitment. The points of controversy – no tenant ballot on tender, the proposal to amend section 105 of the 1985 Housing Act to exempt CCT from tenant consultation, and parcelling stock to provide attractive portfolios for tenderers – are being raised by respondents. This initiative will be in place in all housing authorities by the end of the decade.

In some areas, existing management will successfully tender, either as the authority or a management buyout organisation. Bar further local government structural reforms and departmental name changes, services will be delivered in a similar way as previously, albeit under the constant threat of competition. In other areas, housing associations, either singly or in consortia, will be managing council homes. It is no secret that associations are the preferred agencies, even though several have professed distaste, seeing themselves as partners rather than competitors.

Do tenants actually want new managers? There appears to be little evidence of widespread dissatisfaction, which can be deduced by considering the failure to date of Tenants' Choice.

The 1989 Glasgow study, *The nature and effectiveness of housing management in England and Wales*, revealed higher than expected levels of satisfaction with existing management. Will tenants get a better deal? If the most significant factor in tender acceptance is cost, then if lower management charges are proposed by a non-council bidder, it is likely that rents will be lower than otherwise. But what of quality? Lower costs do not necessarily equate with value for money. Although councils will remain firmly as clients, it is far more difficult to enforce quality through contract compliance legal mechanisms than if the workforce is part of the council, if only because organisational objectives differ.

Much debate has centred around the statement that tenants will not be balloted on the final choice of contractor: it seems to conflict with the emphasis on accountability in the Citizen's Charter, and with official desire to promote tenant involvement. But this objection turns out to be invalid. The question of council housing management is a matter not just for existing tenants, but for all chargepayers: the properties are in common ownership, and the authority has to exercise stewardship on behalf of its entire local electorate and future tenants. Therefore there is as little justification for giving tenants a veto over which agency should manage properties as over the allocations system.

There is no reason why tenants should not exercise the Right to Manage proposed in the consultation document, but that is a distinct issue. If the new managers turn out to be bad, then the council, as client and legal representative of tenant as well as more general interests, can reflect legitimate customer dissatisfaction and sack the contractor, just as council staff can be taken to task if they provide poor service.

The exclusion of individual consultation over the final choice of contractor is, however, at odds with the spirit of customer consciousness. Even if no heed is paid to opinions expressed in the consultation period, tenants, as the ultimate recipient of management, should have the right to be heard. Some commentators appear to have confused 'consultation' with 'veto': listening does not compel action. 'Consultation' implies 'ballot' only if legislation says it does in a specific context, which is ruled out in this case.

A more significant concern is that, having broken up the stock into attractive management parcels, councils may well be left with the most difficult to manage estates which nobody else wishes to service. Two things flow from this: first, the creation or underlining of 'sink' estates, with tenants stigmatised by the general knowledge that no one else wants to manage them, with the problems following from such alienation identified by Anne Power in her Priority Estates Project work. Second, this residualisation will further demoralise council staff and exacerbate turnover and recruitment problems, which will do nothing for the quality of housing management. Equity in quality of service delivery, surely a principle worth preserving, may be hard to sustain.

The aim that all tenants should receive a high quality of management, contained in the Council Tenant's Charter, entails the careful monitoring of the various management agencies. Local authorities are best placed to undertake this role – and CCT will be justified only if they are allowed to do so. This quality guarantee role is entirely consistent with the view that councils should be enablers rather than providers, and it is hoped that government will insist that adequate monitoring apparatus be put in place well before CCT is introduced into housing management.

PSLG, August 1992

Questions

1. What were the main issues raised by the D.o.E. paper *Competing for quality in housing management*?
2. Do tenants need or want new managers?
3. What are the arguments for and against balloting tenants on the choice of contractor?

Involving tenants in compulsory competitive tendering

In May 1994, a conference organised by the Chartered Institute of Housing, along with the Association of Metropolitan Authorities, the Association of District Authorities, and the Tenant Participation Advisory Service, considered tenant involvement in compulsory competitive tendering (CCT). It was a timely reminder for councils contemplating an April 1996 tendering start that there is now a statutory duty to consult and inform tenants at all stages prior to letting contracts, and that, unlike the case for other CCTs, there must be evidence that their views have been taken into account.

Sir George Young, Minister for Housing, Inner Cities and Construction, stressed that CCT provides an ideal opportunity for providers and users to work in partnership in deciding on contract specifications and, in particular, quality standards. Indeed, the philosophy of responding to customer concerns seems to have affected the D.o.E., which has changed regulations several times in the light of representations, and results from the pilot authorities – Rochdale and Westminster – which examined issues of tenant consultation before management agreement and involvement in monitoring respectively.

The recent welcome decision to exempt councils subject to structural reorganisation following impending local government reform from CCT for 24 months after reorganisation was underlined. But the most significant statement was his outline of the government's view of what tenant involvement should entail, drawing on guidance issued in March 1994. This entails a comprehensive framework for involvement at different levels depending on tenant desire to engage with the council; flexibility in how individual authorities involve tenants; and locally designed structures through which consultation and participation take place reflecting the circumstances and views of local authorities and their tenants. Difficulties in consulting a dispersed, rural tenantry could be dealt with by a 'modicum of imagination', and it was stressed that there were no 'no-go' areas.

The cost of participation falls to housing revenue accounts. The D.o.E. made special grants available to 18 councils in the pilot programme designed to boost tenant involvement, but no across-the-board commitment was made for the future. It was claimed that the cost in pilot authorities was low, at a bargain 2 1/2p per tenant per week. Rents will presumably rise for other reasons – for example, subsidy withdrawal! Participation in drawing up specifications was seen as a first step towards tenant management through the Right to Manage. Finally, it was suggested that tenant involvement in CCT, as in other areas of the housing service, helps give people a greater stake in their estates, as well as providing residents with a enhanced understanding of the difficulties their landlords have in allocating resources and management. This mirrors the philosophy of reducing alienation between tenants and managers which underlies similar government initiatives such as the Priority Estates Project.

It is hard to disagree with any of this: it is reassuring to hear that tenant consultation should be taken seriously, and helps diminish the argument that tenants should be given a veto over the authority's appointment of a given contractor, which was in any case ruled out in the Leasehold Reform, Housing and Urban Development Act 1993. In authorities where there are already active tenants' associations or similar bodies, and where there is genuine motivation to engage with the council to ensure good quality standards for management, there is little doubt that CCT will provide a catalyst for further tenant involvement or management. It is equally clear that much groundwork is essential in areas with no such traditions to enable meaningful tenant involvement.

Robina Goodlad, a Senior Lecturer from the University of Glasgow and co-author of the chapter on tenant involvement in the recently launched Association of District Councils/Chartered Institute of Housing manual on CCT and local authority housing, identified eight key stages of tenant involvement in CCT: policy and planning, contract packaging, contract specification, selection of tenderers, tender evaluation, contractor selection and award of contract, monitoring and enforcement, and review. All of these require training to ensure that tenants are on a level playing field with professionals, in order to bring about true empowerment; and consultants like TPAS have a valuable role as 'honest brokers' in bringing officials and tenants together, especially where there may have been mistrust.

It was stressed that tenants had a right to feedback as to the extent to which their views had influenced policy, and Marianne Hood, of TPAS, even offered the services of that organisation in taking to court as a test case any council that blatantly disregards tenant views.

The thrust of the conference was that tenant involvement is an integral part of CCT even without the possibility of ballot, and that councils disregard this at their peril. Hopefully, the day when tenants are regarded as customers in the fullest sense has now arrived, even if partly through a policy which may place housing management at a further remove from democratic control.

PSLG, July 1994

Questions

1. To what extent can tenants' views be taken into account in deciding how and who runs council housing services?
2. How is such participation financed and facilitated?
3. What are the key stages of tenant involvement in CCT, and what form of training might be required to make it effective?

Housing companies: are they the way forward?

At its June 1992 conference, the Chartered Institute of Housing launched a White Paper, *Housing: The first priority*, stating its view as to how social housing should be provided and managed. It opined that around 100 000 affordable homes must be produced annually in England alone to meet demand, against a decline of 1.3 million in the number of houses to rent in Britain over the past decade.

One intriguing proposal is that of local housing companies. Any method of securing housing investment for social housing which avoids increasing the Public Sector Borrowing Requirement (PSBR) might find sympathy in the Treasury, the determinant of public spending.

A local housing company is envisaged as an 'arm's length' enterprise, set up at the behest of a council, to which stock and management duties could be transferred. Its board would contain a larger number of councillors than permitted under the rules imposed by the 1989 Local Government and Housing Act, to ensure local accountability, and yet its financial operations would be outside public sector definitions.

Such a company would not buy in the way that housing associations do under voluntary transfer. Under large-scale voluntary transfer (LSVT), associations usually purchase at Net Present Value: the difference between the projected stream of income over the period of the purchase loan, and expenditure, taking account of sales and acquisitions, at today's prices. The company would take on ownership of the outstanding debt, which could be done in conjunction with transfer of titles, leaving the authority housing debt-free, albeit without a capital receipt.

Companies would then borrow against the stream of rental income and possibly asset sales. Private lenders would then need to satisfy themselves only about rent and other income profiles when considering loans, rather than just increasing or declining asset values. There would be no necessary call on public resources.

A number of things must happen before such a proposal could be realised. First, there is the issue of councillor representation. There are good reasons to maintain a substantial local authority presence on such boards. Transfer associations, which are the main alternative to companies, are not democratic organisations in the sense that councils are. The management of housing built and allocated under the public domain to meet community needs should entail more than token democratic community representation.

Second, if assets are transferred at outstanding debt, the price for such a discount should equitably be a greater degree of public control than is the case where best consideration has been obtained. However, this entails that the rules set out in the 1989 Act, which would define such a company as controlled or influenced, need amendment, otherwise its finances would be treated in the same way as a local authority, which would obviate the point of the exercise. On the other hand, it would be absurd to treat a company with little or no involvement in public expenditure as a council: but it is important that this point is not lost on legislators.

Third, the transfer issue requires further examination. Councils are under a general duty to ensure they get best consideration for assets disposed of. Exceptions can be and have been made in relation to land and property sales to housing associations, but such exceptions are subject to consent. Even if presented as mere transference of debt, such transactions are likely to be treated as disposals. Unless you are a recent mortgagor suffering from negative equity, it is rare that the value of housing is less than outstanding debt. Unless such housing companies are to be mere managing agents, then if a general consent is not given to such under-value disposals, local authorities attempting such transactions could be acting *ultra vires*, with serious legal consequences.

The advantages to all parties over retaining stock with councils or voluntary transfer justify the resolution of these issues. First, such companies would be free from public sector spending rules, and would therefore be able to invest in social housing without the constraint of cash limits, unlike councils. Second, they would remain democratically accountable through councillor representation, unlike LSVT associations. Third, the comparatively low level of outstanding debt inherited from councils would mean that rents could be kept down, without the need to finance the usual loan to pay for market-value purchase. Fourth, following on from the previous point, the housing benefit burden would be less than where a higher price has been paid for transfer, with higher debts to service through rents. This would obviate the need to claw back receipts from transfers to pay for the spiralling housing benefit bill, which has been suggested in some quarters.

This option should be further examined at the highest level, representing as it does a way of reducing calls on the PSBR at a time of economic difficulty, and, as significantly, a method of producing badly needed affordable housing.

PSLG, November 1992

Questions

1. Why must local housing companies fall outside the Public Sector Borrowing Requirement to be of use in generating new social housing?
2. Why might there be need for legislative changes to facilitate such organisations?
3. What are the essential differences between Large Scale Voluntary Transfer and local housing companies?

Housing companies

Local housing companies: new opportunities for council housing, published by the Joseph Rowntree Foundation in March 1993, claims that over £16 billion could be released for social housing through transfers to 'local housing companies' falling outside public expenditure definitions. The authors, Steve Wilcox of Cardiff University, and John Perry of the Institute of Housing, argue that, in addition to releasing the asset value of council housing, which transfer companies would use as security to attract private finance, the effect on public expenditure and hence the Public Sector Borrowing Requirement (PSBR) would be broadly neutral, whilst the constitution of the companies would ensure local accountability.

The main transfer scenarios proposed are for cases where value exceeds debt, and where the reverse is true. Two models envisage transfer at Net Present Value (NPV) as accepted hitherto by the D.o.E. for large-scale voluntary transfers (LSVTs). NPV calculations involve assessing the difference between income and expenditure over the life of a loan at today's values. In the first case, exemplified mainly by shire districts where stock is in generally better condition, transfers at NPV would continue, either to registered housing associations as presently, or to 'local housing companies' with full debt redemption assured. The company route is preferred, as tax revenue would offset any additional cost to the public purse due to switching over to the different housing subsidy regime which exists for private sector housing benefit. If the HA route were chosen, Treasury clawback of 20 per cent of receipts would broadly offset such costs.

In the second case, typified by metropolitan authorities with stock often in poor repair, it is proposed that councils transfer at NPV, retaining outstanding debt, which would continue to attract central government subsidy. It is claimed that this continued cost would be largely offset by VAT and other tax income from the new companies, as well as reduced loan subsidy liability, thus avoiding the need for Treasury clawback.

Other models examined were transfers at historic debt, and on a revenue payment basis. The former would be inappropriate where value exceeds debt, as it would fall foul of the requirement that councils should obtain best consideration for assets. The latter model, where capital value is converted to periodic instalments, is far from straightforward and has yet to be fully articulated, and is therefore difficult to assess or justify, although it should perhaps be examined further.

It is the claimed lack of local accountability of current LSVT bodies as much as public expenditure constraints placed on council and association activities which leads the authors to favour transfer to 'local housing companies', which would have higher council representation on their boards than the 20 per cent allowed on the management committees of registered associations.

At present, higher levels would entail associations becoming 'controlled or influenced companies' under the 1989 Local Government and Housing Act, subject to the same financial constraints as councils labour under, thus eroding many advantages of transfer.

It is suggested that up to 50 per cent of company board members should be council representatives, thus preserving local accountability. It is claimed that the activities of such bodies would fall outside public expenditure rules, and hence would not add to PSBR burdens. Such companies might therefore have a freedom to invest in social housing lacking in the local authority sector: nor would they be subject to the cap on the Approved Development Programme.

However, with the high council representation levels suggested, it is unclear why they and their financial activities should be reckoned outside the public domain: associations adopting such a membership policy certainly would not be. Legislation would be required to exempt such companies from the 1989 Act rules. If so, legislators might as well permit greater council involvement (albeit of a minority nature) in existing associations, and remove their private finance activities from public sector accounting limits, rather than sanctioning the creation of yet more social housing agencies. Housing associations have established credibility with private lenders, which new companies do not. The movement is well understood by institutional investors and central government alike. Associations also have the development and management skills to ensure that social housing is provided efficiently and appropriately; they have also built good working relationships with councils. And any tax gain to the Treasury would presumably have to be paid for by 'housing company' tenant rent hikes, hardly preserving the notion of affordability.

The quantity of social housing which an organisation can deliver is of greater importance than excessive worry over representativeness (though good housing associations do liaise with local communities, often more effectively than local bureaucrats or members, despite the undeniable fact that their boards are not directly elected). Best practice would involve government accepting the financial sense of the proposal, whilst enacting legislation with respect to housing associations as suggested, to ensure the survival of social housing without recourse to unnecessary duplication.

Questions

1. How would public accountability be ensured through the use of local housing companies?
2. In which cases would local housing companies be a more realistic option from the viewpoint of both debt redemption and social housing production than other forms of transfer from council ownership?

Business planning and housing associations

Committee members and officers of associations seeking Housing Corporation registration should note the increasing attention paid to financial and personnel systems. This is reflected in the Housing Corporation's *Criteria for registration of a housing association*, December 1991 edition, which stated: 'many associations will wish to prepare a full business plan, and have this professionally validated ... this information will be scrutinised by the finance staff of the Corporation.' Although business planning is not yet a condition of registration as in Scotland, recommendations often become requirements.

All successful organisations set aims and objectives, comparable respectively to the end of a ladder and its rungs, and, to pursue the analogy, design strategies to climb that ladder without falling off or having to buy a new one. Business planning involves the rational pursuit of ends via a series of operations understood and consented to at all levels of the organisation, and monitoring its progress in helping to achieve goals.

An independent angle on the nature of business planning comes from the Local Government Management Board, which published *The application of business planning* in February 1991. Although targeted at councils, it has general application. Key managers, it says, must reach agreement on the value of the approach; then the concept is explained to others in management positions. A briefing session follows where managers set priorities, and begin to consider the nature of the plan.

Evidence relevant to realising agreed objectives is then collected and collated, so that different forward options can be formulated. Typically, this will take the form of a 'strengths and weaknesses analysis' followed by an assessment of available resources in the light of the prevailing business environment. This would include the impact of current and likely legislative change, and changing attitudes amongst influencing forces – for example, financial institutions. The alternative options are then examined against human and financial resources already identified, and a business plan finalised, including an action statement and monitoring apparatus. Finally, the plan is confirmed with any management at a more senior tier than that devising the plan, and with committee or board members.

Some organisations have attempted such a strategy unaided, but there are disadvantages. Management may be too involved to see fundamental problems in organisational structures, resulting in unclear aims, objectives and inappropriate change methods. Second, the business planning process is a very useful but delicate tool which is best introduced by agencies with considerable experience before it can be self-managed, which is the ultimate objective. A specialist consultant can be used to avoid in-fighting and hidden agendas which might throw

the process off course. By acting as an 'honest broker' of views, the consultant can articulate the legitimate concerns of all personnel, so that their
views can be taken on board, allowing them to retain ownership of the plan.
There is also the need to get it right first time – there may not be a second
chance!

The Manor Consulting Group (TMCG) is a management consultancy with
considerable experience of business planning in both public and private sectors,
and is committed to the philosophy of intra-organisational consent. John Bailey,
a partner, highlights TMCG's approach:

The planning process is a part of overall management. Whether we are discussing internal reorganisation or customer awareness, positive change comes only through the application of the three Cs: co-operation, commitment and communication. Management
pyramids in local authorities and housing associations are becoming flatter and more
devolved, so it's important that everybody should own the plan for meeting agreed objectives. Agreement is crucial to the successful implementation of change strategies. Our
role is not to prescribe aims, but facilitate movement towards them.

TMCG believes that once its business plans have been devised, an association should be able to operate, re-evaluate and if necessary redesign them as
needs change: it is a way of management life rather than a one-off genuflection
which will banish all sins forever!

Apart from the Corporation's expectation that associations should prepare
business plans, there are other vital reasons for doing so. Financiers, when deciding whether and how to lend, expect organisations to demonstrate not only
cash flow and asset-worthiness, but the sort of operational structures which will
cope with periods of both environmental calm and turbulence. The voluntary
housing movement is increasingly dependent upon private finance, therefore
highlighting the business planning issue. Then there is the crucial partnership role
played by associations working with local authorities and others to produce
affordable social housing. It is unlikely that productive links, or lasting results,
will be achieved unless each partner knows and believes in the other's aims,
and, perhaps more importantly, believes that it can carry out its plans to mutual
benefit. Again, business planning, with its emphasis on rational decision-making
and the making explicit of sound but often unexpressed ideas, can assist in mutual
understanding. Also, it provides a valuable opportunity for officers and members
to work together in a constructive, structured way to define development and
management objectives.

For all these reasons, whether associations are newly formed, seeking registration, or reviewing policies, it is recommended that assistance be sought to
ensure that organisations measure up to the challenges implicit in today's social
housing field.

PSLG, March 1993

Questions

1. Outline the main stages of business planning. Why is it important that housing associations develop them?

2. How might business planning strategies strengthen the decision making structure of an organisation?
3. How can consultants assist in the process of business planning?

Home ownership: the housing association connection

A constant in government housing policy over the past 14 years has been the
promotion of home ownership, instanced by the Right to Buy, retention of mortgage interest tax relief, and a variety of low-cost home ownership schemes, using
housing associations as the dominant vehicle. It is expected that by 1995/96, 29
per cent of the Housing Corporation's Approved Development Programme cash
will be allocated to shared ownership, significantly up on this year's [1994's] 18
per cent, when around £190 million was allocated. Many councils are examining their nominations policies to ensure maximum benefit from the programme
through release of scarce social rented housing as eligible tenants take advantage of 'low cost' initiatives.

Associations have been building for low-cost home ownership since the 1970s.
The dominant component has hitherto been new-build shared ownership,
whereby properties are sold on a part-rent part-buy basis to social tenants and
applicants on association and council waiting lists. Essentially, the association
grants a long lease to the purchaser for a percentage, usually 50 per cent or
more, of the property's value, and holds the remainder as a legal charge, with
the occupiers paying rent on the unsold equity to cover loan costs, management and maintenance. The purchaser's legal status as owner entails the usual
repair and insurance obligations. In some cases, councils have made land available at undervalue or at no cost at all in order to reduce project and therefore consumer costs; land discounts for such schemes leave Housing Association
Grant (HAG) rates unaffected.

Planning guidance, specifically PPG3 (Land for Housing) highlights the need
for planning authorities to consider quotas for affordable housing both generally and at site level, and should lead to a more focused approach to enabling
low-cost initiatives.

In April 1992, the government relaunched Do It Yourself Shared Ownership
(DIYSO), first fielded in 1983. A variant of traditional shared ownership, it entails
applicants finding properties on the open market, with the association then buying them and selling a share to the purchaser, charging rent to cover outgoings
and acquisition costs not met by grant and the shared owner's contribution.
Although take-up has been relatively modest so far, there is now significant interest following an aggressive publicity campaign. Wise authorities have tapped into
this scheme by cementing links with DIYSO associations, thus releasing social
lets.

The advantages to the consumer of DIYSO over traditional shared ownership are choice and mobility; and the initiative may well stimulate a still quiet
property market. The housing market is still a buyer's field: there is ample opportunity to purchase at relatively low prices, with revenue costs lessened by recent
falls in interest rates. Also, DIYSO purchasers are not limited to the geographical area usually served by the association, thus they can use this route to ensure

that they end up where they want to be, subject to valuation constraints.

DIYSO could help stimulate market movement – good news for current owners wishing to sell and for those whose livelihood depends upon the paraphernalia associated with home-moving.

Some caution is required. First, new purchasers, perhaps unused to the budgeting entailed by home ownership, are entering at a time of very low interest rates and therefore lowish repayments. Care must be taken by associations and those referring clients to such organisations that budgets are examined, and the implications of ownership fully explained, as it is likely that rates will rise again, and many purchasers may be very 'marginal' in that they can only just afford the deal now. Second, DIYSO purchases are likely to be of second-hand, perhaps older, properties, which characteristically have higher maintenance costs and general outgoings than newer homes; buyers should be made aware of this aspect when expressing an interest. And some lenders have shown themselves wary of lending on shared ownership largely because they are unused to lending over such low percentages of valuations and are understandably worried about recouping their investment in an uncertain market should default occur, although there is no evidence of higher default amongst shared owners than any other category. None of these difficulties is insuperable: proper initial advice and lender education should ease such concerns.

To ensure a coherent role for shared ownership in local housing policy, authorities would do well to secure realistic quotas for nominations from their tenants, based upon previous experience and screening of eligible tenants, possibly entailing an incomes survey, to establish effective demand. A case could then be made to the Housing Corporation through regional offices for appropriate allocations to marry grant to estimated take-up. Such a policy not only helps meet the legitimate aspiration of many towards owner-occupation, but relieves housing stress, and deserves support.

PSLG, January 1994

Questions

1. What are the advantages for those purchasing on a shared ownership basis, and what benefits could this bring to those awaiting social housing for rent?
2. What is the distinctive nature of Do It Yourself Shared Ownership? To what extent could it affect a housing market in decline?
3. What are the dangers of pursuing an increased low-cost home ownership policy at the expense of rented development?

References and useful books

Chapter 1

References

Cullingworth Committee (1969) *Council Housing: Purposes, Procedures and Priorities*. Central Housing Advisory Committee/HMSO, London.
Department of Social Security (1992) *Social Security: The Government's Expenditure Plans 1992–93 to 1994–95*. Cm 1914. HMSO, London.
Department of the Environment (1992) *Homelessness Statistics*. HMSO, London.
Department of the Environment (1992) *Housing and Construction Statistics*. HMSO, London.
Wilcox, S. (1993) *Housing Finance Review 1993*. Joseph Rowntree Foundation, York.

Useful books

Cope, H. (1990) *Housing Associations: Policy and Practice*. Macmillan, London.
Gauldie, E. (1994) *Cruel Habitations*. Allen & Unwin, London.
Smith, M. (1989) *Guide to Housing*. Housing Centre Trust, London.

Chapter 2

References

Department of the Environment (1994) *Housing and Construction Statistics, March Quarter 1994 Part 2*. HMSO, London.
Housing Corporation (1994) *The Housing Corporation's proposals for Introducing a System of Three Year Contractural Review of Special Needs Housing Revenue Funding*. Housing Corporation, London.

Useful books

Aughton, H. and Malpass, P. (1990) *Housing Finance: A Basic Guide*. SHELTER, London.
Garnett, D., Reid, B. and Riley, H. (1994) *Housing Finance*. Chartered Institute of Housing/Longman, London.
Hills, J. (1991) *Unravelling Housing Finance*. Clarendon Press, Oxford.

Chapter 3

References

Department of the Environment (1980–91). *P1 (E) Returns*. HMSO, London.
Department of the Environment (1991). *Housing Act 1985 Part Three: Code of Guidance*. HMSO, London.
Department of the Environment (1991). *Housing Subsidy and Accounting Manual*. HMSO, London.

Useful books

Austerberry, H. and Watson, S. (1983) *Women on the Margins: A Study of Single Women's Housing Problems*. Housing Research Group, City University, London.
Niner, P. (1989) *Homeless in Nine Authorities: Case Studies of Policy and Practice*. Department of the Environment, London.
Thornton, R. (1990) *The New Homeless*. SHAC, London.

Chapter 4

References

Bowen, G. (1978) *Survey of Fringe Bodies*. Civil Service Department, London.
Department of the Environment (1994) *Annual Report 1994: The Government's Expenditure Plans 1994–95 to 1996–97*. HMSO, London.
Housing Corporation (1993) *Housing Associations in England 1993*. London: Housing Corporation.
Housing Corporation (1993) *The Next Three Years: The Housing Corporation's Plans and Priorities 1994–1997*. Housing Corporation, London.
National Federation of Housing Associations (1990). *Committee members' handbook*. NFHA, London.
National Federation of Housing Associations (1995) *NFHA Yearbook, 1995*. NFHA, London.

Useful books

Burrows, L. (1989) *The Housing Act 1988*. SHELTER, London.
Cope, H. (1989) *Housing Associations: Policy and Practice*. Macmillan, London.
Fraser, R. (1991) *Working Together in the 1990s*. Institute of Housing, London.

Chapter 5

References

Cullingworth Committee (1969) *Council Housing: Purposes, Procedures and Priorities*. HMSO, London.
Department of the Environment (1989) *The Nature and Effectiveness of Housing Management in England and Wales*. A report to the D.o.E. by the Centre for Housing Research, University of Glasgow. HMSO, London.
Report of the Royal Commission on Local Government in England (chairman: Lord Redcliffe-Maude) (1968). Cmnd 4040. HMSO, London.
Seebohm Committee (1968) *Local Authority and Allied Social Services*. Cmnd 3703. HMSO, London.
Widdicombe Committee (1986) *The Conduct of Local Authority Business*. Cmnd 9797. HMSO, London.

Useful books

Malpass, P. and Murie, A. (1990) *Housing Policy and Practice*. Macmillan, London.
Power, A. (1991) *Housing Management: A Guide to Quality and Creativity*. Longman, Harlow.
Smith, M. (1989) *Guide to Housing*. Housing Centre Trust, London.
Ward, M. (1990) *The Local Government and Housing Act 1989: A Guide to the Housing Aspects*. Chartered Institute of Housing, Exeter.

Chapter 6

References

Chartered Institute of Housing/Royal Institute of British Architects (1983) *Homes for the Future*. CIH/RIBA, London.
Coleman, A. (1985) *Utopia on Trial*. Hilary Shipman, London.
Metropolitan Police (1995) *Secured by Design*. HMSO, London.
Ministry of Housing and Local Government (1961) *Homes for Today and Tomorrow*. HMSO, London.
Newman, O. (1976) *Defensible Space*. Architectural Press, London.
Royal Borough of Kensington and Chelsea (1992) *Unitary Development Plan: Deposit Copy*. Royal Borough of Kensington and Chelsea, London.

Useful books

Dunmore, K. (1992) *Planning for Affordable Housing: A Practical Guide*. Chartered Institute of Housing and House Builders Federation, London.
Fraser, R. (1991) *Working Together in the 1990s*. Chartered Institute of Housing, London.
National Federation of Housing Associations (1992) *Development After the Act: The HA Development Programme 1989/90*. NFHA, London.
Page, D. (1993) *Building for Communities*. Joseph Rowntree Foundation, York.
Telling, A.E. (1990) *Planning Law and Procedure*. Butterworths, London.

Chapter 7

References

Association of District Council/Chartered Institute of Housing (1994) *CCT and Local Authority Housing*. ADC/CIH, London.
Chartered Institute of Housing (1992) *Housing, the First Priority*. CIH, Coventry.
Department of the Environment (1989) *The Nature and Effectiveness of Housing Management in England and Wales*. A report to the D.o.E. by the Centre for Housing Research, University of Glasgow. HMSO, London.
Department of the Environment (1992) *Competing for Quality in Housing*. HMSO, London.
Housing Corporation (1991) *Criteria for Registration of a Housing Association*. Housing Corporation, London.
Local Government Management Board (1991) *The Application of Business Planning*. LGMB, Luton.
Power, A. (1991) *Housing management: A Guide to Quality and Creativity*. Longman, Harlow.
Wilcox, S. *et al.* (1993) *Local Housing Companies: New Opportunities for Council Housing*. Joseph Rowntree Foundation, York.

Useful books

Donnison, D. and Maclennan, D. (1991) *The Housing Service of the Future*. Chartered Institute of Housing/Longman, London.
Passmore, J. and Fergusson, S. (1994) *Customer Service in a Competitive Environment*. Chartered Institute of Housing, Coventry.

Index